A Delicate Balance:

Church, State, and the Schools

Martha M. McCarthy
Indiana University

A Publication of the Phi Delta Kappan Educational Foundation
Bloomington, Indiana

cover design by Nancy Rinehart

Contents

Preface v

One: Introduction... 1
Historical Context 1
    Old World Church-State Conflict 2
    Colonial Church-State Relations............................... 3
    Religion and Education: Historical Nexus 5
Legal Framework 7
    Rules of Judicial Review....................................... 8
    Application of the First Amendment to State Action 10
    Judicial Criteria Applied in First Amendment
        Church-State Cases 11
Conclusion 15

Two: Religious Observances and Activities
    in Public Schools.. 21
Bible Reading and Prayer 21
Student Religious Clubs.. 26
The Fine Line Between Teaching About Religion and
    Teaching Religious Beliefs 30
Religious Holiday Observances.................................. 34
Display of Religious Symbols 36
Teachers Wearing Religious Garb 37
Religious Influences in Commencement Exercises 39
Distribution of Religious Literature............................. 41
Conclusion 42

Three: Religious Exemptions from Public
    School Programs 52
Exemptions from Mandatory Schooling 52
Exemptions from Mandatory Immunization 54
Exemptions from School Observances............................ 56
Exemptions from Curricular Offerings 59
Exemptions from Regulations Governing Student Athletes 64
Excusal from Public School for Religious Observances 65
Conclusion 69

Four: Religious Challenges to the Public School
    Curriculum.. 76
Challenges to Course Offerings 76
The Creationism-Evolution Dispute 80
Censorship of Instructional Materials 84
Alleged Establishment of the Religion of Secular Humanism........... 89
Conclusion 92

Five: Rental, Shared-Time, and Released-Time Arrangements.. 101
Proprietary Rental Arrangements 101
Shared-Time or Dual-Enrollment Programs......................... 103
Released Time for Religious Instruction 108
Conclusion 112

Six: State Aid to Parochial Schools 117
Transportation Aid 117
Loan of Textbooks... 120
Other Types of Parochiaid 123
Diagnostic, Therapeutic, and Remedial Services 125
State-Prescribed Tests and Record Keeping Services 128
Tax Relief for Parents of Nonpublic School Students 129
Conclusion 132

Seven: Governmental Regulation of Parochial Schools 141
The State's Regulatory Authority................................. 141
    State Regulation of Religious Schools 143
    State Regulation of Home Education Programs 149
Application of Federal Policies to Religious Schools 153
    National Labor Relations Act 153
    Federal Unemployment Tax Act 153
    Civil Rights Act of 1870 155
    Civil Rights Act of 1871 156
    Tax-Exempt Status of Religious Schools Engaging in
        Racially Discriminatory Practices 157
Conclusion 160
Eight: Some Concluding Observations....................... 169

Preface

In this book I have attempted to provide a comprehensive analysis of legal developments pertaining to church-state-school relations through July 1983. I have examined governmental and individual interests and judicial interpretations of the rights of parents, children, and school authorities. While focusing primarily on current legal issues and their implications for the future, some background information is included to provide a historical context.

It is my sincere belief that by becoming better informed about the legal principles involved, all citizens can take a more reasoned approach in solving the volatile current church-state controversies involving education. Thus, this book was written with a wide audience in mind—educators, parents, legal scholars, and others interested in the evolution of the law governing church-state-school relations. I have tried to present the material in nontechnical language, but all topics are thoroughly documented to facilitate using the book as a reference tool.

The book is organized topically. The three chapters following the introductory chapter focus on judicial interpretations of the role of religion in connection with public schools. Chapter 5, covering topics that pertain both to public and parochial education, is followed by two chapters that address governmental relations with sectarian schools. A brief concluding chapter addresses implications of recent legal developments. Although each chapter is designed to stand on its own, some judicial rulings are treated from different perspectives in more than one chapter. Also, the applicable principles of law span some topics. For example, the legal reasoning applied by courts in connection with a topic such as devotional activities in public schools may appear in cases pertaining to other issues such as state aid to religious schools. Therefore, to gain a full understanding of the complex interrelationships involved, the reader is encouraged to read the entire text.

I have made every effort to present developments objectively, covering opposing arguments and their rationales. I have attempted to portray what the law is, rather than what it should be, and to identify areas where the governing legal principles are in a state of flux. However, I freely acknowledge my position that constitutional liberties demand scrupulous protection by the courts.

Religious freedom is very important to me, and the fact that my personal beliefs are held by the Protestant mainstream does not diminish my concern for the constitutional rights of those in the minority. Indeed, while my academic interest in constitutional law provided the impetus for this project, my sincere commitment to the protection of individual civil rights sustained my interest throughout the months of research.

My prefatory remarks would not be complete without mentioning some individuals who have assisted me in the preparation of this book. Patricia Walters, a doctoral student at Indiana University, devoted hours to the task of proofreading chapters and checking case cites and other references. Her help was invaluable. Also, Nita Coyle deserves recognition for her tireless efforts in typing the numerous drafts of this manuscript. Nita and I have been a team in all my writing endeavors. My parents also have made a substantial contribution to this book as well as to all my professional activities. They provided support and encouragement and assisted in proofreading the chapters.

The assistance of my husband, George Kuh, cannot be measured. He serves as my most important critic, and he devoted many hours to reviewing drafts of this material and making helpful suggestions. Without his patience, understanding, and support, this book could not have been written. Finally, my children, Kari and Kristian, played a very special role throughout the project. To them I dedicate this book, with hope that their freedom to learn, to make religious choices, and to practice their beliefs will be assured.

Martha M. McCarthy
June 1983

Chapter One

Introduction

The relationship between religion and government has created extensive controversy in the history of this nation, and some of the most volatile church-state disputes have involved education. Two fundamental beliefs in our democratic society are the encouragement of universal education and the protection of religious liberty. Sensitive legal questions have arisen when the state's interest in assuring an educated citizenry has collided with parental interests in directing the upbringing of their children according to specific religious values. Also, the tension between the free exercise of religious beliefs and restrictions on governmental advancement of religion has been particularly acute in school settings. To understand fully the implications of current church-state controversies involving schools, a brief discussion of their historical and legal context is necessary.

Historical Context

Conflicts between the church and state and among religious sects have been a dominant theme in the western world. Wars have been fought, minority sects have been persecuted, rulers have been dethroned, and migrations have been precipitated by sectarian issues. Without question, religious concerns have been a powerful force in shaping the course of history.

The sentiments that found expression in the First Amendment to the U.S. Constitution emerged from a heritage of religious persecution and strife. Justice Prescott of the Maryland high court observed in 1966:

> . . . the problem to be considered and solved when the First Amendment was proposed was not one of hazy or comparative insignificance, but was one of blunt and stark reality, which had perplexed and plagued the nations of Western Civilization for some 14 centuries, and during that long period, the union of Church and State in the government of man had produced neither peace on earth, nor good will to man.[1]

1

Old World Church-State Conflict

The historical struggle to secure religious freedom and governmental independence from the church has been well documented. The early Christians were certainly martyrs for their faith, with many being thrown to lions because they openly questioned the superior jurisdiction of the state over God:

> The officials of the Roman Empire in time of persecution sought to force the Christians to sacrifice, not to any of the heathen gods, but to the Genius of the Emperor and the Fortune of the City of Rome; and at all times the Christian's refusal was looked upon not as a religious but as a political offense.[2]

In 313 A.D. the early persecution of Christians officially ceased with the Edict of Milan, which proclaimed "universal toleration of all religions" and "absolute freedom of worship."[3] Later in the fourth century, Christianity became the established church of Rome.

However, religious strife and persecution was only redirected rather than eliminated. The Christian church soon asserted not mere equality with the state, but superiority. There was substantial controversy in some Roman provinces between civil officials and Catholic bishops regarding their respective spheres of authority.[4] Thomas Aquinas observed that "the State . . . must be subordinated to the Church. Church and State as two swords which God has given to Christendom for protection; both of these, however, are given by him to the Pope and, the temporal sword by him handed to the rulers of the State."[5]

The Middle Ages were characterized by sectarian conflict; the religious crusades from 1096 until 1270 engaged practically all of continental Europe and England in costly and cruel warfare in attempts to regain possession of the Holy Land. Motivated by religious zeal, monarchs and nobility fought beside Christian clergy in unsuccessful campaigns to drive the Muslims from Jerusalem. Some of the armies were comprised primarily of young children, many of whom died in battle.[6]

The Christian church reached the height of its supremacy over the state in western nations during the thirteenth century.[7] Those who questioned the tenets of the established church were subjected to persecution and sometimes death. Indeed, many heretics were burned at the sake for their religious infidelity.[8] Historians have noted that Christians, in their efforts to eradicate dissenters, inflicted far greater brutality than they had experienced from infidels.[9]

With the advent of the Reformation, the concept that church and state were inseparable remained dominant, but new options regarding the nature of the established church appeared. Also, the concept that secular leaders could use religion to carry out political policy gained increasing support, thus calling into question the notion of church supremacy, which had prevailed for centuries.

All school children study about the intense struggle in England when King Henry VIII rebuked papal authority and established the Church of England.[10] After his death, Queen Mary attempted to reestablish Catholicism and acquired the nickname "Bloody Mary" for her treatment of Protestants who refused to convert. When Queen Elizabeth I ascended to the English throne, the Anglican church and the supremacy of the state over religion became well established. Laws were passed imposing substantial fines on all persons failing to attend the Church of England. David Montgomery has observed that both Protestants and Catholics "believed it a duty to convert or exterminate the other, and the alternative offered to the heretic was to 'turn or burn'."[11]

England was not the only site of church-state controversy during this period. It was inconceivable at that time that church and state could exist independently of each other, so most conflicts focused on determining what should be the established church. The Thirty-Years' War, which started as a civil war between Protestants and Catholics in the German states and spread throughout Europe, ended in 1648 with the Peace of Westphalia. The treaty authorized each German state to "profess its existing religion, whether Catholic, Lutheran, or Reformed."[12] However, other religions were not to be tolerated, and "the power of the reigning princes to 'reform' their states by driving out dissenters was restrained rather than abolished."[13] This period has been characterized as follows:

> In efforts to force loyalty to whatever religious group happened to be on top and in league with the government of a particular time and place, men and women had been fined, cast in jail, cruelly tortured, and killed. Among the offenses for which these punishments had been inflicted were such things as speaking disrespectfully of the views of ministers of government-established churches, non-attendance at those churches, expressions of non-belief in their doctrines, and failure to pay taxes and tithes to support them.[14]

By the latter 1700s no country in Europe had completely severed the state from sectarian concerns or had established freedom of worship. Religious inquisitions were conducted by many governments, with the Spanish Inquisition exemplifying the most severe religious intolerance.[15] In almost every country there was a state-supported or at least state-preferred religion. Holland was the most progressive in its toleration for all faiths.[16] In 1784 James Madison summed up the centuries of bloody religious battles in Europe: "Torrents of blood have been spilled in the world in vain attempts of the secular arm to extinguish religious discord, by proscribing all differences in religious opinions."[17]

Colonial Church-State Relations

At the time of the American Revolution, strong religious values permeated the colonies. Indeed, the Declaration of Independence concludes with:

> And for the support of this Declaration, with a firm reliance on the Pro-
> tection of Divine Providence, we mutually pledge to each other our Lives,
> our Fortunes, and our sacred Honor.[18]

Unlike Europe, America has not experienced religious wars, but this country has not been immune to religious strife. Many of the original colonists came to the New World to flee religious persecution; yet, the deeply ingrained tradition of a state-established religion also travelled across the Atlantic. The individual's right to exercise religious beliefs was far from an accepted notion during the colonial period.[19] Roger Williams and Anne Hutchinson were among the best-known individuals who were banned from their colonies for religious reasons. In New York all settlers were required to support the Dutch Reformed Church; Quakers and Baptists were subjected to persecution. In New England, for all practical purposes, the Calvinist Congregational Church was the established religion, and in Virginia all ministers were required to perform canons of the Church of England.[20] Taxes were imposed to support sectarian institutions in a majority of the colonies at the time they declared their independence from England.[21]

Discrimination against minority faiths most often was political, resulting in the denial of voting privileges or the opportunity to hold public office. For example, in Pennsylvania only those who professed a belief in Jesus Christ could hold office, and civil servants in New Jersey were required to take an oath against the Pope. There were other types of religious persecution in colonial America, such as the Massachusetts witch trials.[22] Leo Pfeffer has noted that the range of religious tolerance varied among the colonies, with the proprietary colonies being the most progressive.[23] However, the limited tolerance that did exist usually excluded certain sects such as Catholics and Jews.

The primary efforts to secure religious toleration and a separation of church and state in America came from colonial leaders in Virginia. In 1785 James Madison wrote his famous *A Memorial and Remonstrance*, in which he offered a reasoned plea for removing sectarian concerns from civil government. Madison argued against the government requiring citizens to contribute even "three pence" of property for sectarian ends.[24] Several years earlier, Thomas Jefferson had placed before the Virginia legislature *An Act for Establishing Religious Freedom*, which proclaimed that "to compel a man to furnish contributions of money for the propagation of opinions which he disbelieves is sinful and tyrannical."[25] This bill finally was enacted into law in 1786, replacing the tax levy to support the Anglican Church.

Both Madison and Jefferson relied heavily on the theory of church-state separation espoused by John Locke who maintained that "the care of souls cannot belong to the civil magistrate."[26] Locke's philosophy provided a third alternative to the Erastian and theocratic theories on church-state relations that were in vogue in the latter eighteenth century. Those adhering to the Erastian theory, named after the German philosopher Erastus, claimed state superiority over the church; religion should be used to advance state interests.

The theocratic theory was grounded in the opposing notion that the church is superordinate and the state should be used to further ecclesiastical interests.[27] Locke's theory eventually prevailed in the United States, but support for this philosophy was by no means universally accepted at the time the U.S. Constitution was written.

When the convention met in Philadelphia to draft the Constitution, the treatment of the church-state question generated considerable controversy. There were competing fears of governmental imposition of religion and of governmental abolishment of religion. Some sentiment was expressed that states should retain the right to enact laws supporting sectarian institutions and that language should be avoided that might be construed as favoring those who disavow religion.[28] After lengthy debate, the delegates did not include in the proposed Constitution any provision regarding religious freedom, but two states would not ratify the Constitution until the first ten amendments, the Bill of Rights, were included as part of the document.

The first of these amendments stipulates in part that "Congress shall make no law respecting the establishment of religion or prohibiting the free exercise thereof." The wording of the religious freedoms in this amendment was influenced by Madison but did not contain his proposed restriction on state interference with religious liberty. Madison felt that state governments, with their parochial orientations, were more likely than the federal government to deprive religious minorities of their rights. However, other framers of the Bill of Rights were not willing to place such restrictions on state authority.[29] Nonetheless, the First Amendment called for substantial protection of religious liberty from federal interference, providing a bold departure from the prevailing doctrine in most Western nations.

Religion and Education: Historical Nexus

The growth of universal schooling in this nation was strongly influenced by sectarian concerns. Indeed, religious training provided the initial impetus for education during colonial days. Churches sought to advance Christianity through knowledge of the Bible. The first compulsory school attendance law, enacted in Massachusetts in 1642, was designed in part to assure that children learned to "read and understand the principles of religion."[30] A few years later, Massachusetts passed its famous "deluder Satan" law providing for the establishment of public schools:

> Sec. 1. It being one chief project of the old deluder, Satan, to keep men from the knowledge of the scriptures, . . . that learning may not be buried in the grave of our fathers in the church and commonwealth, the Lord assisting our endeavors, it is therefore ordered . . . that every township in this jurisdiction, after the Lord has increased them to the number of fifty householders, shall then forthwith appoint one within their town to teach all such children as shall resort to him to write and read, . . .[31]

In the southern and middle colonies, schools that existed usually were operated by the local churches and clergy. Often grants of public land were made for the establishment of these parochial schools. While the New England colonies were the most progressive in creating town-supported schools open to all children, such schools also maintained strong religious ties. Local ministers played an important role in selecting teachers, and the instructional program was oriented toward religious teaching. The *New England Primer*, widely used toward the end of the seventeenth century, taught the alphabet using examples from the Bible such as: "A—In Adams's fall, we sinned all."[32]

With the establishment of the new nation, which granted to the citizenry more rights and obligations than any country previously had attempted to do, education began to be viewed from the perspective of the needs of the state as well as the church. Several colonial leaders championed universal education, asserting that an enlightened citizenry is essential to governmental welfare. For example, George Washington recommended in his "Farewell Address:"

> Promote then as an object of primary importance, institutions for the general diffusion of knowledge. In proportion as the structure of a government gives force to public opinion, it is essential that public opinion should be enlightened.[33]

Similarly, Thomas Jefferson declared that "if a nation expects to be ignorant and free, in a state of civilization, it expects what never was and never will be."[34] Even before the adoption of the U.S. Constitution, the Congress of the Confederation authorized federal land grants for schools, noting that religion, morality, and knowledge should forever be encouraged.[35]

However, the Constitution itself is silent regarding education. Thus, the authority to provide for education is among the powers reserved to the states or to the people under the Tenth Amendment. Although recognizing the importance of education to individual and collective well-being, states were slow to exert leadership in supporting and monitoring public schools, leaving such matters to local communities. As a result, the tradition of local control of education became well ingrained in this country. It was not until the nineteenth century that state education systems were established, primarily through the efforts of educational leaders such as Horace Mann in Massachusetts and Henry Barnard in Connecticut.[36] Today states vary as to the specificity of state-prescribed standards for public schools, but all states in their constitutions address the legislature's responsibility to establish a tax-supported educational system.[37]

Every state also requires compulsory school attendance for children between certain ages and imposes penalties on parents for noncompliance with these mandates. In the early twentieth century, a few states attempted to go even further by enacting laws requiring children to attend *public* schools. However, in 1925 the U.S. Supreme Court invalidated such a law in Oregon, reasoning that it interfered with the rights of private schools and with parental rights to direct the upbringing of their children.[38] Thus, this decision clearly established that parochial schools have a right to exist and parents have a right to select a school for their children that reinforces their religious beliefs. But the scope of the state's authority to regulate such alternatives to public education, which is discussed in chapter 7, remains controversial.

The proper relationship between religion and public education also has continued to generate debate. Protestantism exerted a pervasive influence on the public school curriculum well into the twentieth century. For example, *McGuffey's Eclectic Readers*, written by William McGuffey, a Protestant minister, sold over a million copies between 1836 and 1920. Ellwood Cubberly estimated that about half of the American students during this period "drew their inspiration and formulated their codes of morals and conduct from this remarkable set of Readers."[39]

The change in the public school curriculum from a heavy reliance on sectarian materials and teaching practices to the adoption of a more secular curriculum has been gradual, and religious elements have not been totally eliminated. There is some sentiment that the increasing secularization of the curriculum has come about not because of a commitment to maintain separation of church and state but because of disputes among various religious sects as to which of their tenets would be emphasized in the curriculum.[40] Walter Berns has noted that controversies among denominations over sectarian influences in public schools have "resembled the earlier struggles to disestablish state churches."[41] Minority sects fought to remove religion from the school curriculum when the tenets of their faith did not receive state endorsement. For example, Catholics objected to Bible reading in public schools mainly because of the version of the Bible (King James) being read. According to Pfeffer, the "triumph of the secularization of the public school was in no small measure due to the persistence of . . . Catholic parents in refusing to sacrifice their claims of conscience by yielding to a settlement that was entirely satisfactory to the Protestant majority."[42]

Church-state issues involving schools continue to stimulate controversy. Indeed, during the past decade the issues have become more varied, complex, and emotionally charged. Alexis de Tocqueville noted in 1835 that "scarcely any political question arises in the United States that is not resolved, sooner or later, into a judicial question.[43] This observation certainly holds true regarding church-state issues involving schools; litigation in this area has increased dramatically in recent years.

Legal Framework

Historically most church-state conflicts pertaining to schools were settled in the local community; individuals did not usually seek judicial intervention to redress their grievances. Religious controversies were not viewed primarily in terms of constitutional rights, but rather in terms of majority rule. The dominant sect determined basic community norms, including the place of sectarian instruction in the school curriculum.

As communities became more heterogeneous through urbanization and increased mobility of the populace, local consensus regarding the values that schools should instill was no longer assured. Some groups, fearing that traditional American values (primarily Protestant) would be lost in a pluralistic society, pressed for legislation to codify their version of "appropriate" beliefs. Otto Hamilton, who studied challenges to Bible reading in public schools from 1854 until 1924, reported that state laws mandating religion in the curriculum were defended as necessary to teach moral values and thus to protect the general welfare.[44]

It was not until the mid-twentieth century that the judiciary assumed a more active posture in protecting the individual's constitutional rights. Recognizing that the Bill of Rights was intended to remove certain subjects from political debate, courts required state and local governments to justify legislative infringements on personal freedoms.[45] Since that time, courts have played a seminal role in shaping the law through their interpretations of constitutional and statutory provisions.

Because of the important function of the judiciary in delineating what the law is, much of this book focuses on judicial interpretations of First Amendment religious guarantees and comparable provisions of state constitutions as they have been applied in school settings. To provide a framework for this discussion, the remainder of this chapter offers a brief overview of the rules of judicial review and the legal principles applied by courts in addressing church-state controversies.

Rules of Judicial Review

In 1803 Chief Justice Marshall, speaking for the U.S. Supreme Court, declared that the Supreme Court is the final arbiter of the nature and limits of the federal Constitution and that the Court's interpretation of this document is the supreme law of the land.[46] It is somewhat awesome when we realize that the scope of our First Amendment freedoms as well as our other constitutional rights ultimately resides with the collective judgment of the nine individuals on the Supreme Court. These justices attempt to maintain consistency in applying legal doctrine by relying on precedents, but judgments must be made and new doctrines formulated. Since justices are human, subject to biases and social influences, the Court's interpretations of religious protections have not been totally unaffected by shifts in societal sentiments regarding the appropriate church-state relationship.[47]

While the judiciary has the final word in *interpreting* the law, it cannot *initiate* legislation; courts are limited to exercising judicial review. In 1936 Supreme Court Justice Brandeis summarized the rules that the judiciary is expected to follow. He noted that it is a "cardinal principle: that a legislative enactment will not be judicially invalidated if there is a possible interpretation of the statute that does not implicate constitutional guarantees.[48] He also observed that the Supreme Court will not address a federal constitutional question if there is some other ground, such as an interpretation of a federal or state law, on which the controversy can be resolved. When the Court must interpret a federal constitutional provision, it "will not formulate a rule of constitutional law broader than is required by the precise facts" in the controversy before it.[49]

An important rule of judicial review is that the courts will not judge the constitutionality of legislation in "a friendly, non-adversary proceeding."[50] Article III of the Constitution stipulates that the federal court's power is limited to settling actual "cases" and "controversies" that are brought before it.[51] Courts are not empowered to invalidate unconstitutional practices simply because they may be aware that such practices exist. An actual case must be brought before the judiciary by a party who has standing to initiate the suit.

The issue of "standing to sue" has particular implications for certain types of church-state disputes. In 1982 the Supreme Court ruled that Americans United for Separation of Church and State did not have standing to initiate an establishment clause suit in connection with the administrative transfer of federal surplus property to a religious college under the Property and Administrative Services Act.[52] The five member majority found that Americans United lacked standing to challenge the transfer in federal court because its members had not suffered any actual or concrete injury beyond a "generalized grievance" about the use of their tax dollars.[53] The majority distinguished congressional action pursuant to its taxing and spending powers[54] from the administrative act in question, reasoning that taxpayers lack standing to challenge the latter.

The majority conceded that the concept of "standing" has not been "defined with complete consistency" by the Supreme Court in prior cases,[55] but stated that "the expenditure of public funds in an allegedly unconstitutional manner is not an injury sufficient to confer standing, even though the plaintiff contributes to the public coffers as a taxpayer."[56] Observing that the taxpayers claimed no personal injury beyond the alleged First Amendment violation, the majority reasoned that standing is not measured by the intensity of the litigant's interest in preserving the "constitutional principle of separation of church and state:"[57]

> Their claim that the government has violated the Establishment Clause does not provide a special license to roam the country in search of governmental wrongdoing and to reveal their discoveries in federal court. The federal courts were simply not constituted as ombudsmen of the general welfare.[58]

While it is too early to realize the full implications of this decision, it may have an impact on future church-state controversies involving schools. Individuals seeking access to federal courts to challenge educational policies and practices as impairing First Amendment religious freedoms will have to prove that the practices have resulted in actual personal injury rather than "the psychological consequence presumably produced by observation of conduct with which one disagrees."[59] Such injury may not be too difficult to substantiate in situations where students, parents, or teachers are directly affected by unconstitutional state action (e.g., devotional activities in public schools). But standing in federal court may be more difficult to establish in other church-state disputes, such as challenges to governmental aid to parochial schools. The Supreme Court (or at least a majority of its members) may be indicating that the federal judiciary should not become involved in some of the volatile, current, church-state controversies.[60]

Application of the First Amendment to State Action

The First Amendment and the other nine amendments included in the Bill of Rights originally were directed toward the federal government. Our founding fathers were quite skeptical of a powerful central government and were much less fearful of state encroachment on individual liberties. Thus, as noted previously, the First Amendment did not specifically prohibit individual states from establishing a religion or interfering with the free exercise of religious beliefs. In 1845 the United States Supreme Court declared:

> The Constitution makes no provision for protecting the citizens of the respective states in their religious liberties; this is left to the state constitutions and laws; nor is there any inhibition imposed by the Constitution of the United States in this respect on the states.[61]

States were free to establish religious tests for public office, to provide direct aid to religious institutions, and to mandate sectarian instruction in public schools if they so desired. Although all states ultimately followed the federal lead in guaranteeing religious liberty in their respective constitutions, it was assumed that the First Amendment did not obligate them to do so. Indeed, several states had state-supported religions long after the U.S. Constitution was adopted and had laws on the books that placed political restrictions on certain sects, primarily Catholics and Jews.[62] The opinion that the First Amendment applied only to the federal government continued well into the twentieth century.

However, during the past several decades the Supreme Court has interpreted the Fourteenth Amendment as prohibiting state encroachment on fundamental liberties protected by the Bill of Rights. In a significant 1940 decision, *Cantwell* v. *Connecticut*, the Court recognized that the Fourteenth Amendment renders "the legislatures of the states as incompetent as Congress" to enact laws interfering with First Amendment religious guarantees.[63] Subsequently, this conclusion has been reiterated on numerous occasions.

Thus it has been firmly established that First Amendment religious protections apply to state as well as federal action. This development holds particular significance for church-state controversies involving schools because education is primarily a state function. Since 1940 plaintiffs have not had to rely on state law in challenging school policies and practices that allegedly interfere with their religious liberties. If they can establish standing to sue, they can use the First Amendment in contesting acts of the state as well as the federal government.

Judicial Criteria Applied in First Amendment Church-State Cases

Although the religious guarantees embodied in the First Amendment might appear straightforward, they have created problems for the judiciary for over two centuries. This nation is even "more litigious than religious,"[64] and delineation of the proper relationship between government and religion has proved an awesome judicial task. If the state becomes too assertive in safeguarding establishment clause prohibitions, it may approach disavowing religion, which would impair free exercise rights. On the other hand, if the state becomes too accommodating toward religious beliefs, there may be a danger of advancing religion in violation of the establishment clause. Indeed, the protections included in the two clauses "are cast in absolute terms, and either of which, if expanded to a logical extreme, would tend to clash with the other."[65]

The term "separation of church and state," which was first introduced by Thomas Jefferson, does not appear in the First Amendment; nonetheless, many citizens as well as judges have accepted Jefferson's metaphor as the law of the land. Supreme Court Justice Rutledge stated in 1947 that the First Amendment was not designed merely to prohibit governmental imposition of a religion; it was designed to create "a complete and permanent separation of the spheres of religious activity and civil authority. . . ."[66] Walfred Peterson has observed that "one of the United States' greatest contributions to the art of government was the idea and practice summed up by the phrase, 'separation of church and state'."[67] The sentiment often has been voiced that the best interests of both religion and government are served by keeping civil and sectarian affairs discrete.[68] Governmental acts that suggest state sponsorship of religion or threaten an individual's freedom of religious choice have been viewed as particularly threatening in connection with educational institutions because of the vulnerability of children.[69]

Yet, the Supreme Court has recognized on several occasions that total separation between church and state "is not possible in an absolute sense."[70] In 1952 Justice Douglas declared that "we are a religious people whose institutions presuppose a Supreme Being."[71] He further noted the many references to God in our laws and public rituals such as "prayers in our legislative halls; the appeals to the Almighty in the messages of the Chief Executive; the proclamations making Thanksgiving Day a holiday; [and] 'so help me God' in our courtroom oaths."[72] Several years later when the Supreme Court barred Bible reading from public schools, Justice Goldberg commented in a concurring opinion:

11

> Neither government nor this Court can or should ignore the significance
> of the fact that a vast portion of our people believe in and worship God
> and that many of our legal, political and personal values derive historical-
> ly from religious teachings. Government must inevitably take cognizance
> of the existence of religion and, indeed, under certain circumstances the
> First Amendment may require that it do so.[73]

Lower courts have also endorsed several practices that do not suggest total separation of church and state. For example, religious observances by astronauts during the Apollo moon flight and the issuance of a postage stamp bearing the image of the Madonna have been upheld.[74] In addition, courts have sanctioned the display of the Ten Commandments on a municipal court-house lawn and the use of "In God We Trust" on currency.[75]

Because the First Amendment does not elaborate on what type of govern-mental action respects the establishment of religion or interferes with the free exercise of religious belief, the judiciary has been called upon to give meaning to these provisions. The Supreme Court has attempted to identify the ap-propriate governmental neutrality that neither advances religion nor exhibits hostility toward sectarian concerns. In 1968 the Court stated that "the First Amendment mandates governmental neutrality between religion and religion, and between religion and nonreligion."[76] However, the Court also has recognized that the concept of neutrality is far easier to state than to apply.[77]

The Supreme Court has tended to view the two religion clauses of the First Amendment as independent mandates. Accordingly, it has developed separate tests for assessing the legality of governmental action under the establishment and free exercise clauses. These tests, discussed below, are frequently referred to throughout this book.

Establishment Clause Criteria. The establishment clause prohibits govern-mental action that *respects* the establishment of a religion in that such action is a step toward that end.[78] Traditionally the Supreme Court used two criteria in assessing claims under the establishment clause. In 1963 the Court noted:

> The test may be stated as follows: What are the purpose and the primary
> effect of the enactment? If either is the advancement or inhibition of
> religion then the enactment exceeds the scope of legislative power as cir-
> cumscribed by the Constitution. That is to say that to withstand the stric-
> tures of the Establishment Clause there must be a secular legislative pur-
> pose and a primary effect that neither advances nor inhibits religion.[79]

Since states usually can substantiate a secular purpose for legislation, under the above test the constitutionality of challenged state action generally has hinged on an assessment of the primary effect of the provisions.

However, in 1970 the Supreme Court introduced a third criterion in establishment clause cases: Does the challenged governmental action foster ex-cessive governmental entanglement with religion?[80] In a 1971 case, *Lemon* v. *Kurtzman*, this new standard was first applied in an education case.[81] In subse-quent church-state litigation, the judiciary has applied this tripartite test in

12

evaluating establishment clause claims, and legislation has been invalidated if it has failed to satisfy any one of the three criteria.

If an establishment clause violation is found, the appropriate remedy is a prohibition of the unconstitutional activity. An excusal provision does not neutralize the constitutional defect. For example, when Bible reading in public schools was declared in violation of the establishment clause, this activity was barred from public education.[82] The mere excusal of offended students from the observance was not considered sufficient to safeguard establishment clause guarantees.[83]

If school authorities should continue a practice, despite a clear Supreme Court ruling that the activity abridges the establishment clause, students or teachers might be successful in obtaining damages for the suffering they have experienced from the impairment of their constitutional rights.[84] School authorities are not expected to be prophets and anticipate changes in judicial interpretations of constitutional provisions,[85] but they are expected to adhere to *well established* principles of law.

Free Exercise Criteria. Different judicial standards are used to evaluate free exercise in contrast to establishment clause claims. Under the First Amendment, the government cannot regulate an individual's beliefs, but it can place restrictions on certain conduct based on beliefs. In 1940 the Supreme Court stated that protection of the freedom to believe is "absolute," but "conduct remains subject to regulation for the protection of society."[86] Most free exercise claims have arisen because governmental action has interfered with practices that are either dictated by or prohibited by the individual's religious faith. The judiciary has used a balancing test to evaluate such claims.

This balancing test, outlined in detail by the Supreme Court in *Wisconsin v. Yoder*,[87] involves a three-part analysis. First the judiciary assesses whether or not the activity interfered with by the state is motivated by and rooted in a legitimate and sincerely held religious belief.[88] Finding such a sincere and legitimate belief, the Court then evaluates whether or not practices dictated by this belief have been impaired by the governmental action, and if so, to what extent. If the plaintiff substantiates such an impairment, the Court then evaluates whether the state action serves a compelling interest that justifies the burden imposed on the free exercise of religious beliefs. Applying these criteria, the judiciary must make sensitive judgments as to what constitutes a sincere belief and a burden on its free exercise and what type of governmental interest is necessary to override free exercise rights.

Not only do courts apply different criteria to assess free exercise in contrast to establishment clause claims, but also the remedies differ for violations of the two clauses. While the remedy for a free exercise impairment may entail an exemption from the offensive practice, the practice itself would not have to be eliminated as would be true with establishment clause violations. For example, a school board might be ordered to excuse certain students from a secular school activity that interferes with their free exercise of beliefs, but the school

13

would not be required—or perhaps even allowed—to ban the activity from the curriculum simply to conform to religious beliefs.

Students have been the central targets of religious controversies involving schools, but traditionally parents and school authorities have been the key actors in the disputes. Courts have balanced parental and state interests asserted on behalf of children. However, during the past two decades, judicial attention has also focused on delineating the rights of students themselves.[89] Thus, the child has become a more important actor—although still not an equal partner—in the interest triad. Courts seem increasingly reluctant to view students as merely the objects of the balancing process between parental and governmental interests. Referring to students' free exercise rights, Supreme Court Justice Douglas declared in 1972 that "it's the student's judgment, not his parents', that is essential if we are to give full meaning to what we have said about the Bill of Rights, and the right of students to be masters of their own destiny."[90]

Tension Between the Religion Clauses. Although the dual aspects of the religion clauses are intended to ensure the unitary guarantee of religious liberty, the inherent tension between the free exercise and establishment clauses has been troublesome for the courts. In some cases the judiciary must decide whether the government's obligation to adhere to establishment clause prohibitions or the individual's right to exercise religious beliefs should prevail. Some of the most complex legal questions are raised when students' rights to attend public school in an environment free from state sponsorship of religion are pitted against claims that accommodations to religious beliefs are required to protect free exercise rights.

The Supreme Court to date has declined to specify a hierarchy of First Amendment religious freedoms. However, there is some sentiment that the establishment clause is intended mainly "to implement" the free exercise clause, so the former must be subordinated to the latter if they clash.[91] In 1963 Justice Brennan stated in a concurring opinion that "the logical interrelationship between the Establishment and Free Exercise Clauses may produce situations where an injunction against an apparent establishment must be withheld in order to avoid infringement of rights of free exercise."[92]

Yet, there is a competing theory grounded in the notion that governmental action that serves to advance religion violates the First Amendment regardless of whether the action is intended to accommodate free exercise rights.[93] Several federal appellate courts have reasoned that in connection with public schools, the free exercise of beliefs must be subordinated to establishment clause prohibitions.[94] These courts have viewed the constitutional ban against state sponsorship of religion as an overriding consideration that justifies some minimal impairment of free exercise rights. Until the Supreme Court clarifies the relationship and possible hierarchy between the two religion clauses, the precise parameters of an individual's religious liberties will remain unclear.

Conclusion

Against a backdrop of centuries of religious conflict and persecution, the framers of the U.S. Constitution attempted to safeguard religious liberties by the provisions included in the First Amendment. Individual states followed the federal lead by including similar protections in their respective constitutions. However, judicial interpretations of these provisions have evoked continual controversy. Chief Justice Burger of the U.S. Supreme Court captured the judicial dilemma in 1971 when he observed that courts "can only dimly perceive the lines of demarcation in this extraordinarily sensitive area of constitutional law."[95]

Because of the perceived significance of schools in shaping the values of young people, it is not surprising that educational settings have generated some of the most significant church-state conflicts. One commentator has observed: "Today it is in the area of schooling that the controversies are the most frequent, the most litigious, the most enduring, and the most given to legal and political machinations."[96] Church-state disputes involving schools have accelerated in recent years, spanning diverse topics. Indeed, with the exception of desegregation, no other school topic has contributed cases as regularly to the Supreme Court's docket. Many cases have focused on sectarian influences in public schools, such as student-initiated prayer periods, the teaching of creation-science, and the observance of religious holidays. Other controversies have involved the state's relationship to parochial schools, such as state regulation of nonpublic schools, state aid to such schools, and tax relief for parents of parochial school students. Church-state issues have also been raised in connection with requests for student exemptions from public school activities and claims that the curriculum should be altered to conform to religious doctrine. The remainder of this book is devoted to an analysis of these and related topics, the applicable principles of law, and implications of recent legal developments.

Footnotes

1. Horace Mann League of the United States v. Board of Public Works, 220 A.2d 51, 60 (Md. 1966).

2. Francis Legge, *Forerunners and Rivals of Christianity from 330 B.C. to 330 A.D.* (New Hyde Park, N.Y.: University Books, 1964), p. xxiv.

3. *See* Tudor v. Board of Educ., 100 A.2d 857, 859 (N.J. 1953).

4. *See* Horace Mann League of the United States v. Board of Public Works, 220 A.2d 51, 56 (Md. 1966).

5. M. Searle Bates, *Religious Liberty: An Inquiry* (New York: International Missionary Council, 1945), p. 140, quoting from W. Willoughby, *The Nation of the State*, p. 47.

6. *World Book Encyclopedia*, s.v. "Crusades."

7. However, the supremacy of the church in the Holy Roman Empire was not unchallenged. Leaders such as Charlemagne in France (eighth century), Henry IV in Germany (eleventh century), and Henry II in England (twelfth century) contested papal authority, but ultimately the church prevailed. According to Pfeffer, Pope Innocent III, in the thirteenth century, represented "the apex of the church's supremacy over state in Europe." Leo Pfeffer, *Church, State and Freedom* (Boston: Beacon Press, 1967), p. 19. Pope Innocent proclaimed that the Lord left to the Pope authority not only for the church, but also for the world. *See* Tudor v. Board of Educ., 100 A.2d 857, 860 (N.J. 1953).

8. *See* Henry Lea, *A History of the Inquisition in the Middle Ages* (New York: Harper & Brothers, 1888), pp. 459-561.

9. *See* Lea, *ibid*; Pfeffer, *Church, State and Freedom*, pp. 23-30.

10. *See* David Montgomery, *The Leading Facts of English History* (Boston, Mass.: Ginn & Co., 1895), pp. 195-201.

11. *Ibid.*, p. 207.

12. Tudor v. Board of Educ., 100 A.2d 857, 860-61 (N.J. 1953), quoting Innes, *Church and State: A Historical Handbook*, p. 157.

13. *Id.*

14. Everson v. Board of Educ., 330 U.S. 1, 9 (1947).

15. The religious inquisition in Spain was abolished in 1808, reestablished for a short period and finally eliminated in 1834. *See Encyclopedia Americana*, s.v. "Inquisition."

16. Tudor v. Board of Educ., 100 A.2d 857, 861 (N.J. 1953).

17. Joseph Blau, *Cornerstones of Religious Freedom in America* (Boston: Beacon Press, 1949), p. 85.

18. *See* Charles Beard, Mary Beard, and William Beard, *New Basic History of the United States* (New York: Doubleday and Co., 1944), p. 495.

19. For a discussion of church-state relations during the colonial period, *see* Pfeffer, *Church, State and Freedom*, pp. 71-90.

20. *See* Tudor v. Board of Educ., 100 A.2d 857, 861-62 (N.J. 1953).

21. Tom Clark (former Supreme Court Justice), "Religion and the Public Schools" (Speech delivered in Orlando, Florida, 1970). Reprinted by the Religious Instruction Association, Fort Wayne, Indiana, 1970. *See also* Pfeffer, *Church, State and Freedom*, p. 141.

22. The witch hunt in Salem, Massachusetts, in 1692 was the most famous. *See Encyclopedia Americana*. s.v. "Witchcraft."

23. Pfeffer, *Church, State and Freedom*, pp. 89-90. The proprietary colonies were Maryland, Pennsylvania, and Rhode Island.

24. James Madison, *Memorial and Remonstrance Against Religious Assessments*, ¶ 3, 1785. *See* Pfeffer, *Church, State and Freedom*, pp. 111-12.

25. Thomas Jefferson, *An Act for Establishing Religious Freedom*, ¶ 3, 1786. *See* Pfeffer, *ibid.*, pp. 113-14.

26. Mario Montuori, *John Locke, A Letter Concerning Toleration* (The Hague: Martinus Nijhoff, 1963), p. 19.

27. *See* Kern Alexander, *School Law* (St. Paul, Minn.: West Pub. Co., 1980), p. 170.

28. *See* Walter Berns, *The First Amendment and the Future of American Democracy* (New York: Basic Books, Inc., 1976), pp. 3-6, 33.

29. *Ibid.*, p. 5.

30. Samuel Brown, *The Secularization of American Education* (New York: Columbia University Press, 1912), p. 17.

31. R. L. Finney, *A Brief History of the American Public School* (New York: Macmillan Co., 1946), p. 4.

32. Pfeffer, *Church, State and Freedom*, p. 325.

33. Laurence Cremin, *The American Common School* (New York: Columbia University Press, 1951), p. 29.

34. *Ibid.* In the twentieth century the judiciary often has reiterated these sentiments in noting the crucial role of education in preserving a democratic form of government. *See*, for example, Plyler v. Doe, 102 S. Ct. 2382, 2397 (1982); Wisconsin v. Yoder, 406 U.S. 205, 221 (1972); Brown v. Board of Educ. of Topeka, 347 U.S. 483, 493 (1954).

35. *See* W. Vance Grant and Leo Eiden, *The Digest of Education Statistics 1980* (Washington, D.C.: National Center for Education Statistics, 1980), p. 175.

36. *See* Ellwood Cubberly, *The History of Education* (Boston: Houghton Mifflin Co., 1948), pp. 689-91.

37. *See* Martha McCarthy and Paul Deignan, *What Legally Constitutes an Adequate Public Education?* (Bloomington, Ind.: Phi Delta Kappa, 1982), Appendix B, for a list of all state constitutional provisions pertaining to the legislative duty to provide for public education. *See also* Lee Garber, *Education as a Function of the State* (Minneapolis, Minn.: Education Test Bureau, 1934), pp. 4-11. Based on an analysis of the proceedings of 37 state constitutional conventions, Garber summarized the major state purposes for establishing public education as: (a) protecting the political safety and well-being of the state, (b) promoting the economic well-being of the state, (c) promoting the elimination of evils such as crime and pauperism, and (d) promoting the well-being of the individual.

38. Pierce v. Society of Sisters, 268 U.S. 510 (1925).

39. Ellwood Cubberly, *Public Education in the United States: A Study and Interpretation of American Educational History*, rev. ed. (Boston: Houghton Mifflin Co., 1934), p. 294.

40. *See* Berns, *The First Amendment and the Future of American Democracy*, pp. 66-67; Pfeffer, *Church, State and Freedom*, pp. 335-38.

41. Berns, *ibid.*, p. 66.

42. Pfeffer, *Church, State and Freedom*, p. 335.

43. Alexis de Tocqueville, *Democracy in America*, rev. ed. (New York: Alfred A. Knopf, 1945), p. 280.

44. Otto Hamilton, *The Courts and the Curriculum* (New York: Teachers College Press, 1927), p. 113. Other examples of attempts to legislate traditional values were state laws requiring all students to attend public schools and requiring instruction to be in the English language.

45. *See* Tinker v. Des Moines Independent School Dist., 393 U.S. 503 (1969); West Virginia State Bd. of Educ. v. Barnette, 319 U.S. 624 (1943).

46. Marbury v. Madison, 5 U.S. (1 Cranch) 137 (1803).

47. *See* Committee for Public Educ. and Religious Liberty v. Regan, 444 U.S. 646, 662 (1980). *See also* Walfred Peterson, *Thy Liberty in Law* (Nashville, Tenn.: Broadman Press, 1978), p. 118.

48. Ashwander v. Tennessee Valley Authority, 297 U.S. 288, 346-48 (1936) (Brandeis, J., concurring).

49. *Id.* at 348.

50. *Id.* at 347.

51. U.S., *Constitution*, Art. III, sec. 2.

52. Valley Forge Christian College v. Americans United for Separation of Church and State, 102 S. Ct. 752 (1982). *See also* Americans United for Separation of Church and State v. School Dist. of the City of Grand Rapids, 546 F. Supp. 1071 (W.D. Mich. 1982).

53. *Id.*, 102 S. Ct. at 764.

54. In 1968 the Supreme Court held that taxpayers had standing to challenge the alleged unconstitutional congressional expenditure of categorical funds to aid sectarian schools. The Court reasoned that taxpayer status creates sufficient standing in suits alleging that congressional spending powers have been exercised in violation of constitutional restrictions on those powers (e.g., establishment clause prohibitions). *See* Flast v. Cohen, 392 U.S. 83 (1968).

55. 102 S. Ct. at 760. Compare Flast v. Cohen, *id.*, with Frothingham v. Mellon, 262 U.S. 447 (1923). In Doremus v. Board of Educ., 342 U.S. 429 (1952), the Supreme Court concluded that taxpayers did not have standing to bring a federal suit challenging a state law authorizing Bible reading in public schools. However, in Abington Township v. Schempp, 374 U.S. 203 (1963), the Court invalidated an almost

identical provision, reasoning that children and parents of children directly affected by such devotional activities had standing to sue in federal court.

56. 102 S. Ct. at 761.

57. *Id.* at 765.

58. *Id.* at 766-67.

59. *Id.* at 765. However, in May 1982 a Missouri federal district court concluded that taxpayers had standing to challenge the provision of services to private school students under Title I of the Elementary and Secondary Education Act of 1965, 20 U.S.C. § 241a *et seq.* Wamble v. Bell, 538 F. Supp. 868 (W.D. Mo. 1982).

60. *See* Thomas Flygare, "Supreme Court Makes Filing Church/State Lawsuits more Difficult," *Phi Delta Kappan* 63 (April 1982):561; Leslie Gerstman, "Valley Forge Christian College v. Americans United for Separation of Church and State," *West's Education Law Reporter* 5 (1982):339-49.

61. Permoli v. First Municipality of New Orleans, 44 U.S. 589, 609 (1845).

62. Maryland permitted taxation for the support of religion and denied civil office to non-Christians until 1818. Massachusetts had a state established church until 1833. A provision of the North Carolina Constitution, disqualifying for public office any person denying a belief in God or the truth of the Christian religion, was finally eliminated in 1868. *See* Pfeffer, *Church, State and Freedom*, p. 141; Jesse Choper, "The Religion Clauses of the First Amendment: Reconciling the Conflict,; *University of Pittsburgh Law Review* 41 (1980):676.

63. Cantwell v. Connecticut, 310 U.S. 296, 303 (1940).

64. George Will, "Opposing Prefab Prayer," *Newsweek*, 7 June 1982, p. 84.

65. Walz v. Tax Commission, 397 U.S. 664, 668-69 (1970).

66. Everson v. Board of Educ., 330 U.S. 1, 31-32 (1947) (Rutledge, J., dissenting).

67. Peterson, *Thy Liberty in Law*, p. 120.

68. *See* text with note 9, chapter 8.

69. *See* Leo Pfeffer, *Religious Freedom* (Skokie, Ill.: National Textbook Co., 1977), p. 172; text with note 17, chapter 8.

70. Lemon v. Kurtzman, 403 U.S. 602, 614 (1971). *See also* School Dist. of Abington Township v. Schempp, 374 U.S. 203 (1963); Engel v. Vitale, 370 U.S. 421, 434 (1962). In 1983 the Supreme Court endorsed state support for a chaplain to open Nebraska legislative sessions with a prayer, Marsh v. Chambers, 51 U.S.L.W. 5162 (July 5, 1983).

71. Zorach v. Clauson, 343 U.S. 306, 313 (1952).

72. *Id.* at 312-13 (1952).

73. School Dist. of Abington Township v. Schempp, 374 U.S. 203, 306 (1963) (Goldberg, J., concurring).

74. O'Hair v. Paine, 312 F. Supp. 434 (W.D. Tex. 1969), *aff'd* 432 F.2d 66 (5th Cir. 1970), *cert. denied*, 401 U.S. 955 (1971); Protestants and Other Americans United for Separation of Church and State v. O'Brien, 272 F. Supp. 712 (D.D.C. 1967).

75. Anderson v. Salt Lake City Corp., 475 F.2d 29 (10th Cir. 1973), *cert. denied*, 414 U.S. 879 (1973); Aronow v. United States, 432 F.2d 242 (9th Cir. 1970). However, the California Supreme Court held that the display of a lighted cross on a city hall during the Christmas season abridged First Amendment religious freedoms, Fox v. City of Los Angeles, 587 P.2d 663 (Cal. 1978).

76. Epperson v. Arkansas, 393 U.S. 97, 104 (1968).

77. *See* Roemer v. Board of Public Works, 426 U.S. 736, 747 (1976).

78. Lemon v. Kurtzman, 403 U.S. 602, 612 (1971).

79. School Dist. of Abington Township v. Schempp, 374 U.S. 203, 222 (1963).

80. Walz v. Tax Commission, 397 U.S. 664, 674 (1970).

81. 403 U.S. 602, 612-13 (1971).

82. *See* School Dist. of Abington Township v. Schempp, 374 U.S. 203 (1963).

83. *See* Engel v. Vitale, 370 U.S. 421, 431 (1962).

84. *See* Abramson v. Anderson, No. 81-26W (D. Iowa 1982), text with note 9, chapter 2.

85. *See* Wood v. Strickland, 420 U.S. 308 (1975).

86. Cantwell v. Connecticut, 310 U.S. 296, 303-4 (1940).

87. 406 U.S. 205 (1972).

88. *Id.* at 214.

89. *See generally* Chester Nolte, "Home Instruction in Lieu of Public School Attendance," in *School Law in Changing Times*, ed. M. A. McGhehey (Topeka, Kans.: National Organization on Legal Problems of Education, 1982), pp. 11-12; Martha McCarthy and Nelda Cambron, *Public School Law: Teachers' and Students' Rights* (Boston: Allyn and Bacon, 1981), chapters 8-11.

90. Wisconsin v. Yoder, 406 U.S. 205, 245 (Douglas, J., dissenting).

91. John Moore, "The Supreme Court and the Relationship Between the 'Establishment' and 'Free Exercise' Clauses," *Texas Law Review* 42 (1963):196.

92. Abington Township v. Schempp, 374 U.S. 203, 247 (1963) (Brennan, J. concurring). *See also* Widmar v. Vincent, 102 S. Ct. 269 (1981); text with note 45, chapter 2.

93. *See* Choper, "The Religion Clauses," pp. 690-91.

94. *See* text with note 51, chapter 2.

95. Lemon v. Kurtzman, 403 U.S. 602, 612 (1971).

96. David Tavel, *Church-State Issues in Education*, Fastback 123 (Bloomington, Ind.: Phi Delta Kappa, 1979), p. 1.

Chapter Two

Religious Observances and Activities in Public Schools

T he Bible was one of the primary instructional tools in colonial American classrooms. While the introduction of other curricular materials eventually eliminated the necessity to rely on the Bible, religious materials and observances (primarily Protestant) retained a place in many public school classrooms through the mid-twentieth century. Routinized devotional activities in public schools were particularly common in the South and Northeast. Following the lead of the U.S. Supreme Court under Chief Justice Warren, in the 1960s the judiciary assumed a more assertive posture in protecting public school students from religious indoctrination. However, many controversial issues remain as to what constitutes permissible religious accommodations in contrast to unconstitutional advancement of religious beliefs in public education.

This chapter focuses on judicial interpretations of free exercise rights and establishment clause prohibitions in connection with devotional observances and activities in public schools. Specifically, the following topics are addressed: Bible reading and prayer, student religious clubs, the distinction between teaching *about* religion and *instilling* religious beliefs, religious holiday observances, the display of religious symbols, the wearing of religious garb, religious activities in connection with graduation exercises, and the distribution of religious literature.

Bible Reading and Prayer

The constitutionality of prayer and Bible reading in public schools generated conflicting state court rulings during the latter nineteenth and early twentieth centuries.[1] Although such devotional activities were judicially banned in several states, prayer and Bible reading were a regular part of opening exercises in many of this nation's public schools until 1962. That year, in *Engel* v. *Vitale*, the Supreme Court struck down the daily recitation over the school public address system of a prayer composed by the New York Board of Regents. The Court declared that the "the constitutional prohibition against laws respecting an establishment of religion must at least mean that in this country it is no part of the business of government to compose official prayers for any group of American people to recite as a part of a religious program carried on by government."[2] The Court further noted that the voluntary participation of students did not reduce the constitutional infirmity; "the indirect coercive pressure upon religious minorities to conform to the prevailing officially approved religion is plain."[3]

The following year, in *Abington Township* v. *Schempp*, the Supreme Court invalidated Bible reading in public school classrooms and reiterated that *state sponsorship* of devotional activities, irrespective of the voluntary nature of participation, abridges the establishment clause of the First Amendment.[4] Rejecting the assertion that a brief reading from the Bible poses a relatively minor encroachment on First Amendment freedoms, the Court observed that "the breach of neutrality that is today a trickling stream may all too soon become a raging torrent."[5]

Despite the Supreme Court's strong statements in *Engel* and *Schempp*, there was widespread resistance to the judicially imposed ban on prayer and Bible reading in public education.[6] In some situations educators openly defied the Court's mandate or attempted to comply with the letter, but not the intent, of the prohibition. Some school districts retained prayers, while removing references to God or Jesus from the verses. For example, in 1966 the federal judiciary was called upon to address the constitutionality of an Illinois school district's practice of having kindergarten students say the following verse prior to their morning snack each day:

> We thank you for the flowers so sweet;
> We thank you for the food we eat;
> We thank you for the birds that sing;
> We thank you for everything.

The federal district court concluded that the verse was not religious, and therefore its use was permissible under the establishment clause. However, the Seventh Circuit Court of Appeals disagreed. Even though the reference to God had been eliminated from the last line, the appellate court concluded that the verse constituted a prayer and its daily recitation abridged the First Amendment.[7]

Current practices may not be consistent with the law, but the law is clear in that state-imposed prayer in public schools (even though nondenominational and with voluntary participation) violates the establishment clause. Indeed, if school authorities sanction such devotional activities, teachers and students may have a valid basis to secure damages for the impairment of their clearly established rights.[8] In a recent Iowa case, a teacher was successful in obtaining $300 in damages for "emotional distress" resulting from exposure to prayers led by the principal during school assemblies.[9]

Engel and *Schempp* left little doubt that if public school teachers or administrators read the Bible or recite prayers to students, they do so in contravention of the First Amendment.[10] However, the Supreme Court rulings in the early 1960s left several issues unresolved. Can public schools provide a daily period for silent prayer or student-initiated overt prayer? Can student religious clubs hold meetings that are partly devotional in public schools? Does the free exercise clause require such accommodations or does the establishment clause forbid them? What constitutes the appropriate governmental neutrality toward religion in this domain? These questions have generated a substantial body of litigation, and to date, only partial answers have been provided.

There is general agreement that individuals have a free exercise right to pray silently in public schools, and in other forums for that matter. In fact, it would be difficult—if not impossible—to place constraints on silent prayer or even to monitor whether such silent devotionals were taking place. However, if an individual disrupts the school program (e.g., elects to pray silently instead of taking an examination), school authorities would be justified in placing restrictions on the time and place—but not content—of silent devotionals.

Many states, by law, permit a designated period of daily silent meditation in public schools. Indiana law is typical in providing that public school teachers (if so directed by the school board) must conduct a brief period of meditation at the opening of each school day.[11] As long as students are not instructed to pray, courts in general have accepted that the practice of starting the school day with a moment of silent reflection has a secular purpose in that it calms students.

However, laws calling for a period of silent meditation *or prayer* have generated conflicting judicial rulings. In 1976 a Massachusetts federal district court upheld such a statute as having an incidental relationship to religion because students remain free to have secular or sectarian thoughts during the period of silence.[12] But similar laws authorizing a period of silent meditation or prayer in public schools have recently been struck down in Alabama, Tennessee, and New Mexico as masking a legislative intent to establish daily prayer in public education.[13] Recognizing that meditation per se is not barred from public schools, the courts found that the purpose of the contested laws was to encourage students not only to remain silent, but also to pray.

Even more controversial has been the legality of various types of *overt* student-initiated devotional activities. In 1965, two years after the *Schempp* decision, the Second Circuit Court of Appeals rejected an assertion by parents that the First Amendment *requires* a state to allow student-initiated prayers in public schools.[14] But the appeals court did not address whether the establishment clause *permits* such activities. Thus, there have been numerous efforts at both state and local school district levels to permit various types of student-initiated prayer. These efforts are not surprising since national polls have indicated that a majority of Americans favor some type of prayer in public education.[15]

Most of the courts that have addressed the constitutionality of student-initiated devotional activities have not allowed the practices.[16] For example, in 1971 the Massachusetts high court struck down a school committee's resolution making time available for religious observances prior to the start of school.[17] The court held that the voluntary participation of teachers and students in the devotional activities was immaterial; the fact that they were conducted under the auspices of the public school violated the establishment clause. More recently, the same court invalidated a Massachusetts statute that would have allowed a daily period for overt prayer led by student volunteers in public schools.[18] The Court rejected the contention that having students conduct the devotionals would eliminate school sponsorship of the religious activities.

The U.S. Supreme Court has not yet rendered an opinion on the constitutionality of student-initiated voluntary prayer. However, late in 1981 it declined to review an Arizona case in which the Ninth Circuit Court of Appeals struck down a public school's attempt to permit student-initiated prayers in school assemblies.[19] Also, early in 1982 the Supreme Court affirmed, without an opinion, a decision of the Fifth Circuit Court of Appeals in which a Louisiana voluntary prayer law was invalidated.[20] Since the Supreme Court was not inclined to overturn either appellate decision, it might be inferred from these cases that voluntary student-initiated prayer in public schools runs afoul of the establishment clause.

In the Ninth Circuit case, *Collins* v. *Chandler Unified School District*, school officials had given permission to the student council to open assemblies (attended on a voluntary basis) with a prayer selected by a student member. School authorities argued that their action constituted a reasonable accommodation to the students' exercise of religious beliefs, rather than impermissible school sponsorship of devotional activities. They asserted that the school must make such an accommodation to satisfy the "benevolent neutrality" demanded by the First Amendment. However, the federal judiciary disagreed. Applying the tripartite test, the federal district court concluded that the practice did not have a secular purpose, served to advance religion, and created excessive entanglement because of the teacher involvement required during the assemblies. Thus, the court permanently enjoined school officials from "permitting, authorizing, or condoning the saying of public prayers" by students at school assemblies.[21]

Affirming the lower court's holding, the Ninth Circuit Court of Appeals declared that there is "no meaningful distinction between school authorities actually organizing the religious activities and officials merely 'permitting' students to direct the exercises."[22] The appeals court noted that all students must either listen to the prayer or forego an opportunity to attend a major school function: "It is difficult to conceive how this choice would not coerce a student wishing to be part of the social mainstream, and, thus, advance one group's religious beliefs."[23]

The Fifth Circuit case involved a Louisiana law that allowed a daily period of one minute for a student-led prayer, or in the absence of a student volunteer, a teacher-led prayer. The federal district court upheld the law as a legitimate accommodation to religion, but the appellate court reversed the decision. Recognizing prayer as the "quintessential religious practice for many of the world's faiths," the federal appeals court reasoned that the law did not have a secular purpose and served to advance religion.[24] A few months later the appeals court reiterated this reasoning in striking down a Texas school district's voluntary prayer policy under the establishment clause.[25]

Despite these rulings, state legislatures continue to consider, and even enact, voluntary prayer bills. For example, an Alabama law calling for voluntary overt prayer in public schools was passed in 1982 and immediately was challenged under the First Amendment. In January 1983, the federal district court judge gained national attention by upholding the law and declaring that the Supreme Court has misinterpreted the establishment clause as applying to state action.[26] Earlier, when the judge enjoined implementation of the prayer statute pending a review of the case, he emphasized that verbal prayer is constitutionally protected speech, subject only to time, place, and manner restrictions. He declared that "a student or teacher should be able to pray at school whenever it would be permissible for him to speak."[27] The Eleventh Circuit Court of Appeals disagreed and struck down the law as advancing religion in clear violation of the establishment clause.

Efforts to secure legislation allowing prayer in public education have not been confined to the state level. There also has been substantial federal activity in this regard. In April 1979 the Senate rejected an amendment to the bill establishing the Department of Education that would have prohibited the federal judiciary from banning voluntary prayer periods in public schools.[28] The following year the Senate passed a bill that included a provision prohibiting federal courts from reviewing challenges to voluntary prayer in public schools and buildings.[29] Although this measure died in the House Judiciary Subcommittee, which held seven public hearings but did not report the bill, pro-prayer forces in Congress have not given up. In 1981 and 1982, riders to bills were introduced that would prohibit the use of federal funds to challenge programs of voluntary school prayer and limit federal court jurisdiction in this domain.[30] While such measures have not yet been enacted into law, congressional activity in this arena seems destined to continue.

President Reagan has also made his position clear that voluntary prayer should be allowed in public education. In a White House ceremony marking National Prayer Day in May 1982 he announced a proposed constitutional amendment to allow school prayer, and thus "reawaken America's religious and moral heart."[31] The proposed amendment, which has been introduced in Congress by Senator Strom Thurmond of South Carolina, provides: "Nothing in this Constitution shall be construed to prohibit individual or group prayer in public schools or other public institutions. No person shall be required by the United States or by àny State to participate in prayer."[32]

Since the proposed amendment merely would remove federal constitutional prohibitions against overt prayer in public schools, it still would allow states to bar such devotional activities. George Will has asserted that the adoption of the amendment would not settle the dispute over school prayer, but would instead relocate the argument: "All 50 states, or perhaps all 3,041 county governments, or perhaps all 16,214 school districts would have to decide whether to have 'voluntary prayer'."[33] It seems likely that most school boards would elect to reinstitute prayer in public schools if given such an option, with the prayers selected reflecting the dominant religion of each community.[34]

The proposed amendment has elicited praise from the Moral Majority and the Southern Baptist Convention[35] but has drawn criticism from many religious groups. In New York, for example, six religious organizations including the National Council of Churches and the American Jewish Congress issued a statement denouncing the amendment. The statement declared that religion "does not need, and should not have, the sponsorship or support of government."[36] Furthermore, the statement warned that "experience teaches us that efforts to introduce religious practices into public schools generate the very irreligious tension and conflict that the First Amendment was designed to prevent."[37]

Although the proposed amendment did not come to a vote in Congress in 1982, President Reagan has indicated that he will continue to press for adoption of the amendment. Since Congress must approve the provision, which then must be ratified by 38 states before becoming part of the Constitution, lengthy and volatile public debate on the measure seems imminent. If such an amendment is adopted, the Supreme Court will be faced with the awesome task of reconciling its provisions with the establishment clause of the First Amendment.[38]

Student Religious Clubs

Many public high schools permit student clubs to hold meetings in classrooms after school hours or at a scheduled period during the school day. A relatively unlitigated issue involves the constitutionality of using public schools for such meetings if the advancement of religious values is among the purposes of the student organization.[39] Organizations such as the Fellowship of Christian Athletes and youth groups sponsored by the Young Men's Christian Association (YMCA) and Young Women's Christian Association (YWCA) often are among student groups that have been allowed to hold meetings in public high schools. Since these clubs have secular as well as religious purposes, it might be assumed that as long as the school-related functions are purely secular, the establishment clause is not implicated. However, because these clubs purport to advance Christian beliefs, it might be argued that the public school is placing its stamp of approval on particular religious beliefs by permitting the groups to use school facilities. In the absence of judicial rulings to the contrary, it seems likely that many school districts will continue to allow such clubs to meet in public schools.

An issue that has been litigated on several occasions involves the constitutionality of student religious clubs holding devotional meetings in public school facilities. Unlike YMCA and YWCA groups, these student religious clubs do not claim that they have a secular as well as religious purpose; their primary aim is to advance sectarian beliefs. To date, the judiciary has not allowed such religious clubs to hold meetings under the auspices of the public school.[40]

In 1981 the United States Supreme Court declined to review a case, *Brandon* v. *Board of Education of Guilderland Central School District*, in which the Second Circuit Court of Appeals upheld a school board's action barring a student religious group from holding prayer meetings in a high school classroom before the opening of school.[41] Student members of the club challenged the board's decision as impairing their free speech and association, free exercise, and equal protection rights. The federal district court, and subsequently appellate court, rejected all three assertions.

The district court observed that, in the abstract, a policy permitting any student group to use school facilities might be grounded in the legitimate secular purpose of encouraging extracurricular activities. However, the court reasoned that the use of public school property for prayer meetings, even though restricted to before school hours, "would have the fatal primary effect of advancing religion both by the use of tax-supported property for religious purposes and the appearance created of State support for the dissemination of religious doctrine."[42] The court also concluded that such a practice would involve excessive governmental entanglement with religion. The court noted that despite the fact that the prayer meetings were to be planned and conducted by students, school authorities would have to provide some supervision for the meetings.

Regarding the students' claim that their free speech and association rights were impaired by the board's action, the court reasoned that the right to assemble and express religious points of view is limited by overriding establishment clause considerations in public school settings. The court further held that the school's refusal to allow the prayer meetings did not abridge equal protection rights because the Fourteenth Amendment does not require that a religious organization be treated in the same manner as other student groups.

Affirming the lower court's holding, the Second Circuit Court of Appeals declared that the First Amendment does not require—or even allow—such an accommodation to the exercise of religious beliefs. The court noted that public high school students have access to community religious facilities and can engage in group prayer meetings away from campus before or after school. Moreover, the court held that even if the students' free exercise rights were minimally impaired, there was a compelling state interest in "removing from the school any indication of sponsoring religious activity," which justified denying the use of public school facilities for the prayer meetings.[43] Even the "symbolic inference" that the "state has placed its imprimatur on a particular religious creed" is "too dangerous to permit."[44] The appeals court declared that while public school students have free expression rights, these rights do not extend to the expression of religious views.

The week before declining to review the *Brandon* case, the U.S. Supreme Court rendered an opinion in *Widmar* v. *Vincent*, which involved the constitutionality of student religious groups holding meetings on college campuses.[45] In *Widmar*, the federal district court had endorsed the University of Missouri-Kansas City (UMKC) policy barring student religious groups from holding devotional meetings in university facilities. The court's rationale was quite similar to that espoused by both the district and appellate courts in *Brandon*.[46] However, the Eighth Circuit Court of Appeals reversed the decision, thereby invalidating the university's policy. Subsequently, the Supreme Court affirmed the Eighth Circuit ruling, resting its opinion on free speech rights. A comparison of the Supreme Court's reasoning in *Widmar* with the Second Circuit Appellate Court's reasoning in *Brandon* suggests that application of First Amendment freedoms is different in institutions of higher education than in public elementary and secondary schools.

The Supreme Court held that college campuses constitute an open forum and that any infringement on student access to this forum to express views—including religious views—must be justified by a compelling state interest. The university's distinction between permissible speech "about" religion and impermissible religious worship was rejected as "judicially unmanageable."[47] Finding no compelling justification for the content-based distinction among types of speech, the Court concluded that student religious clubs must be allowed to hold meetings in UMKC facilities.

Acknowledging that compliance with establishment clause prohibitions constitutes a compelling state interest, the Supreme Court concluded that a neutral policy, allowing *all* student groups the same access to campus facilities, would withstand the tripartite test. Such an equal access policy has a secular purpose, neither advances nor inhibits religion, and avoids excessive governmental entanglement with religion. Rejecting the assertion that an equal access policy would "confer any imprimatur of State approval on religious sects or practices," the Court reiterated the appellate court's conclusion that such a policy "'would no more commit the University . . . to religious goals,' than it is 'now committed to the goals of the Students for a Democratic Society, the Young Socialist Alliance,' or any other groups eligible to use its facilities."[48] Even if religious groups should gain some benefits from an equal access policy, the enjoyment of mere "incidental" benefits was not found to violate the establishment clause. The Supreme Court declared that UMKC's interest in achieving *greater* separation of church and state than required by establishment clause prohibitions "is limited by the Free Exercise Clause and in this case by the Free Speech Clause as well."[49]

Several factors distinguish institutions of higher education from elementary and secondary schools, which perhaps explain the judiciary's differential application of establishment clause prohibitions. There are obvious differences in the respective students as to their maturity and vulnerability to indoctrination. The Supreme Court has noted on several occasions that college students are less impressionable than younger pupils, and therefore less stringent application of establishment clause restrictions may be necessary.[50] In addition, the decision to pursue higher education is voluntary, whereas elementary and at least part of secondary schooling is compulsory in all states. Also, public elementary and secondary students have ample opportunity to exercise their religious beliefs away from school, whereas college students often reside on campus, which then becomes their total community. Furthermore, less faculty involvement is required in supervising student organizations on college campuses than in elementary and secondary schools.

Since the Supreme Court found no establishment clause violation in *Widmar*, it avoided the issue of whether free speech and free exercise or establishment clause considerations should prevail when in conflict. However, it might be inferred from the Court's opinion that the protection of students' free expression rights is the overriding concern in institutions of higher education. As long as religious worship involves expression, it enjoys free speech protection, at least on state-supported college campuses. To reconcile *Widmar* with the appellate court's reasoning in *Brandon*, one must assume that a double standard exists. A distinction between religious expression and other types of speech is *required* by the establishment clause in public secondary schools,[51] but a content distinction among types of speech *cannot* be made for college students.

In future litigation, proponents of voluntary prayer periods in public schools will likely rely on *Widmar* in asserting that pupils have a free speech right to engage in devotional activities.[52] The Supreme Court has recognized that high school as well as college students have a constitutional right to express their views in a nondisruptive manner;[53] thus, it might be argued that religious expression, like other forms of speech, deserves protection in public schools as well as on college campuses. If the Supreme Court should adopt the logic that speech cannot be distinguished on the basis of content in public education, the impact would be significant. Justice White, dissenting in *Widmar*, pointed out that "apart from its content, a prayer is indistinguishable from a biology lesson."[54] He further asserted that by eliminating the distinction between religious worship and other protected speech, "the Religion Clauses would be emptied of any independent meaning in circumstances in which religious practice took the form of speech."[55]

Under such a precedent, it would appear that any type of student-initiated devotional activities—as long as they involve expression—would be protected by the free speech clause. While the Supreme Court has not yet endorsed this reasoning in connection with elementary and secondary schools, it seems likely that it will be called upon to clarify the application of its *Widmar* ruling beyond university settings. Of course, this issue will become moot if the proposed constitutional amendment, allowing voluntary prayer in public schools, becomes part of the U.S. Constitution.

The Fine Line Between Teaching About Religion and Teaching Religious Beliefs

Because teachers have a captive audience in public schools, their actions have been carefully scrutinized to ensure that the classroom is not used as a forum to indoctrinate religious beliefs. Choper has noted that the academic study of religion cannot "take the form of teaching 'that religion is sacred' nor present religious dogma as factual material."[56] The establishment clause prohibits teachers from using their position of authority to influence students' freedom of religious or conscientious choice.

In an early case, the Iowa Supreme Court invalidated an arrangement whereby public school students were subjected to sectarian instruction conducted by Catholic nuns. The Court stated:

> If there is any one thing which is well settled in the policies and purposes of the American people as a whole, it is the fixed and unalterable determination that there shall be an absolute and unequivocal separation of church and state, and that our public school system . . . shall not be used directly or indirectly for religious instruction, and above all that it shall not be made an instrumentality of proselytizing influence in favor of any religious organization, sect, creed, or belief.[57]

More recently the New Mexico Supreme Court similarly enjoined Catholic nuns from using their position as public school teachers to proselytize students.[58]

In several cases teachers have been dismissed for crossing the line from teaching about religion to proselytization. For example, a New York tenured teacher was dismissed based on evidence that she had tried to recruit students to join her religious organization.[59] Moreover, she had conducted prayer sessions in her office, offered to transport pupils to religious meetings, and used her classroom to promote the tenets of her religious faith. The New York appeals court concluded that such actions were in clear violation of the establishment clause and constituted valid grounds for dismissing the teacher.

In an Indiana case, a professor at a state university was dismissed for insisting on reading the Bible aloud at the beginning of his classes.[60] When instructed to stop the practice, he refused, asserting a free exercise right to engage in the activity. The Indiana appeals court rejected this assertion and upheld dismissal. The court emphasized that the professor was not discharged because of his *beliefs* but rather because of his unconstitutional *acts*.[61] Although the state was not a direct participant in the professor's devotional activities during class, the court concluded that the state had placed the individual in his position of authority and would be guilty of violating the establishment clause if the religious observances were allowed to continue.

In a recent Pennsylvania case, a state court upheld the dismissal of a public school teacher for refusing to comply with the superintendent's directives to cease religious activities in the classroom.[62] Evidence substantiated that the teacher had been opening both morning and afternoon sessions of his fourth-grade class with the Lord's Prayer and a Bible story. After parental complaints, he did excuse two students who objected to the activities and eventually eliminated the afternoon devotionals. However, he continued to say a prayer in the morning and read a story from the Bible. The teacher was warned several times to stop such conduct and, upon refusal, was terminated. He contested his dismissal on free exercise grounds, and the court held that a public school teacher's right to free exercise of religion does not give him the right to conduct religious activities in the classroom. The court noted: "It is well established that the freedom to hold religious beliefs is absolute; conduct in consequence of such beliefs, however, may be regulated or even prohibited by the state in the interest of peace, order, and tranquility in society."[63] An individuals use of the "power, prestige, and influence" of his position as a public school teacher to lead devotional activities is clearly proscribed by the establishment clause.[64]

Teachers also cannot advance their religious beliefs by selectively disregarding aspects of the state-prescribed curriculum that conflict with their sectarian values. For example, a Chicago kindergarten teacher was dismissed for refusing to teach patriotic topics.[65] The teacher, who interpreted literally the Biblical prohibition against worshiping graven images, refused to teach about the American flag, the observance of patriotic holidays, and the importance of various historical leaders such as Abraham Lincoln. She asserted a free exercise right to omit such instruction, which she alleged was tantamount to idolatry. Upholding the dismissal, the Seventh Circuit Court of Appeals noted that although the teacher enjoys freedom to believe, she has "no constitutional right to require others to submit to her views and to forego a portion of their education they would otherwise be entitled to enjoy."[66] The court further recognized that if all teachers were allowed to design their own curriculum based on their personal beliefs, students would receive a "distorted and unbalanced view" of history.[67]

While it is unconstitutional to proselytize students in public schools, it is permissible to teach the Bible and other religious documents from a literary, cultural, or historical perspective. Indeed, if no mention of religion were allowed in public schools, an accurate portrayal of historical events would not be possible. For example, it would be difficult to teach about the settlement of Florida or the Southwest without including the significant role played by Spanish Catholic missions. When the Supreme Court banned daily Bible reading from public schools, it emphasized that the academic study of religion was not being invalidated. Justice Clark stated for the majority:

[I]t might well be said that one's education is not complete without a study of comparative religion or the history of religion and its relation-

31

ship to the advancement of civilization. It certainly may be said that the Bible is worthy of study for its literary and historic qualities. Nothing we have said here indicates that such study of the Bible, or of religion, when presented objectively as part of a secular program of education, may not be effected consistently with the First Amendment.[68]

In a concurring opinion, Justice Brennan also noted that "it would be impossible to teach meaningfully many subjects in the social sciences or humanities without some mention of religion."[69]

However, the line between teaching *about* religion and teaching religious tenets is not always clear. Religion is considered an important aspect of American life and is often emphasized in history and literature courses. J. V. Panoch has observed that "a school may sponsor a study of what is practiced but may not sponsor a practice of what is studied."[70] In conveying information about the past and present religious influences in society, educators will move into forbidden territory if they present particular religious values in an indoctrinative manner.

Courses that purportedly focus on the academic study of religion also cannot be used as a ploy to advance sectarian beliefs. In 1981 the Fifth Circuit Court of Appeals struck down an Alabama school district's elective course in Bible literature as having the primary effect of advancing religious doctrine in violation of the establishment clause.[71] The court concluded from the evidence that the course was not restricted to the literary and historical study of the Bible as claimed. Instead, it consisted of instruction presented from a fundamentalist Christian perspective. The school district was enjoined from teaching the course in its present form and prohibited from using the text, *The Bible for Youthful Patriots*, in any future courses that might be developed.

Other Bible study courses also have generated litigation, and courts have been asked to provide guidelines for permissible instruction in this area. A Tennessee federal district court invalidated two Bible Study programs offered in the Chattanooga and Hamilton County elementary schools, concluding that the programs served to advance the Christian religion rather than to expand students' awareness of religion from a historical or literary perspective.[72] The school boards were enjoined from teaching the courses, pending proof that the indoctrinative features of the courses had been removed. The court held that for the courses to withstand constitutional scrutiny, materials could not be selected by the evangelical Bible Study Committee, and materials fostering particular religious beliefs would have to be eliminated. Furthermore, minimum standards for selection of the teachers of such courses would have to be established, and nonschool personnel could not participate in the selection, training, or supervision of the instructors. After school officials submitted revised plans for the courses, they were allowed to implement the programs for one year, at which time the court reviewed tapes of the sessions.[73] Based on the evidence in the tapes, the federal district court endorsed the revised city program but enjoined continuation of the county program, reasoning that the latter still conveyed a religious rather than academic message in violation of the establishment clause.[74]

In a West Virginia school district, weekly classes purportedly teaching public school students about religion similarly were challenged as advancing the Christian faith.[75] Instructors for the classes were not school district employees but were members of the Weekday Religious Education Council. Students, whose parents had not signed permission cards, were placed in study halls in lieu of the religious instruction. The federal district court observed that the excusal provision suggested that the instruction was more indoctrinative than academic. It reasoned that if the instruction were actually *about* religion, all children could be expected to participate as part of their regular instructional program. Enjoining the school district from continuing the religious instruction, the court indicated that the classes could be redesigned (i.e., using public school teachers and eliminating indoctrination) to withstand constitutional scrutiny.

A course in the Old and New Testament was the source of controversy in a Utah school district. The course was part of the school's released-time program for students to receive religious instruction at a nearby Mormon seminary. The released-time program was not at issue, but the award of high school credit to students taking the course was attacked under the establishment clause. The federal district court and subsequently the Eighth Circuit Court of Appeals held that the arrangement in which credit was granted for the secular aspects of the course necessitated excessive governmental entanglement with religion in violation of the establishment clause.[76]

Some question the "tenuous" assumption that schools can actually distinguish teaching religious beliefs from teaching *about* religion.[77] In a comparative study of religions, there may be a tendency to emphasize a particular faith or to discount the légitimacy of minority sects. Moreover, courses that can withstand establishment clause scrutiny might still implicate free exercise rights. For example, courses pertaining to the Bible as literature, to remain academic, would likely entail subjecting the scriptures to usual literary criticism. This might offend some students who believe that the Bible is sacred and should be interpreted literally.

Bible study courses have not been the only source of controversy; the school's role in teaching moral values has also been subject to assertions that the state is unconstitutionally instilling particular sectarian beliefs. It is generally agreed that public schools do attempt to transmit certain values such as honesty, self-control, brotherhood, responsibility, and respect for authority. However, since many of these values are also fundamental teachings of specific religions, the distinction between moral education and religious education is sometimes ambiguous.

Choper has reasoned that certain recognized values "are common to all segments of our society, irrespective of religious faith or philosophic school" and can be taught through nonsectarian means.[78] Also, in 1963 Supreme

Court Justice Brennan observed that it "has not been shown that readings from the speeches and messages of great Americans, for example, or from the documents of our heritage of liberty," cannot accomplish the purpose of teaching moral values without relying on sectarian materials.[79] But more troublesome issues are raised by claims that such a nonreligious approach to values advances the antitheistic faith of secular humanism in violation of the establishment clause.[80] Courses pertaining to values clarification and similar topics have been vulnerable to this charge. Thus, public schools appear to be caught in the crossfire between the competing assertions that values taught from a traditional religious perspective as well as values taught from a nontheistic viewpoint abridge First Amendment freedoms.

Religious Holiday Observances

As with many of the topics discussed in this chapter, controversies over religious holiday observances in public schools illustrate the tension between the free exercise and establishment clauses. Is the observance of religious holidays in public schools permissible—or perhaps even required—to accommodate the free exercise of beliefs? Or are such observances prohibited as an unconstitutional advancement of religion? Can such holidays be observed from a cultural and historical rather than religious perspective?

The Supreme Court has not given clear answers to these questions, and until recently lower courts had provided little guidance in this arena. However, in 1980 the Eighth Circuit Court of Appeals upheld a school board's policy allowing religious holiday observances in public schools, and the Supreme Court declined to review the decision.[81] While no court has *required* schools to engage in such activities, at least one federal appellate court has *permitted* school districts to do so.

This case, *Florey* v. *Sioux Falls School District*, involved a dispute that started in 1977 when two kindergarten classes presented a Christmas assembly for parents. One of the most controversial aspects of the program was a Christmas quiz in which the students responded to questions about the birth of Christ and the meaning of Christmas. After complaints about this program and other Christmas assemblies, the school board adopted a policy and regulations concerning the observance of religious holidays. The policy stipulates that one of the school district's "educational goals is to advance the students' knowledge and appreciation of the role that our religious heritage has played in the social, cultural and historical development of civilization."[82] Rules designed pursuant to this policy provide in part that: 1) holidays with both a religious and secular basis can be observed; 2) religious music, art, literature and drama can be used in the curriculum and at school-sponsored functions "if presented in a prudent and objective manner;" and 3) religious symbols that are part of a religious holiday can be displayed temporarily as a teaching aid.

Several students and parents challenged the policy and rules as unconstitutionally advancing religion because they allow the singing of songs such as "Silent Night" and "Joy to the World" and the display of symbols such as the Nativity scene. Applying the tripartite test to the controversial guidelines, the federal district court, and subsequently Eighth Circuit Court of Appeals, found no establishment clause violation. The appeals court reasoned that the policy and rules have the secular purpose of improving the overall instructional program. As to the second test, the court acknowledged that it would be "literally impossible to develop a public school curriculum that did not in some way affect the religious or nonreligious sensibilities of some of the students or their parents."[83] Concluding, however, that school authorities must only ensure that the *primary* effect of their action neither advances nor impedes religion, the court held that the board policy meets this standard. The court noted that the Christmas quiz formerly used in the district "exceeded constitutional bounds" and would not be permitted under the board's new rules.[84]

In rejecting the contention that the policy and rules foster excessive governmental entanglement with religion, the appellate court reasoned that they have the opposite effect in that they "provide the means to ensure that the district steers clear of religious exercises."[85] The court also was not persuaded that the policy impairs free exercise rights. Noting that students may be excused from the activities if they choose, the court recognized that schools are not "compelled to sift out of their teaching" everything that might be objectionable to some segment of the school population.[86]

The appellate court broadly interpreted the permissible "study" of religion as including the "objective" observance of religious holidays. It concluded that much of the art, literature, and music associated with Christmas has acquired cultural importance that is no longer strictly religious. The court reiterated the federal district court's conclusion that without the opportunity to perform religious works which "have developed an independent secular and artistic significance," students might receive "a truncated view of our culture."[87]

While the majority opinion was endorsed by two members of the appellate panel, the third justice issued a strong dissent. He argued that the Christmas holiday has "no *inherent* secular basis" and that Christmas observances openly promote specific religious sects to the disadvantage of others: "Those persons who do not share those holidays are relegated to the status of outsiders by their own government; those persons who do observe those holidays can take pleasure in seeing . . . their belief given official sanction."[88]

The *Florey* decision did not provide a final resolution of the First Amendment issues associated with religious holiday observances in public schools.[89] Nonetheless, since the Supreme Court declined to review the appellate court's ruling, this case has been viewed by some as signaling a more permissive judicial attitude toward such religious activities in public education. While certain seasonal observances such as Santa Claus, evergreen trees, Frosty the Snowman, and colored Easter eggs have generally been accepted because of their incidental religious connotations, symbols and hymns tied more directly to sectarian doctrine may also be permissible under the *Florey* precedent.

Display of Religious Symbols

As with holiday observances, the line between permissible and impermissible activity is not always clear in regard to the display of religious symbols in public schools. There is general consensus that religious symbols can be displayed temporarily in a comparative religion course as long as the symbols are used for instructional purposes. However, the permanent display of symbols such as the Ten Commandments or the motto, "In God We Trust," has been more controversial.

In 1967 the New Hampshire Supreme Court concluded that a legislative resolution requiring a plaque with the phrase "In God We Trust" to be posted in all public educational institutions did not compromise First Amendment freedoms.[90] The court noted that the phrase has historical significance as a national motto and appears on coins, currency, and public buildings as well as in patriotic songs. The court reasoned that the phrase does not promote particular religious tenets and therefore does not respect the establishment of religion.

Until 1980 the constitutional status of posting the Ten Commandments in public schools was ambiguous, reflected by conflicting lower court opinions on this issue. A North Dakota federal district court struck down a statute requiring the posting of the Ten Commandments as lacking a secular purpose and advancing the Christian religion in violation of the establishment clause.[91] In contrast, a Kentucky trial court upheld a state law requiring the Ten Commandments to be posted in all public school classrooms.[92]

The latter case, *Stone* v. *Graham*, involved a statute enacted in 1978, which placed a duty on the Kentucky Superintendent of Public Instruction to ensure that a durable copy of the Ten Commandments, of set specifications, was displayed on the wall of all public school classrooms within the state. Each copy was to contain the following notation in small print at the bottom: "The secular application of the Ten Commandments is clearly seen in its adoption as the fundamental legal code of Western Civilization and the Common Law of the United States."[93] The law also stipulated that the copies were to be purchased through voluntary contributions made to the state treasury for that purpose. Upholding the constitutionality of the challenged law, the Kentucky trial court reasoned that the Ten Commandments contain a code of conduct which is appropriate for school children to learn regardless of their specific religious beliefs. The Kentucky Supreme Court justices split evenly on this issue, thereby leaving the trial court's holding intact.

In 1980 the U.S. Supreme Court in a five-to-four decision summarily reversed the Kentucky high court ruling, thereby invalidating the controversial law.[94] The Court rejected the trial court's conclusion that an "avowed secular purpose" suffices to satisfy the prohibition against establishing a religion.[95] The majority reasoned that the primary purpose for posting the Ten Commandments was plainly religious as three of the Commandments outline "religious duties of believers." The Court distinguished the impermissible posting of religious texts from the permissible use of religious literature in the study of history, civilization, and comparative literature. The majority found no educational rationale, but rather a sectarian purpose, for displaying the Ten Commandments. The effect, if any, of their posting would be "to induce the school children to read, meditate upon, perhaps to venerate and obey, the Commandments."[96] Neither the printed disclaimer on each copy nor the fact that the copies were financed by private contributions convinced the majority that the First Amendment infringement was minimized.

Yet, the Supreme Court decision did not immediately end the controversy in Kentucky. Although the state attorney general directed school officials to remove the copies of the Ten Commandments, some school districts refused, contending that the Supreme Court merely invalidated their *mandatory* posting. The Supreme Court was petitioned to clarify its ruling, but it declined to do so.[97] After school boycotts and threats to defy the state directive, most Kentucky school districts eventually removed the controversial posters. However, religious groups have not given up and have printed the Ten Commandments and the Lord's Prayer on the front and back of 40,000 folders to be given to students.[98] Thus, despite the Supreme Court ruling, the Ten Commandments may find their way into Kentucky Schools.

Teachers Wearing Religious Garb

The issue of a teacher's right to wear religious attire has generated conflicting court opinions. Most of the cases have involved the public school's employment of Catholic nuns who have asserted a right to wear distinctive habits associated with their religious order. They have argued that public employment should not be conditioned on attire in the absence of proselytization of students or sectarian teaching. Those challenging the wearing of religious garb by public school teachers have claimed that such attire creates a subtle religious influence on vulnerable children, who comprise a captive audience.

Several courts have concluded that the establishment clause is not abridged by public school employees wearing religious garb. In an early (1894) case, the Pennsylvania Supreme Court found no constitutional violation in connection with public school teachers wearing religious habits.[99] Also, the Supreme Court of North Dakota concluded that the wearing of religious attire by public school teachers does not present a threat of state advancement of religion because it does not involve sectarian teaching. The court noted: "Whether it is wise or unwise to regulate the style of dress to be worn by teachers in our public schools or to inhibit the wearing of dress or insignia indicating religious belief is not a matter for the courts to determine."[100] A Kentucky appellate court similarly reasoned that the wearing of religious garb or emblems does not violate the First Amendment.[101]

However, other courts have recognized the state's authority to enact legislation prohibiting public school teachers from wearing religious dress. For example, in response to the Pennsylvania Supreme Court decision mentioned above, the state legislature enacted a statute barring religious garb among public school teachers and imposing a fine on school board members in any school district permitting the practice. Upholding the constitutionality of the statute, the Pennsylvania Supreme Court reasoned that the right to wear religious garb is not "absolute and . . . free from legislative control."[102] The court further declared that a teacher's right "to clothe himself in whatever garb his taste, his inclination, the tenets of his sect, or even his religious sentiments may dictate is no more absolute than his right to give utterance to his sentiments, religious or otherwise."[103]

Similarly, the New York high court ruled in an early case that the state superintendent of instruction had the authority to forbid public school teachers from wearing religious garb.[104] The court reasoned that the prohibition was in accord with public policy of the state, and held that teachers refusing to stop wearing religious attire after sufficient notice would forfeit all rights to subsequent compensation under their contracts with the public school district. The New Mexico Supreme Court also upheld a state board of education resolution prohibiting religious attire, noting that "there can be little doubt" that the effect of religious garb worn by teachers in the presence of public school pupils "would be to inspire respect, if not sympathy, for the religious denomination to which they so manifestly belong."[105] The court concluded that the wearing of such attire creates a religious atmosphere and silently promulgates sectarianism in violation of public policy, even though it does not involve the teaching of denominational doctrine.[106]

While most litigation on this topic has taken place in state courts, in 1974 the Seventh Circuit Court of Appeals addressed the legality of teachers wearing religious attire in a public school that was housed in a facility that had formerly been a Catholic school.[107] The court upheld the lease arrangement that allowed the public school district to close an old inadequate high school and move the students into the modern facility leased from the Catholic diocese. However, the court ordered the removal of religious influences in the new environment, including the wearing of habits by nuns who were employed as public school teachers. The United States Supreme Court subsequently declined to review the appellate court's decision.

The law is clear that individuals cannot be denied public school employment because of their religious beliefs or their affiliation with a religious order, but the extent to which the state can control their attire while teaching in a public school remains somewhat ambiguous. From the litigation on this topic, it appears that the wearing of religious garb by public school personnel presents a minimal infringement of the establishment clause unless accompanied by other sectarian influences. However, several courts have recognized that states have the authority to implement policy by enacting legislation or regulations prohibiting public school teachers from wearing religious attire.

Religious Influences in Commencement Exercises

The judiciary has appeared more receptive toward baccalaureate services and prayers during the graduation ceremony than toward routinized devotional activities—even though student-initiated—in public schools. Unlike the assertion that religious holiday observances should be allowed in public schools because of their cultural and historical meaning, there is no contention that an invocation or baccalaureate service is instructional rather than religious. Instead, such activities are defended primarily because of their transient nature. Choper has observed that such one-time events, which are a small segment of the graduation program, pose a minimal threat of religious inculcation and make "fairly unpersuasive the 'stamp of approval' argument . . . advanced in connection with daily religious exercises in public schools."[108]

In 1973 a Pennsylvania federal district court upheld the constitutionality of an invocation and benediction delivered by a minister during the graduation ceremony. Distinguishing the challenged practices from daily devotional activities, the court noted that the former "are ceremonial and are in fact not a part of the formal, day-to-day routine of the school curriculum to which is attached compulsory attendance."[109] The court found no establishment clause violation in the ceremony's indirect and incidental benefit to religion. Since participation in the graduation program was voluntary, the alleged impairment of free exercise rights was also considered to be without merit. Plaintiffs subsequently brought suit in state court, and the Pennsylvania Supreme Court reiterated the reasoning of the federal district court in interpreting state constitutional religious protections as well as the First Amendment. The United States Supreme Court declined to review the latter decision.[110]

A Virginia federal district court similarly reasoned that the mere use of an invocation and benediction during the graduation ceremony lacks the "repetitive or pedagogical function of the exercises which characterized the school prayer cases."[111] Observing that "the measure of constitutional adjudication is the ability and willingness to distinguish between real threat and mere shadow,"[112] the court held that such fleeting devotionals in connection with graduation could not serve to inculcate students or to embroil the state in religious matters.

Baccalaureate services have also been judicially endorsed as presenting a minimal First Amendment infringement. For example, an Arkansas federal district court was not convinced that a voluntary baccalaureate service held on school premises on the weekend, with a member of the clergy speaking, posed a sufficient threat to First Amendment religious guarantees to justify judicial intervention.[113] Although conceding that baccaluareate programs are religious in nature, courts have reasoned that such activities, held only once a year after school hours and attended on a voluntary basis, cannot significantly influence students' religious beliefs or benefit sectarian institutions.

Courts have not clarified whether public school graduation exercises can be held in a church. For example, a Wisconsin federal district court noted that the establishment clause does not prohibit school officials from holding secular activities in religious facilities under all circumstances. But the court enjoined plans to hold the public school graduation ceremony in a Catholic church because some students had objected.[114] Acknowledging the importance of attending graduation exercises, the court reasoned that students should not be forced either to miss this function or to compromise their religious faith. The court found immaterial that students planned the ceremony and that only a few students objected to the proposed locale. However, after the ceremony was held, the Seventh Circuit Court of Appeals vacated the lower court's decision and remanded the case without an opinion.

In contrast to the Wisconsin federal district court, the New Mexico Supreme Court upheld a school board's decision to use church facilities for commencement activities.[115] Recognizing that churches offered the only space with sufficient seating capacity for the baccalaureate and commencement exercises, the court endorsed holding these functions respectively in Baptist and Presbyterian churches. The court reasoned that "the holding of these time honored programs in a building where all who desire to attend may be accommodated" provides justification for using church facilities for the activities.[116]

While some ambiguity surrounds the legality of holding the graduation ceremony in a church, the judiciary has rejected the assertion that the free exercise clause places an obligation on public school authorities to alter graduation exercises to accommodate particular religious beliefs of pupils. For example, two Orthodox Jewish students were unsuccessful in forcing a Virginia school board to change the day of the high school graduation ceremony to avoid the Jewish Sabbath.[117] In dismissing the suit, the federal district court reasoned that the free exercise clause does not require such an accommodation; moreover, the establishment clause does not *allow* school districts to alter school activities to cater to the varied religious beliefs of all their students.

Although there has not been extensive church-state litigation involving graduation exercises, in the reported cases the judiciary usually has rejected both free exercise and establishment clause challenges to graduation ceremonies. Courts have not been inclined to find that devotional activities associated with the ceremony abridge the establishment clause and have distinguished these single events from daily religious activities conducted under the auspices of the public school.

However, it is somewhat difficult to reconcile the judiciary's interpretation of establishment clause prohibitions in these cases with legal principles announced in other establishment clause litigation. For example, in disallowing student religious clubs to hold meetings in public school facilities, the judiciary has recognized that even the "hint" that the state has placed its stamp of approval on sectarian activities violates the establishment clause.[118] Surely the school board's decision to hold a baccalaureate service on an annual basis as an integral part of commencement exercises gives more than a hint of state endorsement of the religious nature of the event. Also, the fact that participation is voluntary, which has seemed important in sanctioning religious activities in connection with graduation, has been rejected as justification for other types of devotional activities in public schools.[119] If permissible prayer and religious services associated with commencement are distinguished from impermissible religious activities in the regular school program primarily because of the routinized nature of the latter, it would appear that periodic prayers in school assemblies could be similarly defended.

Distribution of Religious Literature

Many religious sects rely heavily on the distribution of printed materials to spread the tenets of their faith. It is not surprising that public schools, with their captive and impressionable audience, have often been the target of campaigns to distribute sectarian literature. To date, courts have not condoned this activity in public education, but the issue continues to generate legal controversy.

Most of the litigation involving the distribution of religious literature has focused on Gideon Bibles. In 1953 the New Jersey Supreme Court struck down a school district's policy allowing children with parental permission to report to a room at the close of school to receive Bibles furnished by the Gideon Society.[120] Despite the fact that only the children with such permission were present during the distribution, the court concluded from the testimony that there was indirect pressure on all students to participate. Reasoning that the practice served to advance a religious faith, the court struck down the activity under the establishment clause. The U.S. Supreme Court subsequently declined to review the case.

An Arkansas federal district court reached a similar conclusion in 1973 when it struck down a school board's policy allowing the Gideon Society to visit each elementary school annually and present a Gideon Bible to all fifth-grade students.[121] Rejecting as immaterial the argument that students were not required to accept the presentation, the court concluded that the action served to advance religion in violation of the establishment clause. The court also was not persuaded that the distribution was justified because the Bible is a proper book for study from a literary and historical perspective, reasoning that the version of the Bible distributed was designed to spread particular religious beliefs.

A few school cases have involved religious material other than Gideon Bibles. For example, parents contested the distribution of Presbyterian pamphlets in a New Mexico public school. School personnel did not actually distribute the pamphlets, but the material was made available in classrooms, and the supply was periodically replenished. The New Mexico Supreme Court enjoined the the practice as unconstitutionally advancing religion.[122] More recently, the Nebraska federal district court concluded that a school district could prohibit the distribution of sectarian literature in public schools even though it could not impose a blanket ban on the distribution of commercial literature.[123] Reasoning that the prohibition against religious material is required by the establishment clause, the court declared: "In no activity of the state is it more vital to keep out divisive forces than in its schools, to avoid confusing, not to say fusing, what the Constitution sought to keep strictly apart.[124]

In 1979 the U.S. Supreme Court declined to review a complicated Florida case, thus leaving the legal status of religious literature distribution somewhat ambiguous.[125] This case, spanning almost a decade of litigation, involved First Amendment challenges to a state law requiring educators to instill "Christian virtues" in school children and school board policies allowing the distribution of religious literature at designated places in public schools and daily "inspirational" Bible reading and prayer. The federal district court had dismissed the request for injunctive relief, concluding that the plaintiff students had not established that they were threatened with irreparable injury by the schools' practices. Also denying declaratory relief, the court noted that the school board had changed its policies to prohibit morning devotionals and the distribution of Gideon Bibles in schools, and that there was little likelihood of enforcement of the contested state statute.[126]

A panel of the Fifth Circuit Court of Appeals agreed with the trial court's denial of an injunction but concluded that the plaintiffs were entitled to declaratory relief. Noting that morning devotional activities were still being conducted in some schools and that the policy on distribution of religious literature had merely been tabled by the school board, the appellate panel ruled that both practices violate the establishment clause.[127] The panel also held that implementation of the "Christian virtue" statute abridges establishment clause prohibitions. However, upon rehearing before the full appellate court, only the prayer and Bible reading policy was declared invalid.[128] The trial court's denial of relief regarding the other two provisions was affirmed by an evenly divided appeals court. Thus, while all courts involved in the litigation indicated that the distribution of religious literature would violate the establishment clause, the final court order, which the Supreme Court declined to review, did not provide a declaration to this effect.

Conclusion

Traditionally, local school authorities had considerable latitude to design the public school program in conformance with the community's religious values. However, in the 1960s federal courts began playing a more active role in safeguarding constitutional freedoms, including religious liberties. For the past two decades the judiciary has addressed sensitive free exercise and establishment clause issues in assessing the constitutionality of a variety of religious observances and activities in public education.

In general, the courts have concluded that a minor infringement on the free exercise of religious beliefs in public school settings is justified by the over-riding interest in guarding against state-sponsorship of sectarian tenets. Accordingly, the proselytization of students and overt devotional activities have not been allowed in public education. However, the Supreme Court recently has not provided clear guidance in interpreting establishment clause prohibitions. It has declined to review many lower court decisions, thus leaving ambiguity as to its stance on some volatile First Amendment issues such as the constitutionality of religious holiday observances in public schools and student-initiated prayer meetings held before classes begin. The Court has acknowledged that the sharp division among its members on church-state issues may reflect a similar division among Americans in this domain.[129]

Some contend that minor religious accommodations in public education, such as a brief period of prayer, pose a minimal threat of establishing a state religion. But taken together, seemingly insignificant efforts to tailor the public school program to the tenets of the dominant faith may have profound implications for the rights of religious minorities. In 1963 Justice Clark warned that without vigilant judicial protection of religious freedoms, powerful sects "might bring about a fusion of governmental and religious functions or a concert or dependency of one upon the other to the end that official support of the State or Federal Government would be placed behind the tenets of one or of all orthodoxies."[130]

In the absence of strong Supreme Court directives, legislative bodies have become more assertive in proposing measures that strain the wall of separation between church and state. Efforts to reintroduce devotional activities in public schools and to restrict the curriculum in conformance with fundamentalist Christian beliefs have escalated in recent years, and political candidates increasingly have been forced to take positions on religious issues. In spite of the Supreme Court's caution that political divisiveness based on religion is one of the evils that the establishment clause is designed to guard against,[131] devotional activities in public schools have become the focal point of substantial political controversy.[132] With the proposed constitutional amendment to allow prayer in public education, continued political and judicial activity seems assured.[133]

Footnotes

1. Decisions upholding morning devotional activities in public schools included Lewis v. Board of Educ. of the City of New York, 285 N.Y.S. 164 (Sup. Ct., New York County, 1935); Hackett v. Brooksville Graded School Dist., 87 S.W. 792 (Ky. App. 1905); Billard v. Board of Educ. of City of Topeka, 76 P. 422 (Kan. 1904); Moore v. Monroe, 20 N.W. 475 (Iowa 1884); Donahoe v. Richards, 38 Me. 379 (1854). Decisions invalidating such activities included State *ex rel.* Finger v. Weedman, 226 N.W. 348 (S.D. 1929); Herold v. Parish Bd. of School Directors, 68 So. 116 (La. 1915); People *ex rel.* Ring v. Bd. of Educ. of Dist. 24, 92 N.E. 251 (Ill. 1910); State *ex rel.* Freeman v. Scheve, 91 N.W. 846 (Neb. 1902); State *ex rel.* Weiss v. District Bd. of School Dist. No. 8 of Edgerton, 44 N.W. 967 (Wis. 1890).

2. 370 U.S. 421, 425 (1962).

3. *Id.* at 431.

4. School Dist. of Abington Township v. Schempp, Murray v. Curlett, 374 U.S. 203 (1963).

5. *Id.* at 225.

6. *See* William Muir, *Law and Attitude Change* (Chicago: University of Chicago Press, 1973).

7. DeSpain v. DeKalb County Community School Dist., 255 F. Supp. 655 (N.D. Ill. 1966), *rev'd* 384 F.2d 836 (7th Cir. 1967), *cert. denied*, 390 U.S. 906 (1968).

8. In Wood v. Strickland, 420 U.S. 308 (1975), the Supreme Court announced that ignorance of clearly established law cannot be used as a defense under Section 1983 of the Civil Rights Act of 1871 for violating an individual's federal rights.

9. Abramson v. Anderson, No. 81-26W (D. Iowa 1982). The teacher also sought punitive damages, but the court concluded that punitive damages were not warranted in the absence of evidence that the principal's unlawful actions were motivated by malicious and wanton intent.

10. *See* Hall v. Board of School Comm'rs, 656 F.2d 999 (5th Cir. 1981); Mangold v. Albert Gallatin, 438 F.2d 1194 (3d Cir. 1971); text with notes 60, 62.

11. Ind. Code Ann § 20-10.1-7-11 (Burns). However, it should be noted that in January 1983, a New Jersey federal judge enjoined implementation of such a silent contemplation law, reasoning that it is likely to be found unconstitutional under the establishment clause. *See* May v. Cooperman, cited in *Education Daily*, 12 January 1983, p. 3.

12. Gaines v. Anderson, 421 F. Supp. 337 (D. Mass. 1976). *See also* Opinion of Justices, 307 A.2d 558 (N.H. 1973).

13. Jaffree v. Wallace, 705 F.2d 1526, 1535-36 (11th Cir. 1983); Duffy v. Las Cruces Public Schools, 557 F.Supp. 1013 (D.N.M. 1983); Beck v. McElrath, 548 F.Supp. 1161 (M.D. Tenn. 1982).

14. Stein v. Oshinsky, 348 F.2d 999 (2d Cir. 1965), *cert. denied*, 382 U.S. 957 (1965).

15. In national studies conducted at the University of Michigan it was reported that almost 75% of Americans favored public school prayer in both 1964 and 1968. *See* Walfred Peterson, *Thy Liberty in Law* (Nashville, Tenn.: Broadman Press, 1978), pp. 178-79. Studies conducted more recently indicate that a large majority of Americans continue to favor the reintroduction of prayer in public education. *See* Eugene Methvin, "Should Prayer be Restored to Our Public Schools?" *Reader's Digest*, September 1979, p. 88; George Will, "Opposing Prefab Prayer," *Newsweek*, 7 June 1982, p. 84.

16. However, in 1964 a Michigan federal district court upheld a public school program in which students met in a classroom before or after school to read scriptures or say a prayer of their choice. While endorsing the devotional activity, the court did prescribe some guidelines for school officials. Among other stipulations, the court held that the role of teachers in these voluntary devotional sessions must be confined to maintaining order and that no overt prayer or Bible reading could take place during the regular school day. Reed v. Van Hoven, 237 F. Supp. 48 (W.D. Mich. 1965).

17. Commissioner of Educ. v. School Committee of Leyden, 267 N.E.2d 226 (Mass. 1971). *See also* State Bd. of Educ. v. Board of Educ. of Netcong, 270 A.2d 412 (N.J. 1970).

18. Kent v. Commissioner of Educ., 402 N.E.2d 1340 (Mass. 1980). *See also* Opinion of the Justices to the House of Representatives, 440 N.E.2d 1159 (Mass. 1982).

19. Collins v. Chandler Unified School Dist., 470 F. Supp. 959 (D Ariz. 1979), *aff'd in part, rev'd in part*, 644 F.2d 759 (9th Cir. 1981), *cert. denied*, 102 S. Ct. 322 (1981).

20. Karen B. V. Treen, 653 F.2d 897 (5th Cir. 1981), *aff'd mem.*, 102 S. Ct. 1267 (1982).

21. Collins v. Chandler Unified School Dist., 470 F. Supp. 959, 964 (D. Ariz. 1979). *See also* Goodwin v. Cross County School Dist. No. 7, 394 F. Supp. 417 (E.D. Ark. 1973).

22. *Id.* Collins, 644 F.2d at 761. The appellate court affirmed the district court's injunctive order. However, the appeals court reversed and remanded the portion of the lower court's decision denying attorneys' fees to the plaintiff.

23. *Id.* at 762.

24. Karen B. v. Treen, 653 F.2d 897, 901 (5th Cir. 1981).

25. Lubbock Civil Liberties Union v. Lubbock Independent School Dist., 669 F.2d 1038 (5th Cir. 1982), *cert. denied*, 103 S. Ct. 800 (1983).

26. Jaffree v. Board of School Commissioners of Mobile Cty, 554 F. Supp. 1104 (S.D. Ala. 1983), *rev'd sub nom.* Jaffree v. Wallace, 705 F.2d 1526 (11th Cir. 1983). Supreme Court Justice Powell had stayed the federal district court judge's ruling, pending appellate review of the case, 103 S. Ct. 842 (1983).

27. Jaffree v. James, 544 F. Supp. 727, 733 (S.D. Ala. 1982). Other courts have not adopted such an expansive interpretation of free speech protections afforded to religious speech in elementary and secondary schools, but the U.S. Supreme Court

has ruled that religious expression is entitled to free speech protection on college campuses. *See* Widmar v. Vincent, 102 S. Ct. 269 (1981); text with note 47.

28. *See Education Daily*, 11 April 1979, p. 1.

29. The amendment to S450 was introduced by Senator Jesse Helms (North Carolina). *See Education Daily*, 20 August 1980, p. 4.

30. *See Education Daily*, 18 November 1981; *Education Daily*, 11 May 1982, p. 2. *See also* note 133.

31. *Education Daily*, 7 May 1982, p. 1. A month earlier President Reagan had been presented a petition with one million signatures asking for the return of voluntary prayer to public schools.

32. *See Education Daily*, 2 June 1982, p. 1.

33. Will, "Opposing Prefab Prayer."

34. *Ibid.*

35. *See Education Daily*, 22 June 1982, p. 5.

36. "President Calls for Amendment to Allow Prayer in Public Schools," *Louisville Courier Journal*, 7 May 1982, p. A-2.

37. *Ibid.*

38. *See* text with note 2. *See also Education Daily,* 30 July 1982, pp. 3-4, for a summary of the debate at the first Senate Judiciary Committee hearing on the resolution.

39. In an early New York case, a trial court did endorse nonsectarian meetings of such groups at public schools. Lewis v. Board of Educ. of the City of New York, 285 N.Y.S. 164 (Sup. Ct., New York County, 1935).

40. *See* Trietly v. Board of Educ. of the City of Buffalo, 409 N.Y.S.2d 912 (App. Div. 1978); Johnson v. Huntington Beach Union High School Dist., 137 Cal. Rptr. 43 (Cal. App. 1977).

41. 487 F. Supp. 1219 (N.D.N.Y. 1980) *aff'd* 635 F.2d 971 (2d Cir. 1980), *cert. denied*, 102 S. Ct. 970 (1981). Also, in 1983 the Supreme Court declined to review a case in which the Fifth Circuit Court of Appeals struck down a school board's policy allowing student prayer meetings before and after school. Lubbock Civil Liberties Union v. Lubbock Independent School Dist., 669 F.2d 1038 (5th Cir. 1982), *cert. denied*, 103 S. Ct. 800 (1983).

42. *Id.*, 487 F. Supp. at 1229.

43. *Id.*, 635 F.2d at 979.

44. *Id.* at 978.

45. Chess v. Widmar, 480 F. Supp. 907 (W.D. Mo. 1979), *rev'd and remanded,* 635 F.2d 1310 (8th Cir. 1980), *aff'd sub nom.* Widmar v. Vincent, 102 S. Ct. 269 (1981).

46. *Compare* Chess v. Widmar, 480 F. Supp. 907 (W.D. Mo. 1979) *with* Brandon v. Board of Educ. of Guilderland Central School Dist., 487 F. Supp. 1219 (N.D.N.Y. 1980), *aff'd* 635 F.2d 971 (2d Cir. 1980).

47. 102 S. Ct. at 275.

48. *Id.* at 276, citing 635 F.2d at 1317.

49. *Id* at 277.

50. *See* note 49, chapter 6.

51. Brandon v. Board of Educ. of Guilderland Central School Dist., 635 F.2d 971, 980 (2d Cir. 1980). *See also* Karen B. v. Treen, 653 F.2d 897 (5th Cir. 1981); Collins v. Chandler Unified School Dist., 644 F.2d 759 (9th Cir. 1981).

52. *See* Jaffree v. James, 544 F. Supp. 727, 733 (S.D. Ala. 1982); Patricia Lines, "Educational Institutions as Open Forums for Religious Expression," *West's Education Law Reporter* 2 (1982):333-36.

53. Tinker v. Des Moines Independent School Dist., 393 U.S. 503 (1969).

54. Widmar v. Vincent, 102 S. Ct. at 282 (White, J., dissenting).

55. *Id.*

56. Jesse Choper, "Religion in the Schools: A Proposed Constitutional Standard," *Minnesota Law Review* 47 (1963):382.

57. Knowlton v. Baumhover, 166 N.W. 202, 206 (Iowa 1918).

58. Zellers v. Huff, 236 P.2d 949 (N.M. 1951).

59. LaRocca v. Board of Educ. of Rye City School Dist., 406 N.Y.S.2d 348 (App. Div. 1978).

60. Lynch v. Indiana State University Board of Trustees, 378 N.E.2d 900 (Ind. App. 1978), *cert. denied,* 441 U.S. 946 (1979).

61. The court cited Torcaso v. Watkins, 367 U.S. 488 (1961), in which the Supreme Court invalidated a Maryland law requiring notary publics to sign an oath affirming their belief in God. Ruling that employees cannot be discharged for holding a certain belief, the Court recognized that they can be dismissed for *acts* that violate the establishment clause.

62. Fink v. Board of Educ. of the Warren County School Dist., 442 A.2d 837 (Pa. Commw. 1982).

63. *Id.* at 841.

64. *Id.* at 842.

65. Palmer v. Board of Educ. of City of Chicago, 603 F.2d 1271 (7th Cir. 1979), *cert. denied*, 444 U.S. 1026 (1980).

66. *Id*, 603 F.2d at 1274.

67. *Id.*

68. School Dist. of Abington Township v. Schempp, 374 U.S. 203, 225 (1963).

69. *Id.* at 300 (Brennan, J., concurring).

70. J. Vincent Panoch, "Law, Religion and Education Within American Pluralism," *Religion* 16 (April 1979):7.

71. Hall v. Board of School Comm'rs, 656 F.2d 999 (5th Cir. 1981).

72. Wiley v. Franklin, 468 F. Supp. 133 (E.D. Tenn. 1979).

73. *Id.*, 474 F. Supp. 525 (E.D. Tenn. 1979).

74. *Id.* 497 F. Supp. 390 (E.D. Tenn. 1980).

75. Vaughn v. Reed, 313 F. Supp. 431 (W.D. Va. 1970).

76. Lanner v. Wimmer, 662 F.2d 1349 (10th Cir. 1981). *See* text with note 55, chapter 5.

77. David Tavel, *Church-State Issues in Education*, Fastback 123 (Bloomington, Ind.: Phi Delta Kappa, 1979), p. 41.

78. Choper, "Religion in the Schools," p. 378.

79. School Dist. of Abington Township v. Schempp, 374 U.S. 203, 218 (Brennan, J., concurring).

80. For a discussion of secular humanism, *see* text with note 89, chapter 4.

81. Florey v. Sioux Falls School Dist. 49-5, 464 F. Supp. 911 (D.S.D. 1979), *aff'd* 619 F.2d 1311 (8th Cir. 1980), *cert. denied*, 449 U.S. 987 (1980).

82. *Id.*, 619 F.2d at 1319-20 (Appendix).

83. *Id.* at 1317.

84. *Id.* at 1318.

85. *Id.*

86. *Id.*, citing McCollum v. Board of Educ., 333 U.S. 203, 235 (1948).

87. *Id.*, at 1316, citing 464 F. Supp. at 916.

88. *Id.* at 1325-26 (McMillan, J., dissenting), citing Fox v. City of Los Angeles, 587 P.2d 663, 670 (Cal. 1978) (Bird, C.J., concurring).

89. For example, the excusal provision included in the board's guidelines raises troublesome issues. If such assemblies in fact approach religious music and literature from an academic perspective, an excusal provision would seem un-

necessary. Indeed, it might be argued that the excusal provision indicates that the programs are designed to reinforce particular religious beliefs. Moreover, could student members of school band or choral groups be penalized by having their grades lowered for not performing at religious assemblies? For a discussion of this issue, *see* text with note 47, chapter 3.

90. Opinion of the Justices, 228 A.2d 161 (N.H. 1967). *See* Baer v. Kolmorgen, 181 N.Y.S.2d 230 (Sup. Ct., Westchester County, 1958), in which a New York trial court dismissed a complaint by taxpayers challenging the display of the Nativity Scene on the public school lawn during the Christmas holidays. The court noted that the display was erected without the use of public funds or public employees and that the religious symbol could do little to influence students' beliefs as they were not in school at the time of the display. Acknowledging that the creche is "undoubtedly a religious symbol," *id.* at 238, the court reasoned that the required separation of church and state does not mean that "the state should be stripped of all religious sentiment," *id.* at 234, citing Doremus v. Board of Educ., 75 A.2d 880, 888 (N.J. 1950). The court concluded that the school board was not advancing religion, but merely was making a reasonable religious accommodation. *See also* Anderson v. Salt Lake City Corp., 475 F.2d 29 (10th Cir. 1973), *cert. denied,* 414 U.S. 879 (1973), in which the appeals court upheld a private organization's construction of a monolith with the Ten Commandments among other symbols on a courthouse lawn. The court concluded that the display was designed primarily to depict events of historical significance and not to promote religion.

91. Ring v. Grand Forks Public School Dist. No. 1, 483 F. Supp 272 (D.N.D. 1980).

92. Stone v. Graham, No. 78 CI 1300 (Ky. Cir. Ct., Franklin County, 1979), *aff'd* 599 S.W.2d 157 (Ky. 1980), *rev'd* 449 U.S. 39 (1980).

93. Acts 1978, ch. 436 § 1 (effective 17 June 1978); K.R.S. 158.178.

94. 449 U.S. 39 (1980). This decision was rendered one week after the Court declined to review the Eighth Circuit decision upholding religious Christmas observances. *See* text with note 81.

95. *Id.* at 41.

96. *Id.* at 42.

97. *See* Fox v. Crittenden County Bd. of Educ., cited in *Education Daily,* 6 April 1981, pp. 3-5.

98. "Ten Commandments May Ease Into Schools on Students' Folders," *Louisville Courier Journal,* 31 July 1981, p. A-10.

99. Hysong v. School Dist. of Gallitzin Borough, 30 A. 482 (Pa. 1894).

100. Gerhardt v. Heid, 267 N.W. 127, 135 (N.D. 1936).

101. Rawlings v. Butler, 290 S.W.2d 801 (Ky. 1956). *See* Choper "Religion in the Schools," p. 403.

102. Commonwealth v. Herr, 78 A. 68, 72 (Pa. 1910).

103. *Id.*

104. O'Conner v. Hendrick, 77 N.E. 612 (N.Y. 1906).

105. Zellers v. Huff, 236 P.2d 949, 963 (N.M. 1951).

106. *Id.*

107. Buford v. Southeast Dubois County School Corp., 472 F.2d 890 (7th Cir. 1973), *cert. denied*, 411 U.S. 967 (1973).

108. Choper, "Religion in the Schools," p. 405.

109. Wood v. Mt. Lebanon Township School Dist., 342 F. Supp. 1293, 1294 (W.D. Pa. 1972).

110. Wiest v. Mt. Lebanon School Dist., 320 A.2d 362 (Pa. 1974), *cert. denied*, 419 U.S. 967 (1974).

111. Grossburg v. Deusebio, 380 F. Supp. 285, 288 (E.D. Va. 1974).

112. *Id.* at 289.

113. Goodwin v. Cross County School Dist., 394 F. Supp. 417 (E.D. Ark. 1973). *See also* Chamberlin v. Dade County Bd. of Public Instruction, 160 So. 2d 97 (Fla. 1964), *rev'd in part, appeal dismissed in part*, 377 U.S. 402 (1964), in which the Supreme Court dismissed a challenge to a baccalaureate service for lack of a properly presented federal question.

114. Lemke v. Black, 376 F. Supp. 87 (E.D. Wis. 1974), *vacated and remanded*, 525 F.2d 694 (7th Cir. 1975).

115. Miller v. Cooper, 244 P.2d 520 (N.M. 1952).

116. *Id.* at 521.

117. Stein v. Fairfax County School Bd., cited in *Education Daily*, 2 June 1980, p. 4.

118. *See* text with notes 22, 24, and 43.

119. *Id. See also* Engel v. Vitale, 370 U.S. 421, 431 (1962).

120. Tudor v. Board of Educ., 100 A.2d 857 (N.J. 1953), *cert. denied*, 348 U.S. 816 (1954).

121. Goodwin v. Cross County School Dist., 394 F. Supp. 417, 427 (E.D. Ark. 1973).

122. Miller v. Cooper, 244 P.2d 520 (N.M. 1952).

123. Hernandez v. Hanson, 430 F. Supp. 1154 (D. Neb. 1977).

124. *Id.* at 1162, citing McCollum v. Board of Educ., 333 U.S. 203, 231 (1948). However, in 1982 the Fifth Circuit Court of Appeals ruled that a policy, requiring all sectarian or political material distributed on any campus to have prior approval of the district assistant superintendent of administration, was unconstitutional on its face and as applied. The challenge to the policy did not focus on the distribution of religious literature, but rather on the application of the policy to teachers who wanted to distribute leaflets criticizing a proposed teacher competency testing pro-

gram. Hall v. Board of School Commissioners of Mobile, Alabama, 681 F.2d 965 (5th Cir. 1982).

125. Meltzer v. Board of Public Instruction of Orange County, Florida, 577 F.2d 311 (5th Cir. 1978), *cert. denied*, 439 U.S. 1089 (1979). *See also* Brown v. Orange County Bd. of Public Instruction, 128 So. 2d 181 (Fla. App. 1960).

126. For a discussion of the various trial court orders, *see* 548 F.2d 559, 562-67 (5th Cir. 1977).

127. *Id.*

128. 577 F.2d 311 (5th Cir. 1978).

129. Committee for Public Educ. and Religious Liberty v. Regan, 444 U.S. 646, 662 (1980).

130. School Dist. of Abington Township v. Schempp, 374 U.S. 203, 222 (1963).

131. *See* Lemon v. Kurtzman, 403 U.S. 602, 622 (1971).

132. *See Education Daily*, 17 August 1982, p. 5; *Education Daily*, 30 July 1982, pp. 3-4; Will, "Opposing Prefab Prayer;" text with note 23, chapter 4.

133. Although the proposed constitutional amendment did not come to a vote in 1982, it generated considerable debate over the definitions of "prayer" and "voluntary" in hearings before the Senate Judiciary Committee. *See Education Daily*, 19 August 1982, p. 3. Such debate has continued in 1983, and alternatives to the Reagan amendment have been proposed. Also, plans are underway to introduce additional measures in Congress to limit federal courts' jurisdiction over school prayer cases and to allow student groups to hold prayer meetings in public schools after school hours. Moreover, current church-state disputes involving schools are not confined to the legality of traditional religious observances and activities in public education. Allegations that public schools are establishing a religion of "secularism" are creating substantial political controversy. *See* text with note 89, chapter 4.

Chapter Three

Religious Exemptions
from Public School Programs

W ith regularity parents have requested religious exemptions for their children from specific public school observances and activities and even from compulsory education altogether. Many of these requests have resulted in legal disputes involving interpretations of the protections afforded by the free exercise clause. Courts have assessed the sincerity of the asserted religious belief and the scope of governmental infringement on conduct dictated by the belief. These findings have then been balanced against the state's asserted justification for requiring the activity and the impact of the requested exemption on attaining legitimate governmental objectives.

This chapter focuses on judicial application of this delicate balancing process in evaluating the constitutionality of a variety of public school practices challenged as interfering with parental rights to direct the religious upbringing of their children. Specifically, the first five sections address parental efforts to secure religious exemptions for their children from compulsory education laws, immunization requirements, specific school observances, certain curricular offerings, and regulations governing student athletes. The final section deals with legal issues pertaining to the excusal of teachers and students from public school to observe religious holidays.

Exemptions from Mandatory Schooling

In several cases parents have asserted a free exercise right to disregard compulsory education statutes. While the Supreme Court has recognized that parents have a protected right to select private schooling for their children,[1] the state's authority to require a designated amount of education for all citizens has been upheld.[2] In 1950 the Illinois Supreme Court noted that compulsory school attendance laws are not designed "to punish those who provide their children with instruction equal or superior to that obtainable in the public schools," but are intended "for the parent who fails or refuses to properly educate his child."[3] Parental attempts to deny their children an education altogether, even though based on sincerely held religious convictions, have not prevailed.

In an illustrative case, the Virginia Supreme Court rejected parents' assertion that the Bible commanded them to teach their children at home as justification for disregarding the compulsory attendance law.[4] In ruling against the parents, who were not licensed teachers, the court stated that "no amount of religious fervor . . . in opposition to adequate instruction should be allowed to work a lifelong injury" to their children.[5] A Wisconsin appeals court similarly concluded that parents did not have a free exercise right to withdraw their children from public school, where evidence substantiated that the children were not receiving an adequate alternative education. The court observed that "a way of life, however virtuous and admirable, may not be interposed as a barrier to reasonable state regulation of education. . . ."[6] In a recent case, an Alabama appeals court upheld the state compulsory school attendance law against a free exercise challenge by parents who sought to keep their children out of school to protect them from the secular influences in public education.[7]

The one judicially sanctioned exemption from compulsory attendance mandates for religious reasons applies to Amish children who have successfully completed the eighth grade. In *Wisconsin* v. *Yoder* the U.S. Supreme Court reasoned that for the state to prevail in mandating school attendance beyond eighth grade against a claim that such attendance interferes with the practice of a legitimate religious belief, it must be shown that either the requirement does not impair free exercise rights or "there is a state interest of sufficient magnitude to override the interest claiming protection under the Free Exercise Clause."[8] Noting that a determination of what constitutes a religious belief or practice deserving constitutional protection is a very "delicate question," the Court nonetheless concluded that the Amish practice of having adolescents devote their full attention to preparing for their adult roles in the religious community was grounded in a legitimate and sincerely held religious belief.

Turning to an assessment of whether the state had sufficient justification for the burden imposed on the exercise of this belief, the Court recognized that "providing public schools ranks at the very apex of the function of a State."[9] But the Court concluded that an additional one or two years of formal high school for Amish children in place of their long-established program of informal vocational education would do little to advance the state's interest. The Court found no threat of harm to the physical or mental health of the child or to the public health or welfare by granting the exemption. Thus, the state did not carry its burden of showing "how its admittedly strong interest in compulsory education would be adversely affected by granting an exemption to the Amish."[10]

However, the Court was careful to limit its holding to the Amish, noting that this religious sect deserves special consideration because Amish youth are prepared to enter a cloistered agrarian community rather than mainstream American society. The Court stated:

> It is one thing to say that compulsory education for a year or two beyond the eighth grade may be necessary when its goal is the preparation of the child for life in modern society . . ., but it is quite another if the goal of education be viewed as the preparation of the child for life in the separated agrarian community that is the keystone of the Amish faith.[11]

The Court thus considered not only the *sincerity* of the belief but also the *nature* of the faith asserted. Moreover, the Court emphasized that it was not attempting to function as a state legislature or local school board and cautioned lower courts to move "with great circumspection" in balancing the state's legitimate interests against religious claims for exemptions from any educational requirements.[12]

Justice Douglas, however, issued a strong dissent in this case. Arguing that the children rather than their parents should have testified, he contended that this ruling "imperiled" the future of any child who might wish to break away from the Amish tradition.[13] Douglas asserted that if a student "is harnessed to the Amish way of life by those in authority over him and if his education is truncated, his entire life may be stunted and deformed."[14] Despite this admonition, the majority concluded that the parents' free exercise rights were controlling.

While most other parental attempts to avoid compulsory education requirements have not been successful, in recent years First Amendment challenges to the state's authority to regulate the *means* by which children are educated have increased. These challenges generally have focused on parental rights to select alternatives to public education that reinforce their religious values. Courts have been faced with balancing free exercise claims against the state's duty to assure that all children receive an adequate education. Litigation pertaining to governmental regulatory authority over religious academies and home education programs is covered in chapter 7.

Exemptions from Mandatory Immunization

Courts traditionally have upheld the state's authority to require children attending school to be in good health so as not to endanger the well-being of others. Students who have not been properly immunized against communicable diseases have been denied admission to school, which in turn has placed their parents in violation of compulsory attendance mandates. Parents have been fined and in some instances jailed for disobeying the law by refusing to have their children immunized as a prerequisite to school enrollment.

Several state courts have upheld mandatory vaccination, even when in conflict with parents' religious convictions, and have reasoned that an epidemic need not be pending to justify such a requirement.[15] In a typical early case, a parent defended his refusal to have his child vaccinated as "partly religious and partly because he didn't want that poison injected into his child."[16]

Upholding the conviction of the parent for violating the compulsory attendance law, the court declared:

> The defendant's individual ideas, whether "conscientious," "religious," or "scientific," do not appear to be more than opinions. . . . The defendant's views cannot affect the validity of the statute or entitle him to be excepted from its provisions. . . . It is for the Legislature, not for him or for us, to determine the question of policy involved in public health regulations.[17]

More recently, the Supreme Court of Arkansas declared that religious freedom does not mean that parents can "engage in religious practices inconsistent with the peace, safety, and health of inhabitants of [the] state."[18]

During the last few decades, several states have enacted statutes that provide for religiously based exemptions from required immunization, as long as the welfare of others is not endangered. Most of these exemption provisions stipulate that they apply only to members of recognized religious sects. For example, Kentucky law makes an exception for "members of a nationally recognized and established church or religious denomination, the teachings of which are opposed to medical immunization against disease."[19] In 1976 a federal district court ruled that a parent was not entitled to the exemption because he was "philosophically opposed" to having his children immunized.[20] The court was not persuaded by the argument that the law was discriminatory because it granted an exemption to members of religious groups while denying the same privilege to those opposed to immunization on nonreligious grounds.

A few courts have interpreted religious exemption provisions somewhat broadly. For example, the North Carolina Supreme Court concluded that the exemption for members of sects whose teachings oppose immunization should not be interpreted as applying *only* to denominations that actually forbid vaccination.[21] Thus, the court ruled that parents can qualify for an exemption for their children based on sincere religious convictions, even though not grounded in official church doctrine. Also, a trial court interpreted the New York statutory religious exemption as covering individuals who objected to vaccination on genuine and sincere religious grounds regardless of whether they were members of an organized church.[22] The court concluded that despite the statute's wording, which limits exemptions to bona fide members of religious organizations, an individual who genuinely practices tenets of a belief that opposes vaccination, as well as "formal" members of the church, are entitled to the exemption.

In contrast, the Massachusetts high court was not willing to read such an expansive interpretation into a statutory religious exemption and invalidated the provision because it unconstitutionally discriminated against individuals who objected to vaccination based on sincere religious beliefs but who were not members of a recognized denomination.[23] Endorsing the general vaccination requirement, the court suggested that the state legislature could remedy the defect in the religious exemption by expanding its coverage to individuals who objected to immunization based on sincere religious beliefs irrespective of their formal church affiliation. The court noted that under an expanded religious exemption, the state could still retain the "safety valve" of specifying that the exemption would apply only in the absence of an epidemic or emergency. The Maryland high court recently espoused somewhat similar reasoning in striking down a religious exemption from the state law requiring students to be immunized against diphtheria, tetanus, pertussis, polio, measles, and rubella before entering elementary school.[24] The court found that the exemption was unconstitutional since it applied only to members of recognized religious groups.

The New Hampshire federal district court also struck down a religious exemption, concluding that the state law vesting complete discretion in local school boards to determine whether a religious exemption should be permitted was unconstitutionally vague.[25] Since there were no prescribed standards for making this determination, parents were uninformed as to the criteria that would be applied. Although finding that the vague religious exemption violated due process rights, the court upheld the remainder of the law which mandated immunization as a condition of school enrollment.

In a significant 1979 case the Supreme Court of Mississippi struck down the entire concept of a statutory religious exemption.[26] The state had enacted a law, similar to many discussed previously, allowing an exemption from mandatory immunization for bona fide members of recognized religious sects whose teachings require reliance on spiritual means of healing. Parents who objected to immunization for nonreligious reasons challenged the law as denying their equal protection rights. The court agreed and therefore invalidated the exemption. Furthermore, the court noted that a religious exemption defeats the purpose of an immunization requirement, which is to protect all children from exposure to communicable diseases. The court concluded that the state law requiring immunization as a prerequisite to school attendance must be applied equally to all students, regardless of their religious convictions. In 1980 the U.S. Supreme Court declined to review this case, thus leaving the Mississippi high court decision in force.

While the state's authority to mandate student vaccination—even over religious objections—has long been recognized, it has been assumed that states can provide for religious exemptions. However, several recent decisions cast doubt on the legality of such exemptions. Thus, the judiciary may be returning to its traditional position that if the state decides that mandatory vaccination is necessary for general welfare purposes, all children should be treated similarly under the requirement.

Exemptions from School Observances

The major controversy over compulsory participation in school observances has involved the flag salute ceremony. In 1898 New York enacted the first statute requiring this observance in public schools, and by 1940 eighteen other states had statutory provisions to this effect.[27] Although most of the laws did not make participation in the flag salute ceremony mandatory, Kern Alexander has observed that "the reality of the classroom regimentation tended to make such statutory pronouncement unnecessary."[28]

Prior to 1940 several state courts had upheld the authority of school officials to require students to salute the flag. For example, the Georgia Supreme Court ruled that the flag salute is a patriotic rather than religious exercise, and therefore required participation in this observance does not violate free exercise rights.[29] Also, the California Supreme Court upheld the expulsion of students for refusing to salute the flag.[30] The New Jersey Supreme Court declared that those who do not wish to engage in the mandatory flag salute in public school "can seek their schooling elsewhere."[31]

In 1940 the United States Supreme Court finally addressed this issue in *Minersville School District* v. *Gobitis*.[32] Concluding that a Pennsylvania statute requiring the flag salute and pledge of allegiance did not violate free exercise rights, the Court stated:

> Conscientious scruples have not, in the course of the long struggle for religious toleration, relieved the individual from obedience to a general law not aimed at the promotion or restriction of religious beliefs. The mere possession of religious convictions which contradict the relevant concerns of a political society does not relieve the citizen from the discharge of political responsibilities.[33]

However, the *Gobitis* decision did not end the controversy over mandatory participation in patriotic observances by public school pupils. Some states reacted to the ruling by passing laws making the flag salute compulsory, and state courts rendered conflicting decisions regarding the legality of such provisions under state constitutional mandates.[34]

Ultimately the Supreme Court again addressed the issue in 1943, and in so doing it overturned the *Gobitis* precedent.[35] This case emerged after the West Virginia legislature amended its education statutes to require all schools to include instruction "for the purpose of teaching, fostering and perpetuating the ideals, principles and spirit of Americanism, and increasing the knowledge of the organization and machinery of the government."[36] Pursuant to the statutory provision, the state board of education ordered that the flag salute become a regular part of the public school program. Members of Jehovah's Witnesses refused to comply with the order, asserting that the flag salute impaired their religious belief against bowing to any "graven image." They sought a court injunction restraining the state board from enforcing the requirement. After the federal district court granted the injunction, the state board appealed to the U.S. Supreme Court.

In *West Virginia State Board of Education* v. *Barnette* the Supreme Court affirmed the district court's judgement,[37] thereby reversing the position it had assumed only three years earlier. The Court noted that the conflict centered on the state's authority to condition public school attendance on a prescribed observance (and to punish both parent and child for noncompliance) and the individual's asserted right of self-determination involving matters of individual opinion and attitude. Reasoning that refusal to participate in the flag salute ceremony does not interfere with the rights of others to do so or threaten any type of disruption, the Court held that the action of school authorities in compelling this observance "transcends constitutional limitations on their power and invades the sphere of intellect and spirit which it is the purpose of the First Amendment to our Constitution to reserve from all official control."[38] Justice Jackson stated for the Court:

> If there is any fixed star in our constitutional constellation, it is that no official, high or petty, can prescribe what shall be orthodox in politics, nationalism, religion, or other matters of opinion or force citizens to confess by word or act their faith therein. If there are any circumstances which permit an exception, they do not now occur to us.[39]

The Court, however, only prohibited school authorities from *compelling* participation in the flag salute and pledge and did not bar these observances from public schools. If the Court had concluded that this patriotic ceremony somehow advanced religion in violation of the establishment clause, then an injunction against state sponsorship of the activity would have been an appropriate remedy. But the secular nature of the observance was not contested; only its interference with the exercise of certain religious beliefs was at issue. Therefore, the proper relief was for the offended individuals to be excused from participation. Whereas an excusal provision does not remedy the constitutional defect of activities found in violation of the establishment clause (see chapter 2), an exemption from religiously offensive secular activities can satisfy requirements of the free exercise clause.

Following the *Barnette* precedent, lower courts have protected the rights of students not only to decline to participate in the flag salute ceremony, but also to register a silent protest by remaining seated during the observance. In 1966 the New Jersey Supreme Court held that student followers of the Black Muslims, who believe in the religion of Islam, could not be compelled to participate in the pledge of allegiance.[40] In subsequent cases courts have ruled that nonparticipating students cannot be forced to stand or leave the classroom during the flag salute.[41] The Second Circuit Court of Appeals noted that there is no threat of disruption posed by a student seated quietly during the pledge; such silent nondisruptive protest is a type of expression protected by the First Amendment.[42] Of course, if a student should carry the silent protest to an extreme, such as lying down or standing on his hands during the observance,[43] the threat of classroom disruption would justify curtailing the conduct.

Courts have also upheld teachers' rights to refuse to pledge their allegiance as a matter of personal conscience.[44] The Second Circuit Court of Appeals declared that "the right to remain silent in the face of an illegitimate demand for speech is as much a part of First Amendment protections as the right to speak out in the face of an illegitimate demand for silence."[45] However, teachers cannot deny students the opportunity to engage in the flag salute ceremony. They have the right not to participate, but they do not have the right to eliminate this observance from their classrooms.

Although most First Amendment controversies over exemptions from school observances have focused on the flag salute ceremony, the coming decade may witness a new wave of litigation challenging holiday observances. Since the Eighth Circuit Court of Appeals has ruled that holidays with both a secular and religious meaning can be observed "in a prudent and objective manner" in public schools,[46] it seems likely that the scope of students' rights to be excused from such observances will generate First Amendment controversies. For example, if a student music group performs at a Christmas holiday program, could a student's grade be lowered for refusal to participate on religious grounds?

A Missouri student recently attempted to secure damages from a school district, alleging that he unfairly was given failing grades in band and chorus for not attending a Christmas concert.[47] Among other allegations, the student argued that the holiday program unlawfully advanced religion in violation of the First Amendment and that the school could not condition grades on participation in such a program. Rejecting these assertions, the Missouri circuit court judge reasoned that the concert was secular rather than religious in nature. Since band and chorus members were advised at the beginning of the term that unexcused absences from performances would result in failing grades and the student had not notified his instructors of his plan to miss the Christmas concert, the judge concluded that the grade awarded was fair.

This case raises several interesting legal issues which will likely be the focus of future lawsuits. If students are excused without penalty from such holiday programs on religious grounds, are school authorities admitting that the programs are devotional rather than instructional? And if so, would not establishment clause prohibitions be implicated? Or, is an exemption for a student who finds the holiday program religiously offensive simply an appropriate accommodation to free exercise rights, similar to exemptions from patriotic observances? Following the latter logic, it would appear that grades could not be contingent on a student's participation in a holiday assembly. The application of First Amendment principles to these and related issues has not been judicially clarified.

Exemptions from Curricular Offerings

In some states, statutes provide for students to be excused from specific types of instruction that conflict with their religious beliefs. Typically such statutory exemptions pertain to instruction in health or family life and sex education. Indiana law, for example, stipulates that any student who objects to the state-required hygiene course for religious reasons is entitled to be excused, without penalty, from receiving medical instruction or instruction in disease prevention.[48] Similarly, New Jersey's state regulation prescribing instruction in sex education for all students includes a religious excusal provision,[49] and in Hawaii parents can withdraw their children from sex education instruction by submitting a written request to that effect.[50]

Often requests for exemptions have involved instructional assignments or course offerings that are not addressed in statutory provisions or administrative regulations. If school authorities have not granted the specific requests, parents sometimes have sought judicial intervention. In these cases courts have been called upon to balance free exercise rights against the state's interest in maintaining an efficiently operated school in which all students receive an adequate education.

In an early California case, a state appeals court held that students were entitled to be excused from folk dancing because the activity conflicted with aspects of the children's religious training.[51] The court concluded that required participation impaired free exercise rights as well as parental rights to direct the moral upbringing of their children. The court further noted that parents would be entitled to such an exemption for their children even though the request might not be based on a sincerely held religious belief: "These are considerations which may address themselves as well to the minds or consciences of those not connected with any church or other religious society."[52] Recognizing the legitimacy of the school's interest in including folk dancing in the curriculum, the court reasoned that exemptions from the activity must be granted to those students whose parents are conscientiously opposed to dancing.

Until the mid-1970s some school districts as well as universities required male students to participate in officers' training (R.O.T.C.) courses. These requirements generated several lawsuits in which students asserted a free exercise right to be excused from such courses. With the recent reinstatement of registration for the military draft, the issue of R.O.T.C. may surface again in public schools.

In an early (1934) case, *Hamilton* v. *Regents*, the U.S. Supreme Court reasoned that a California land grant college had a compelling reason to require military training in the interest of the welfare of the state.[53] Upholding mandatory R.O.T.C. for male students, the Court declared that if students "elect to resort to an institution for higher education maintained with the state's moneys, then and only then they are commanded to follow courses of instruction believed by the state to be vital to its welfare."[54]

Subsequently, a Georgia federal district court upheld the expulsion of a high school student for his refusal to enroll in mandatory military instruction.[55] The student, whose objection to military instruction was based on his personal belief that killing was repugnant, asserted that the board's action violated his First Amendment right to exercise freely his beliefs. Finding that the student's objection was not based on religious grounds, the court dismissed the free exercise claim. The court noted that although personal beliefs might subsequently entitle the plaintiff to a statutory exemption from military service as a conscientious objector, they do not constitute a religious belief or conviction for First Amendment purposes. Thus, the student could not challenge his required participation in R.O.T.C. on free exercise grounds.

In 1972 the Sixth Circuit Court of Appeals directly addressed a religious challenge to mandatory R.O.T.C. and concluded that free exercise rights were controlling.[56] The controversy focused on the Memphis School Board's policy stipulating that male high school students must take a year of physical education or R.O.T.C. Since physical education was not offered for male students at the plaintiff's school, he alleged that he had to "choose between following his religious beliefs and forfeiting his diploma . . . and abandoning his religious beliefs and receiving his diploma."[57] The appellate court concluded that there was no compelling state justification for the Memphis schools to require students to participate in officers' training if it conflicted with their religious beliefs. Indeed, the optional provision in the policy negated the contention that military training was considered essential for the welfare of the state. The court distinguished this case from *Hamilton*, where students were not obligated to attend the state land-grant college. It noted that the high school conscientious objector was forced to engage in military training "contrary to his religious beliefs, or to give up his public education."[58] The court held that such a choice, in the absence of a compelling state interest, violated the student's First Amendment rights.

A dissenting appellate justice, however, found unpersuasive the distinction between higher education and secondary schools. Asserting that the R.O.T.C. program required of male high school students did not impair free exercise rights, he expressed fears that by allowing the requested exemption, other aspects of the public school curriculum might become vulnerable to similar challenges:

> I see no reason why a conscientious objector, if his liberties are to be so extended, could not with equal plausibility refuse to subject himself to any course which involved the study of military history—for example, a study of the Napoleonic or Punic wars and others of similar character.[59]

Although controversies over officers' training programs have subsided (at least temporarily), other aspects of the public school curriculum have continued to generate litigation under the free exercise clause. Many requests for student exemptions have involved mandatory physical education classes, and courts have been called upon to assess whether the state's interest in requiring physical education instruction is sufficient to override free exercise rights.

In 1962 the Alabama Supreme Court addressed a situation in which a female high school student had been suspended from school for refusing to attend physical education classes.[60] The student asserted that the required attire and some of the exercises offended her religious beliefs. The trial court ordered the student readmitted, with the concessions that she could wear attire deemed modest to her and her parents and that she would not have to participate in the offensive exercises. On appeal, her parents asserted that their child should not have to participate at all in the classes which subjected her to being in the presence of other females whose dress and behavior offended her beliefs. They contended that school authorities were obligated to conduct a separate class composed of those who shared similar objections as their daughter, so she would not appear to be a "speckled bird," ridiculed by classmates. The Alabama Supreme Court upheld the lower court's conclusion that the school's concessions were adequate accommodations to the student's free exercise rights. The court noted that there are inconveniences associated with holding religious or moral beliefs that are not shared by the majority. Each citizen has a right to be a "speckled bird," but "solace for the embarrassment that is attendant upon holding such beliefs must be found by the individual citizen in his own moral courage and strength of conviction, and not in a court of law."[61]

It has generally been assumed that the state can require students to participate in physical education instruction, even though they might be excused from specific activities that offend their religious beliefs. However, in 1978 an Illinois federal district court reached a different conclusion regarding a student's free exercise right to be exempted from physical education classes altogether.[62] The controversy arose after physical education classes were made coeducational pursuant to federal anti-sex discrimination legislation.[63] Student members of the Pentecostal Church objected to their required participation in physical education instruction with members of the opposite sex dressed in alleged "immodest" attire. The plaintiffs themselves were not required to wear the objectionable outfits, but they were mandated by state law to receive physical education instruction. The Pentecostal students refused to participate in the coeducational classes and consequently were suspended from school or placed in study hall, thus losing academic credit needed for graduation. Their parents brought suit, claiming that the school's action violated their rights to direct the upbringing of their children and their children's rights to exercise their beliefs.

Balancing the parents' and students' free exercise rights against the state's interest in mandating physical education, the federal court concluded that the religious freedoms were overriding.[64] The court found no compelling justification for the state-imposed burden on the exercise of beliefs. The court noted that the state had other means available to achieve its objective of providing daily physical education for students that would not impair free exercise rights. The school could provide sex-segregated classes or individual instruction for the offended children. If school resources prohibited these options, the court held that the Pentecostal students could be excused from physical education. Thus, in contrast to the Alabama Supreme Court, the Illinois federal district court reasoned that the individual's free exercise rights prevail over the state's interest in assuring that all students receive instruction in physical education.

Sex education instruction has also been the source of several lawsuits. Most of the religious challenges have involved assertions that the school is not authorized to offer such instruction at all (these cases are reviewed in chapter 4). However, in some of the cases, courts have addressed students' rights to be excused from sex education programs. Indeed, the judiciary often has reasoned that an exemption provision in a sex education requirement negates the legitimacy of a free exercise challenge to such instruction.[65]

Upholding a school board's authority to offer a mandatory health education course including instruction in sex education and family life, a Connecticut common pleas court observed that parents are more likely to be successful in securing instructional exemptions for their children than in seeking the elimination of courses that conflict with their religious beliefs.[66]. The court stated:

> The plaintiffs claim in this court that the practice of teaching the curriculum denies to them the religious freedoms guaranteed by the First Amendment and that therefore the curriculum, as well as the statutory authority under which it is taught, is unconstitutional and void. The burden undertaken by the plaintiffs by making such claims is made greater than if the plaintiffs had claimed that individual rights were being invaded and that individually they seek exemption from the curriculum or some other specific form of alternative relief.[67]

In 1971 a New Jersey superior court directly addressed students' rights to be excused for religious reasons from a course on human sexuality.[68] State Board of Education regulations, giving local districts discretionary authority to decide whether to offer the course, stipulated that no student would be excused from sex education instruction on the basis of conscience. In balancing the governmental interest in compelling students to take the course against the individual's free exercise claim, the court concluded that the latter must prevail. It noted that when the state intrudes upon free exercise rights, it must either produce a compelling justification or pursue its objectives through means that are less burdensome on personal freedoms. Since local districts had the option of declining to offer the course, the court rejected the assertion that the program was considered so essential that exemptions could not be allowed. The court concluded that excusing a few students from the sex education class would not substantially detract from the success of the program.

Despite the judiciary's tendency to respect parental requests for specific public school exemptions based on religious grounds, such requests have not been honored when they have resulted in a disruption of the school or a significant interference with the student's educational progress. Courts have recognized that the judiciary must assess the impact of the requested religious exemption on the "overall regulatory program."[69]

For example, in a New Hampshire case, parents were unsuccessful in obtaining an exemption for their children from health and music courses and from classes where instructional media were used. The federal district court reasoned that the requested exemption would substantially disrupt the

school's instructional program. The court held that the public school is not required "to allow students and parents to pick and choose which courses they
want to attend" based on idiosyncratic religious views.[70] Although the
students were not to be released from academic classes, the court did concede
that they should be excused when audio-visual equipment was used solely for
entertainment purposes.

Exemptions from Regulations Governing Student Athletes

Eligibility requirements for student athletes and training regulations have
been challenged in numerous lawsuits, but only recently have such rules been
contested as impairing free exercise rights. In these cases, students have
asserted a First Amendment right to exemptions from specific regulations that
allegedly interfere with the practice of their religious beliefs. Courts have
weighed the burden imposed by the rule on students' freedom to exercise their
faith against the state's justification for maintaining the rule.

In a recent case, an Illinois federal district court rejected a First Amendment challenge to a coach's rule prohibiting elementary school basketball
players who miss practice (except for illness or death in the family) from
suiting up for the next scheduled game.[71] The plaintiff student had been
denied an excused absence from practice to attend a catechism class once each
week at a Catholic church. Applying the *Yoder* balancing test, the court found
that the legitimate interest in ensuring participation in basketball practice prior
to games outweighed any infringement on the student's free exercise rights.
Evidence indicated that the student could make arrangements to attend
catechism classes that do not conflict with basketball practice. Moreover, the
court reasoned that the requested exemption would place a considerable
burden on the school's basketball program in that proper preparation of all
team members could not be assured. The court also noted that other means to
ensure regular participation in practice were not available; the school could
not arrange practice schedules to accommodate the religious education classes
of all participants.

In another Illinois case, Jewish high school basketball players challenged
the state high school athletic association rule prohibiting the wearing of
headgear during interscholastic basketball games.[72] The students asserted a
First Amendment right to wear yarmulkes because the tenets of Orthodox
Judaism require them to keep their heads covered at all times except when un-
conscious, immersed in water, or in imminent danger. The plaintiff students
contended that they faced a choice between compromising their religious
beliefs or being excluded from interscholastic basketball competition because
of the association's rule. The association defended the prohibition against
wearing headgear during basketball games as necessary for health and safety
reasons.

After reviewing extensive evidence, the federal district court concluded that
the threat of injury resulting from a yarmulke coming loose and falling on the

court is minimal and far less than the potential danger resulting from a player's eyeglasses falling off or from foreign objects being thrown on the court by fans. Recognizing that "any infringement of fundamental freedoms must survive the most exacting scrutiny," the court held that the association's rule burdened the free exercise of religious beliefs in the absence of any compelling justification.[73]

However, in 1982 the Seventh Circuit Court of Appeals vacated and remanded the decision, and the U.S. Supreme Court subsequently declined to review the case. Reasoning that the association rule is based on legitimate safety considerations, the appellate court held that the students did not substantiate that the rule interferes with a prescribed religious obligation. The court noted that the students are not required by their faith specifically to wear yarmulkes fastened with bobby pins and suggested that they might be able to devise a more secure form of head covering that would satisfy the association's safety concern. The appeals court indicated that if the association then refused to relax its rule to accommodate the students' free exercise of religious beliefs, a valid First Amendment claim might be raised. The students have petitioned the appellate court to rehear the case, asserting that the burden should have been placed on the association (rather than on the students) to find a means to ensure the safety of athletes that is less instrusive on free exercise rights.

While regulations applied to student athletes seem likely to generate additional First Amendment litigation, to date courts have not required schools and state athletic associations to excuse students from requirements that allegedly impede the exercise of religious beliefs. Courts in these cases have not been convinced that exemptions were necessary for the students to practice their faith. Thus, the legitimate state interests in maintaining uniform regulations for all student athletes and ensuring the health and safety of participating students have prevailed over the free exercise claims. However, the courts have recognized that if students can establish that a specific school regulation *forecloses* options for them to practice a basic tenet of their religion, school authorities must produce a compelling justification to deny an exemption from the rule.

Excusal from Public School for Religious Observances

The issue of excusing students and teachers without penalty from public school to observe religious holidays is a particularly delicate one. Schools usually are closed when the majority of the students and teachers are observing their religious holidays; thus, most controversies have arisen in connection with minority sects. Courts have been called upon to determine how far school authorities *must* go in accommodating free exercise rights in connection with religious observances and how far they *can* go in this area without unconstitutionally aiding religion. Sensitive questions have been raised regarding what constitutes a legitimate religious observance and a sincere religious belief.

Although most litigation on this topic has involved teachers, a decision pertaining to students was rendered by a federal district court in 1981 and was affirmed without an opinion by the Fifth Circuit Court of Appeals.[74] The controversy focused on an Amarillo, Texas, school board policy that allowed students only two excused absences for attending religious holidays. Students were not given credit for tests and other work missed during unexcused absences. Plaintiff students, members of the Worldwide Church of God, challenged the policy as impairing their free exercise, equal protection, and due process rights. A fundamental tenet of the Church of God is that members must observe seven annual holy days in the local church and abstain from any secular activities on these days. Members also must attend a week-long religious convocation on the Feast of Tabernacles. Failure to observe the holy days and convocation can result in loss of membership in the Church of God.

Applying the *Yoder* balancing test, the federal district court concluded that the belief at issue was religious in nature as opposed to personal or secular, and that the school's policy placed an unquestionable burden on the exercise of that belief.[75] Plaintiff students were forced to abandon a tenet of their religion or suffer a penalty for classwork missed. The court reasoned that the school's interests in ensuring regular school attendance and protecting teachers from extra work were not sufficiently compelling to justify the infringement on the pupils' free exercise rights.

The court also rejected the school's contention that by recognizing the religious holidays of one church the school would be giving preference to a particular religion in violation of the establishment clause: "The Court's holding reflects nothing more than the governmental obligation of neutrality in the face of religious differences, and does not represent that involvement of religious with secular institutions which is the object of the establishment clause to forestall."[76] Finding the policy unconstitutional under the First Amendment, the court did not consider it necessary to address whether the policy also violated equal protection and due process rights.

The judiciary has not, however, condoned excessive student absences for religious reasons. For example, in a Pennsylvania case, parents did not prevail in securing excused absences for their children to stay out of school every Friday, which is the sacred day of the Muslim religion.[77] The state superior court concluded that it is "virtually impossible" to educate a child who is absent one day a week. The child not only misses one-fifth of the instruction but also the continuity of the course of study is interrupted, which is a great disadvantage to the student. Noting that parental control over the child is not exclusive, the court held that the requested religious accommodation would preclude the state from assuring the child an adequate education. Accordingly, the court ruled that the parents were obligated to comply with the state compulsory school attendance requirements.

School employees more often than students have been plaintiffs in cases challenging school policies limiting the number of permissible absences for religious reasons. In addition to First Amendment rights, employees are protected from religious discrimination under Title VII of the Civil Rights Act of

66

1964.[78] In the 1972 amendments to Title VII, Congress stipulated that the protection against religious discrimination includes "all aspects of religious observance and practice, as well as belief, unless an employer demonstrates that he is unable to reasonably accommodate an employee's or prospective employee's religious observance or practice without undue hardship on the conduct of the employer's business."[79] The Equal Employment Opportunity Commission has promulgated guidelines with suggested accommodations such as accepting voluntary substitutes and assignment exchanges, using flexible scheduling, and changing job assignments.[80] The employer can justify the refusal to make such accommodations if more than minimal costs would create an undue burden.[81] Also, employers are not required to alter work schedules for employees' personal preferences rather than sincere religious beliefs.

Many controversies have arisen over the degree of religious accommodations in work schedules required under Title VII. In 1981 the Fourth Circuit Court of Appeals affirmed a federal district court's conclusion that the discharge of a teacher's aide for religious absences violated Title VII. The school board defended its dismissal action by asserting that the aide's beliefs, which included observing the seven-day convocation of the Church of God, were not covered by the act. The federal district court rejected this defense, holding that the plaintiff's "religious interpretation that she must refrain from work . . . to attend a regional Feast of Tabernacles is to to be considered a bona fide religious practice" protected by Title VII.[82] The appellate court concurred with this holding, but disagreed with the district court's conclusion that the aide was entitled only to back pay from the time of her discharge to the end of her one-year contract. Reasoning that Title VII creates a substantive right to nondiscriminatory treatment, the appeals court held that the plaintiff was entitled to back pay (mitigated by interim earnings) from the time of the discharge until a valid offer of reinstatement was made.[83]

The preceding year, a New Jersey federal district court addressed a teacher's dismissal in connection with religious absences.[84] The board asserted that the dismissal was based on the teacher's unauthorized absence for two class periods, but the teacher claimed that the actual reason was his eight prior absences for religious observances. The court concluded that the religious absences were a "substantial motivating factor" in the dismissal decision, which violated the teacher's rights under Title VII.[85] Finding that the absences created no hardship for the school or students, the court ordered the teacher's reinstatement with back pay. However, the court denied the teacher's request for compensatory and punitive damages. The court was not persuaded that the teacher suffered mental and emotional distress or that the superintendent and board acted with a malicious and wanton disregard for his constitutional rights.

In addition to federal requirements, most states also have constitutional or statutory provisions protecting individuals from religious discrimination. The

California constitution, for example, provides that "a person may not be disqualified from entering or pursuing a business, profession, vocation, or employment because of sex, race, creed, color or national or ethnic origin."[86] An elementary teacher challenged his dismissal as impairing the religious protection included in this provision. The teacher, whose requests for unpaid leave for religious observances were rejected by the school board, had accumulated thirty-one unauthorized absences without pay over a four-year period. Subsequently, the teacher was discharged, and the trial court upheld the dismissal. On appeal, the California Supreme Court assessed whether the teacher's absences created an undue hardship for the school district. Noting that additional funds were not required to pay a substitute in lieu of the regular teacher, the court reasoned that to establish a hardship, the school district would have to prove that the teacher's absences had a detrimental effect on the educational program. The court concluded that only a minor inconvenience was created for the district because the teacher had left detailed lesson plans for the substitute, which resulted in minimal disruption for the students involved. The court further noted that the unpaid leave requested by the teacher did not exceed the amount allowed under California law, and that neighboring school districts permitted such absences for religious observances. Accordingly, the teacher's reinstatement was ordered.[87]

However, a Colorado appeals court departed from the prevailing judicial posture by upholding the dismissal of a tenured teacher for similar unauthorized religious absences, reasoning that his teaching duties had been neglected.[88] The teacher had challenged his discharge under Colorado's antidiscrimination law, and the civil rights commission had ordered reinstatement contrary to its hearing officer's recommendation. Reversing the commission's order, the court found that evidence supported the hearing officer's conclusion that the dismissal was justified. The court cited testimony of the hearing officer indicating that the teacher's four unauthorized absences interfered with the academic progress of his students and disrupted the management of the school.[89]

Although most courts have ordered school districts to make reasonable accommodations so that employees can observe religious holidays, paid leave is not required for this purpose. Indeed, paid leave tied specifically to religious observances implicates the establishment clause. A California appeals court ruled that a school district did not abuse its discretion in concluding that a religious observance is not a "personal necessity" for purposes of paid sick leave.[90] The teacher, who was entitled to unpaid leave for religious absences, claimed that such absences were legitimate personal necessities under the district's sick-leave policy. Noting the school board's discretionary authority to determine what constitutes justifiable personal necessities, the court concluded that the board acted within its authority to exclude religious observances from the list. The court inferred that the school board could include religious holidays among the legitimate reasons for use of paid leave, but it was not obligated to do so.

In a New Jersey case, teachers were allowed to use personal leave days for religious as well as other purposes, but the teachers' association sought specific paid leave for religious observances.[91] The state superior court ruled that the establishment clause prohibits the school board from granting such religious leave, and therefore negotiations over this item would be unconstitutional. The court reasoned that if specific leave were designated for religious reasons, the nonreligious employee could never enjoy the proposed benefit. Similarly, in 1976 a California appeals court struck down a proposed order by the governor granting state employees paid leave for three hours on Good Friday for religious worship.[92] The court found that the order did not have a secular purpose and served to advance religion. However, the following year a California school district's collective bargaining agreement, designating Good Friday as a paid holiday for all employees, was judicially endorsed.[93] The appeals court reasoned that the religious observance on that day was incidental to the main purpose of the agreement, which was to afford employees a longer spring vacation. The paid holiday applied equally to all teachers and *was not* expressly tied to religious worship.

Most individual requests by students or teachers to miss school for religious reasons have not reached the litigation stage because they have been handled at the local school or school district level. However, from the few cases that have been decided, it appears that school authorities will be expected to honor reasonable requests for individuals to be absent from school for religious observances as long as the absences do not create substantial hardships for the school or significantly impede students' academic progress. However, courts have recognized that the establishment clause precludes school boards from conferring special benefits on religious grounds, such as paid leave specifically tied to sectarian observances.

Conclusion

In balancing governmental and individual interests, courts have been inclined to honor requests for students to be excused from specific public school activities if the requests have been based on sincere religious beliefs and the exemptions have not unduly interfered with the management of the school or the integrity of the educational program. School authorities have been required to produce compelling justification to deny exemptions from school observances or curricular activities that clearly compromise the exercise of religious beliefs. Similarly, courts have generally held that students and teachers are entitled to reasonable accommodations to enable them to observe religious holidays. However, free exercise rights cannot be used as a basis for completely disregarding compulsory school attendance mandates; the state has an overriding interest in assuring an educated citizenry. The state also has a compelling interest in safeguarding the health of school children, which justifies mandatory immunization as a condition of school attendance.

In assessing the legitimacy of specific requests for religious exemptions from public school activities and requirements, courts consider the hardship that would be placed on the school's program by granting the request. They also evaluate whether there are other means for the individual to practice the religious belief that would not necessitate the exemption. The judiciary has recognized that "the boundary is a narrow one between an exemption from a universal requirement in deference to a particular basic religious belief on the one hand and on the other hand a special preference given because of a discretionary religious practice."[94] Exemptions for the latter have not received judicial endorsement. For example, student athletes have not been excused from rules if they have alternative means to practice their faith that would not require preferential treatment.

In cases involving free exercise claims, courts are thrust into the domain of evaluating the sincerity of religious beliefs and whether specific practices are central to the exercise of those beliefs. While requests for exemptions based on mere personal preference have not been afforded First Amendment protection, some courts have concluded that the free exercise clause protects sincerely held beliefs even though they are not grounded in official teachings of a recognized religious sect. With requests for religious exemptions and accommodations becoming more numerous, it seems likely that courts will be forced to define more precisely what constitutes a religious belief that triggers the balancing process under the free exercise clause.

Once determined that a school practice impairs the exercise of a genuine religious belief in the absence of a compelling justification, school authorities can satisfy their obligation to respect free exercise rights by excusing individuals from the religiously offensive activities or requirements. But public schools are not required to alter their programs in order that excused students do not feel singled out for special treatment. Choper has observed that the state is not obligated to protect children of religious minorities "from the embarrassment and concomitant pressures that nonconformity brings."[95] However, some parents have contended that an excusal provision is insufficient to protect their First Amendment rights and have asserted that curricular offerings offensive to their religious values should be eliminated from the curriculum. These and related claims are addressed in the next chapter.

Footnotes

1. *See* Pierce v. Society of Sisters, 268 U.S. 510 (1925).

2. *See* text with note 3, chapter 7, for a discussion of the state's *parens patriae* role in mandating school attendance for the well-being of the state and the child.

3. People v. Levisen, 90 N.E.2d 213, 215 (Ill. 1950).

4. Rice v. Commonwealth, 49 S.E.2d 342 (Va. 1948). *See also* People v. Harrell, 180 N.E.2d 889 (Ill. App. 1962).

5. *Id.* 49 S.E.2d at 348.

6. State v. Kasuboski, 275 N.W.2d 101, 105 (Wis. App. 1978). *See also* Commonwealth v. Renfrew, 126 N.E.2d 109 (Mass. 1955).

7. Jernigan v. State, 412 So. 2d 1242 (Ala. Crim. App. 1982).

8. 406 U.S. 205, 214 (1972).

9. *Id.* at 213.

10. *Id.* at 236.

11. *Id.* at 222.

12. *Id.* at 235.

13. *Id.* at 245 (Douglas, J., dissenting).

14. *Id.* at 246.

15. *See* McCartney v. Austin, 293 N.Y.S.2d 188 (Sup. Ct., Broome County, 1968); Board of Educ. of Mountain Lakes v. Maas, 152 A.2d 394 (N.J. Super. 1959); Mosier v. Barren County Bd. of Health, 215 S.W.2d 967 (Ky. App. 1948).

16. State v. Drew, 192 A. 629, 630 (N.H. 1937).

17. *Id.* at 632.

18. Cude v. State of Arkansas, 377 S.W.2d 816 (Ark. 1964).

19. Ky. Rev. Stat. § 214.036.

20. Kleid v. Board of Educ. of Fulton, Kentucky Independent School Dist., 406 F. Supp. 902, 903 (W.D. Ky. 1976).

21. State v. Miday, 140 S.E.2d 325 (N.C. 1965).

22. Maier v. Besser, 341 N.Y.S.2d 411 (Sup. Ct., Onondaga County, 1972). The court ordered a trial to determine if the plaintiff's opposition to immunization was grounded in a sincere religious belief.

23. Dalli v. Board of Educ., 267 N.E.2d 219 (Mass. 1971).

24. Davis v. State, 451 A.2d 107 (Md. 1982). Previously, a Maryland appeals court had ruled that a parent opposed to immunization based on "deeply held moral convictions" could not qualify for the statutory religious exemption. Syska v. Montgomery County Bd. of Educ., 415 A.2d 301 (Md. App. 1980), *cert. denied*, 101 S. Ct. 1475 (1981).

25. Avard v. Dupuis, 376 F. Supp. 479 (D.N.H. 1974).

26. Brown v. Stone, 378 So. 2d 218 (Miss. 1979) *cert. denied*, 449 U.S. 39 (1980).

27. *See* Kern Alexander, *School Law* (St. Paul, Minn.: West Pub. Co., 1980), p. 249.

28. *Ibid.*

29. Leoles v. Landers, 192 S.E.2d 218 (Ga. 1937), *appeal dismissed*, 302 U.S. 656 (1937). *See also* People v. Sandstrom, 18 N.E.2d 840 (N.Y. 1939).

30. Gabrielli v. Knickerbocker, 82 P.2d 391 (Cal. 1938).

31. Hering v. State Bd. of Educ., 189 A. 629, 630 (N.J. 1937).

32. 310 U.S. 586 (1940).

33. *Id.* at 594-95.

34. *See* Bolling v. Superior Court, 133 P.2d 803 (Wash. 1943); State v. Davis, 120 P.2d 808 (Ariz. 1942); Matter of Latrecchia, 26 A.2d 881 (N.J. 1942); State v. Smith, 127 P.2d 518 (Kan. 1942).

35. West Virginia State Bd. of Educ. v. Barnette, 319 U.S. 624 (1943).

36. *Id.* at 625.

37. *Id.*

38. *Id.* at 642.

39. *Id.*

40. Holden v. Board of Educ. of Elizabeth, 216 A.2d 387 (N.J. 1966).

41. *See* Lipp v. Morris, 579 F.2d 834 (3d Cir. 1978); Goetz v. Ansell, 477 F.2d 636 (2d Cir. 1973); Frain v. Baron, 307 F. Supp. 27 (E.D.N.Y. 1969).

42. Goetz v. Ansell, 477 F.2d 636 (2d Cir. 1973).

43. *Id.* at 638.

44. *See* Opinions of the Justices to the Governor, 363 N.E.2d 251 (Mass. 1977); Hanover v. Northrup, 325 F. Supp. 170 (D. Conn. 1970).

45. Russo v. Central School Dist. No. 1, 469 F.2d 623, 634 (2d Cir. 1972).

46. Florey v. Sioux Falls School Dist. 49-5, 620 F.2d 1311 (8th Cir. 1980), *cert. denied*, 449 U.S. 987 (1980). *See* text with note 81, chapter 2.

47. Johnson v. Shineman, No. CV381-29CC (Mo. Cir. Ct. 1982), cited in *Nolpe Notes* 17 (July 1982):6. *See also Nolpe Notes* 16 (May 1981):4.

48. Ind. Code. Ann. § 20-10.1-4-7 (Burns).

49. *See* Smith v. Ricci, 446 A.2d 501 (N.J. 1982).

50. *See* Medeiros v. Kiyosaki, 478 P.2d 314, 316 (Hawaii 1970).

51. Hardwick v. Board of School Trustees, 205 P. 49 (Cal. App. 1921).

52. *Id.* at 53.

53. 293 U.S. 245 (1934).

54. *Id.* at 266.

55. Sapp v. Renfroe, 372 F. Supp. 1193 (N.D. Ga. 1974).

56. Spence v. Bailey, 465 F.2d 797 (6th Cir. 1972).

57. *Id.* at 800.

58. *Id.* at 799.

59. *Id.* at 801 (Miller, J., dissenting).

60. Mitchell v. McCall, 143 So. 2d 629 (Ala. 1962).

61. *Id.* at 632.

62. Moody v. Cronin, 484 F. Supp. 270 (C.D. Ill. 1979).

63. Title IX of the Education Amendments of 1972 stipulates that "No person in the United States shall, on the basis of sex, be excluded from participation in, be denied the benefits of, or be subjected to discrimination under any education program or activity receiving Federal financial assistance . . ." 20 U.S.C. § 1681(a) (1976).

64. Moody v. Cronin, 484 F. Supp. 270, 276 (C.D. Ill. 1979).

65. *See* Smith v. Ricci, 446 A.2d 501 (N.J. 1982), *appeal dismissed sub nom.* Smith v. Brandt, 103 S. Ct. 286 (1982); Medeiros v. Kiyosaki, 478 P.2d 314 (Hawaii 1970); text with note 5, chapter 4.

66. Hopkins v. Hamden Bd. of Educ., 289 A.2d 914 (Conn. C.P. 1971), *aff'd* 305 A.2d 536 (Conn. 1973).

67. *Id.* at 921.

68. Valent v. New Jeresy State Bd. of Educ., 274 A.2d 832 (N.J. Super. 1971).

69. *See* Hopkins v. Hamden Bd. of Educ., 289 A.2d 914, 921 (Conn. C.P. 1971).

70. Davis v. Page, 385 F. Supp. 395, 405 (D.N.H. 1974).

71. Keller v. Gardner Community Consolidated Grade School Dist. 72C, 552 F. Supp. 512 (N.D. Ill. 1982).

72. Menora v. Illinois High School Association, 527 F. Supp. 637 (N.D. Ill. 1981), *vacated and remanded* 683 F.2d 1030 (7th Cir. 1982), *cert. denied,* 103 S. Ct. 801 (1983). The students attended a private school but were governed by the association's rule in connection with interscholastic basketball competition. Although the association is not a formal agency of the state government, it regulates and supervises virtually all interscholastic sports in the state. For example, no member school can schedule a game with a nonmember school; thus, nonmember schools are effectively foreclosed from interscholastic competition. Accordingly, the federal district court reasoned the association's regulations constituted "state action" for purposes of the constitutional challenge in this case, 527 F. Supp. at 643-44.

73. *Id.* at 645.

74. Church of God v. Amarillo Independent School Dist., 511 F. Supp. 613 (N.D. Tex. 1981), *aff'd* 670 F.2d 46 (5th Cir. 1982) (per curiam).

75. *Id.* at 616-18.

76. *Id.* at 618.

77. Commonwealth v. Bey, 70 A.2d 693 (Pa. Super. 1950).

78. Title VII prohibits employers with over 15 employees from discriminating on the basis of race, sex, color, national origin, and religion.

79. 42 U.S.C. § 2000e(j) (1976).

80. *See Nolpe Notes* 16 (September 1981):4.

81. *See* Trans World Airlines (TWA) v. Hardison, 432 U.S. 63 (1977), in which the Supreme Court concluded that a requested religious accommodation would place an undue burden on the employer. An airlines maintenance store clerk refused to work on Saturdays and all holy days. The holy days were accommodated, but TWA refused to give the employee every Saturday free. Ruling in favor of TWA, the Court reasoned that weekend work was essential to the job and a transfer of other personnel to assume the Saturday duties would violate the bargained seniority system. *See also* Wondzell v. Alaska Wood Products, Inc., 583 P.2d 860 (Alaska 1978).

82. Edwards v. School Bd. of Norton, Virginia, 483 F. Supp. 620, 625 (W.D. Va. 1980), *vacated and remanded*, 658 F.2d 951 (4th Cir. 1981).

83. *Id.*, 658 F.2d 951. The case was remanded for a determination of damages, with instructions that the school board should be given the opportunity to prove that the plaintiff made insufficient efforts to mitigate damages by securing other employment after her discharge. *See also* Wangsness v. Watertown School Dist. No. 14-4, 541 F. Supp. 332 (D.S.D. 1982).

84. Niederhuber v. Camden County Vocational and Technical School Dist. Bd. of Educ., 495 F. Supp. 273 (D.N.J. 1980).

85. *Id.* at 274. The court cited Mt. Healthy City School Dist. Bd. of Educ. v. Doyle, 429 U.S. 274 (1977), in which the Supreme Court held that if a protected right is a motivating factor in a dismissal decision, the school board must show by a "preponderance" of evidence that it would have reached the same decision without considering the constitutionally protected conduct.

86. Rankins v. Comm'n on Professional Competence, 593 P.2d 852, 853 (Cal. 1979), *appeal dismissed*, 444 U.S. 986 (1979).

87. *Id.*

88. School Dist. #11, Joint Counties of Archuleta and LaPlata v. Umberfield, 512 P.2d 1166 (Colo. App. 1973).

89. *Id.* at 1169.

90. California Teachers' Ass'n v. Board of Trustees of the Cucamonga Elem. School Dist., 138 Cal., Rptr. 817 (Cal. App. 1977).

91. Hunterdon Central High School Bd. of Educ. v. Hunterdon Central High School Teachers' Ass'n, 416 A.2d 980 (N.J. Super. 1980).

92. Mandel v. Hodges, 127 Cal. Rptr. 244 (Cal. App. 1976).

93. California School Empl. Ass'n v. Sequoia Union High School, 136 Cal. Rptr. 594 (Cal. App. 1977).

94. Keller v. Gardner Community Consolidated Grade School Dist. 72C, 552 F.Supp. 512, 516 (N.D. Ill. 1982).

95. Jesse Choper, "Religion in the Public Schools: A Proposed Constitutional Standard," *Minnesota Law Review* 47 (1963):348.

Chapter Four

Religious Challenges to the Public School Curriculum

As indicated in the preceding chapter, courts have often been receptive to parental requests for their children to be excused from various public school observances and activities that conflict with their faith. Reasonable accommodations to sectarian concerns are considered necessary to protect free exercise rights. However, more complex legal issues are involved in requests for the curriculum to be altered for *all* pupils in conformance with particular religious values.

This chapter addresses free exercise and establishment clause considerations in connection with religious challenges to the public school curriculum. The first section deals generally with contested course offerings, and the next two sections focus specifically on the creationism-evolution dispute and efforts to censor instructional materials for religious reasons. In the final section, the alleged establishment of the religion of secular humanism in public schools is explored.

Challenges to Course Offerings

Parents frequently have challenged the inclusion of certain subjects in the public school curriculum as interfering with their rights to direct the religious upbringing of their children. While courts have endorsed parents' rights to be censors for their own children to some extent, the judiciary has not been inclined to allow the curriculum itself to be restricted to satisfy parents' religious preferences. In 1968 the Supreme Court recognized that "the state has no legitimate interest in protecting any or all religions from views distasteful to them."[1]

Indeed, the Court has recognized the impossibility of eliminating all features of the public school curriculum that might conflict with some religious values. In 1948 Justice Jackson offered the following rationale for the Supreme Court's position:

> Authorities list 256 separate and substantial religious bodies to exist in
> the continental United States. Each of them . . . has as good a right as

this plaintiff to demand that the courts compel the schools to sift out of their teaching everything inconsistent with its doctrines. If we are to eliminate everything that is objectionable to any of these warring sects or inconsistent with any of their doctrines, we will leave public education in shreds. Nothing but educational confusion and a discrediting of the public school system can result from subjecting it to constant law suits.[2]

Yet, disgruntled parents have persisted. In fact, parent groups have become better organized and more vocal in seeking school board policies and state legislation to require the public school curriculum to conform to particular religious beliefs.

One of the focal points of parental attacks has been the public school's authority to include sex education in the curriculum. In most states such instruction is incorporated in health courses, and local school boards are usually given discretionary authority to design the specific sex education instructional program. It was reported in 1979 that 30 states had legislation or written policies pertaining to sex education, with most provisions allowing students to be excused from such instruction upon parental request.[3]

However, some parents have not been appeased by an exemption for their own children and have claimed that such instruction per se impairs their constitutional right to direct the upbringing of their children and to exercise religious beliefs. Furthermore, in some cases parents have argued that the teaching of sex education under the auspices of the public school serves to advance antitheistic religious concepts in violation of the establishment clause.[4] Courts to date have rejected such assertions in upholding the state's authority to offer sex education instruction. For example, in 1969 the Maryland federal district court upheld a state board of education bylaw requiring local school systems to provide a comprehensive program of family life and sex education in every elementary and secondary school.[5] The court reasoned that the bylaw was justified as a public health measure and did not involve the state in religious matters or in favoring particular sectarian tenets. The court declared that the state may not prohibit instruction simply because it is deemed antagonistic to some religious sects.

A Connecticut common pleas court similarly dismissed a challenge to sex education instruction, noting that the few parents involved in the suit had not requested exemptions for their children, but instead had undertaken a "sweeping constitutional indictment" against a course supported by the majority.[6] Finding the only legitimate claim to be that some health instruction might conflict with specific religious beliefs, the court held that in the absence of coercion to participate, there was no interference with free exercise rights.[7] The court reasoned that if parents were allowed to regulate the curriculum as their beliefs dictate, a public school system would become "vulnerable to fragmentation whenever sincere, conscientious religious conflict is claimed."[8]

Courts in New Jersey, Hawaii, Michigan, and California similarly have upheld sex education instruction in public schools as justified by the overriding public interest in teaching students important health information.[9] Contentions that parents have an exclusive constitutional right to teach their children information about sex and that sex education impairs the constitutional right to privacy have not prevailed.[10] Recognizing the need for students to be exposed to such instruction, a California appeals court noted that the state cannot "contract the spectrum of available knowledge" by enjoining a school district's course in family life and sex education.[11]

In the most recent ruling on this subject, the New Jersey Supreme Court unanimously endorsed the state's comprehensive sex education mandate in 1982, and the U.S. Supreme Court declined to review the decision.[12] The state board of education's regulations require all school districts to implement a program in family life and sex education by the fall of 1983, but local school boards are allowed discretion in designing the specific curriculum.[13] A parents' group challenged the state mandate as advancing amorality or secular humanism as a religion in violation of the establishment clause. The court disagreed and found nothing in the curriculum guidelines that suggests antagonism toward religion or support of nonreligion. Noting that the controversial program includes an excusal provision, the court also rejected the free exercise claim.

Sex education programs have generated some of the most volatile controversies, but other components of the curriculum have also come under First Amendment attack. For example, instruction in transcendental meditation (TM) has been challenged as advancing religious tenets. While parents have not persuaded the judiciary that sex education unconstitutionally establishes an antitheistic faith, parents have been successful in convincing a federal appellate court that TM instruction in public schools runs afoul of the establishment clause. In the early 1970s a national organization secured federal funding to develop a TM unit for high school use. After five New Jersey schools agreed to pilot the unit as an elective course for seniors, a group of parents brought suit in federal court. The district court and subsequently the Third Circuit Court of Appeals concluded that the Science of Creative Intelligence, upon which TM is based, possesses many attributes of a religion and elevates a particular philosophy to the level of theology.[14] Thus, the judiciary reasoned that by offering the TM unit, the public schools were advancing religion in violation of the establishment clause.

The courts did not accept the argument that the secular purposes of the TM unit (i.e., to reduce tension and improve learning) eliminated the constitutional violation any more than the secular purpose asserted in defense of daily Bible reading (i.e., to calm children at the start of the school day) remedied its constitutional defect.[15] This case is noteworthy in that the judiciary was called upon to make an assessment of what constitutes a religion and is therefore subject to establishment clause prohibitions. It may signal a new wave of First Amendment litigation involving the introduction of various nontraditional philosophies in public schools.[16]

Other aspects of the curriculum are also vulnerable to being challenged as impinging upon religious freedoms. For example, several school districts have recently decided to include an instructional unit about the Holocaust. Although there have been no reported cases on this issue to date, special instructional emphasis on the Holocaust without similar attention to other historical examples of genocide (e.g., the American Indian) might be challenged as singling out a period of history to satisfy the demands of a particular religious group.[17] Such instruction might even be contested by some Jewish parents, asserting that a unit on the Holocaust revives anti-Semitic feelings and discredits the Jewish religion in violation of the First Amendment.

Although courts usually have rejected parents' religiously based challenges to the state's authority to *expand* learning opportunities for students, more troublesome issues are posed in connection with state efforts to *restrict* the curriculum. Fundamentalist religious groups have become increasingly successful in securing legislative backing for their demands that instructional offerings be tailored to Christian beliefs. Are there constitutional constraints on the authority of legislatures and local school boards to prohibit specific subject matter in conformance with dominant values?

In an early case the U.S. Supreme Court invalidated a Nebraska law prohibiting instruction in a foreign language to students who had not successfully completed the eighth grade. Overturning the conviction of a private school teacher for violating the law, the Supreme Court declared that the teacher's right to teach and the parents' right to engage him to instruct their children are protected liberties under the Fourteenth Amendment.[18] The Court found no support for the contention that instruction in a foreign language would be harmful to students, and, indeed, noted that such instruction would seem desirable. Even though this case did not focus on a religious issue, the precedent established is significant in that the Court recognized that the U.S. Constitution places some limits on the state's authority to restrict curricular offerings.

In 1968 the Court directly addressed a state attempt to restrict the public school curriculum for religious reasons.[19] Ruling that Arkansas could not deprive students of useful knowledge by barring the teaching of evolution from the curriculum, the Court declared that the First Amendment "does not permit the State to require that teaching and learning must be tailored to the principles or prohibitions of any religious sect or dogma."[20]

However, in 1974 the Supreme Court affirmed a Michigan federal district court ruling, upholding a state law that prohibits discussion of birth control in public schools.[21] The district court recognized the state's authority to control the public school curriculum by law or delegation of authority to local school boards. The court reasoned that choices must be made as to "which portions of the world's knowledge" should be included in the curriculum, and therefore, the state is within its legal authority to select specific subjects that will be reserved for instruction by the family, church, or other institutions.[22]

The Michigan decision has provided an incentive for fundamentalist religious groups to press for legislation prohibiting instruction that allegedly conflicts with religious values. Bills have been introduced in several states that would bar from the public school curriculum subjects that allegedly do not foster basic Christian tenets.[23] Despite the Supreme Court's strong statement in 1968, it seems likely that efforts to secure statutory restrictions on the public school curriculum in conformance with the dominant religious faith will escalate in the coming decade.

The Creationism-Evolution Dispute

Instruction in public schools about the origin of human life has generated substantial church-state controversy. The creationism-evolution dispute has been the focus of recent national conferences, extensive media coverage, and several lawsuits. This controversy has significant implications regarding the appropriate role of religion in dictating the substance of public school offerings.

Initially, legal activity focused on state efforts to bar instruction in Darwin's theory of evolution because it conflicts with the Biblical account of the origin of life. Evolution embodies the concepts that the universe emerged by naturalistic processes from disordered matter several billion years ago, that present forms of life developed through mutation and natural selection from simpler more primitive organisms, and that the earth's geology is explained by uniformitarianism. In contrast, the Genesis account is characterized by the notions that the universe and life were suddenly created by the Creator's design, that all living things did not develop from a single organism, that the earth's geology is explained by catastrophism including a worldwide flood, and that creation occurred between six and ten thousand years ago.[24]

In the famous *Scopes* "Monkey Trial," the Tennessee Supreme Court in 1927 endorsed a state law prohibiting the teaching of any theory that denies the Biblical version of creation or suggests "that man has descended from a lower order of animals."[25] Upholding the conviction of John Scopes for teaching evolution in violation of the law, the court stated:

> If the Legislature thinks that, by reason of popular prejudice, the cause of education and the study of science generally will be promoted by forbidding the teaching of evolution in the schools of the state, we can conceive of no ground to justify the court's interference.[26]

In 1968, however, the U.S. Supreme Court reached a different conclusion in *Epperson* v. *Arkansas*.[27] As noted previously, the Court invalidated an Arkansas anti-evolution statute under the establishment clause, reasoning that the state could not limit the knowledge made available to students simply to satisfy religious preferences.[28] While the *Epperson* decision clearly established that the state cannot bar evolution from the public school curriculum, it left several issues unresolved.

Recent legal disputes have focused on teaching evolution as fact and introducing the Genesis version of creation in public schools. Can evolution be taught to the exclusion of creationism without impairing free exercise rights? Must the Biblical account be given equal instructional emphasis with evolution? Does a teacher enjoy academic freedom to elect only to teach creationism, even though evolution is not barred from the curriculum? Can the Genesis version be presented *at all* without advancing religious beliefs? These questions raise complex issues as to the hierarchy of First Amendment protections when they are pitted against each other.

In 1975 the Sixth Circuit Court of Appeals struck down a Tennessee statute stipulating that evolution could not be taught as fact and requiring equal emphasis on creationism whenever the theory of evolution was introduced in the curriculum or described in a text.[29] This ruling, however, did not deter other state legislatures from proposing similar measures requiring balanced instruction about the origin of human life. Indeed, during 1980-81, "equal time" provisions were introduced in 15 states,[30] and two of these provisions were enacted into laws.

The Arkansas "Balanced Treatment for Creation-Science and Evolution-Science Act" was signed into law in March 1981 and almost immediately was challenged under the First Amendment. During the nine-day trial, the law was defended as necessary to protect religious freedom and freedom of speech and to prevent the indoctrination of students with evolutionary dogma. The federal district court judge reviewed the legislative history of the statute and ruled that it failed to satisfy the three-pronged test used to evaluate state action under the establishment clause.[31] The judge concluded that there was no evidence of a secular purpose; "it was simply and purely an effort to introduce the Biblical version of creation into the public school curricula."[32] Reasoning that creation-science is religious dogma, the judge reached the "inescapable" conclusion that the *only* real effect of the law was to advance religion. He also found that the act created excessive governmental entanglement with religion because the Genesis account cannot be taught in a secular fashion.

The judge rejected the defendant's attack on evolution as illogical. Recognizing that case law has clearly established that evolution is not a religion and presents no establishment clause violation, the judge noted that even if it were a religion, the establishment clause problem would not be redressed by giving balanced treatment to creation-science. He declared: "If creation-science is, in fact, science and not religion, as the defendants claim, it is difficult to see how the teaching of such a science could 'neutralize' the [alleged] religious nature of evolution."[33]

A Louisiana statute similar to the Arkansas law was struck down by a federal district court judge in November 1982.[34] The judge reasoned that the law usurped the authority granted under the Louisiana Constitution to the State Board of Elementary and Secondary Education. According to the judge, the state legislature is empowered to "establish and maintain" public schools, but not to mandate how a particular course must be taught. The judge confined his ruling to the state constitutional issue and did not address whether the contested law also violates the First Amendment by requiring religious instruction. The state attorney general plans to appeal the ruling to the Fifth Circuit Court of Appeals.[35] A novel feature of the Louisiana controversy is that some legislators and individuals supporting the law unsuccessfully countersued to obtain a federal court order requiring state authorities to enforce the statute.[36]

It is somewhat ironic that arguments similar to those offered in defense of the teaching of evolution are being used to assert that the Biblical account should be included in the curriculum. Proponents of creationism allege that the curriculum is being arbitrarily restricted by omitting the Genesis version as a possible explanation of the origin of humanity. They claim that public school students are receiving an unbalanced view of the beginning of life when they are denied instruction in the Biblical theory, which has as much scientific verification as does evolution.[37] They further contend that a belief in evolution is a matter of faith as is a belief in divine creation. Indeed, some creationists argue that instruction in creation-science does not advance religious tenets, while the teaching of evolution does.[38]

Organizations of scientists recently have taken an activist position in condemning efforts to include the Genesis account in the science curriculum. In 1982 the American Association for the Advancement of Science adopted a resolution denouncing the forced teaching of creationist beliefs in public schools as presenting a "real and present threat to the integrity of education and the teaching of science."[39] The resolution urges citizens, educators, and policymakers to oppose legislation requiring instruction that cannot withstand "the process of scrutiny and testing that is indispensable to science."

Also, educators have become more assertive in denouncing the teaching of creationism. The National Association of Biology Teachers is distributing newsletters to its 6,000 members to keep them informed about the creationist threat to the science curriculum.[40] Some school districts have also taken a stand against creation-science instruction. In June 1982, the New York City million-pupil school district notified three publishers that it would no longer purchase biology textbooks that do not state that evolution is supported by most scientists and that creationism is a supernatural explanation.[41]

Although courts have rejected efforts to bar the teaching of evolution from the public school curriculum, anti-evolution forces did secure a judicial declaration in California requiring evolution to be presented as theory and not fact. In 1981 a superior court judge ordered the California Board of Education to distribute to all school districts guidelines stipulating that evolution cannot be taught as fact.[42] This suit, however, was limited to the narrow question of how evolution must be presented; the court was not asked to decide whether the Biblical version is entitled to equal instructional emphasis. State officials claimed that the ruling merely reaffirmed what educators in the state already knew; evolution is a theory and science is tentative.[43] The state board of education had adopted guidelines to this effect in 1973 and has merely been required to distribute copies of this anti-dogmatism policy to school districts and textbook publishers. Nonetheless, creationists consider this ruling a victory in their efforts to eliminate the dogmatic teaching of evolution in public schools.

Courts have not yet clarified whether the Biblical account of creation belongs in the public school curriculum *at all*, but they have struck down blatant attempts to present the origin of life from the creationist perspective to the exclusion of scientific theories. For example, in 1978 an Indiana superior court judge invalidated the use of a biology textbook with an avowedly creationist orientation.[44] The Indiana state textbook commission had approved for use in biology classes the book, *Biology—A Search for Order in Complexity*, developed by the Creation-Science Research Center. After several school districts adopted the controversial text for biology courses, parents and the Indiana Civil Liberties Union challenged the use of the book as advancing religion. Concluding that the book clearly promotes the Genesis account of creation, particularly in instructions included in the teacher's manual, the judge ruled that the establishment clause prohibits the use of the book as a basic biology text.[45] However, the judge did not bar all discussion of creationism from the curriculum.

More recently the South Dakota Supreme Court upheld the nonrenewal of the contract of a biology teacher for devoting too much instructional time to the Biblical theory.[46] The teacher received repeated warnings to follow the school board's adopted guidelines for teaching biology and to limit his discussion of creationism. After the teacher persisted in violating the guidelines, his contract was not renewed. The teacher challenged the board's action as arbitrary, capricious, and in violation of his due process rights. Rejecting these assertions, the court concluded that the teacher willfully disregarded the board's guidelines and that all procedural requirements were met prior to the board's nonrenewal action. The court emphasized, however, that the teacher's termination was not based on his introduction of the Biblical account of creation in his biology classes; rather, it resulted from his overemphasis on the creationism-evolution dispute to the exclusion of other basic biology concepts.

Thus, the issue of whether creationism can be introduced at all in public schools, and if so, to what extent, remains to be clarified in future litigation. Since courts have concluded that creationism is a religious belief, not science, it might be inferred from rulings to date that the Genesis account can be covered in comparative religion classes, but not in the public school science curriculum. The American Civil Liberties Union recently asked Michigan's attorney general to order public school districts to stop teaching creation-science in compliance with a resolution of the state board of education.[47] If the Michigan controversy generates a lawsuit, it might ultimately result in judicial clarification of the constitutional status of teaching the Biblical account of creation in public schools.[48]

Censorship of Instructional Materials

There is a mounting movement to eliminate public school curriculum materials and library books that allegedly conflict with the Christian faith. Few aspects of the public school program remain totally untouched by recent censorship activities. It was estimated in 1980 that approximately 200 organizations were involved in efforts to purge public schools of "immoral, anti-Christian" materials and course offerings.[49] During the 1980-81 school year, over 900 book banning cases were reported to the Office for Intellectual Freedom of the American Library Association, up from 300 reported in 1978-79.[50] Also, in a 1981 survey of 2,000 elementary and secondary school administrators and librarians, almost 20% of the administrators and almost 30% of the librarians reported at least one challenge to curricular materials in their schools in the preceding two years. About a third of these challenges were reported to have been initiated by school personnel.[51]

Attempts to remove books from classrooms and libraries and to tailor curricular offerings and methodologies to particular religious and philosophical values has led to a substantial number of judicial rulings. With the multiple actors and interests involved in censorship disputes, the issues do not lend themselves to simplistic resolution. Most would agree that schools *do* transmit values, but there is little consensus regarding *which* values should be transmitted or *who* should make this determination. Many of the censorship efforts have been religiously motivated, but curriculum disputes have also involved other social and political issues.[52]

In one of the most widely publicized censorship cases, a West Virginia federal district court upheld the Kanawha County School Board's authority to adopt an English series that some parents asserted was Godless, communistic, profane, and generally inappropriate for students.[53] The parents asserted that the controversial materials undermined their religious beliefs and established the religion of secular humanism in the public schools. Rejecting these claims, the court endorsed the board's authority to determine curricular materials. However, this ruling did not deter school boycotts and public demonstrations in Kanawha County. Indeed, eventually the protesting parents were successful in changing the composition of the school board—and subsequently the English curriculum—through the political process.

To date courts have not been inclined to allow mere parental displeasure over course content to dictate the public school curriculum. In 1978 a Massachusetts federal district court judge stated: "With the greatest of respect to . . . parents, their sensibilities are not the full measure of what is proper education."[54] The Second Circuit Court of Appeals also has recognized that the judiciary must ensure that community prejudices do not infringe upon individual freedoms since the "will of the transient majority can prove devastating to freedom of expression."[55] One commentator has observed that "courts have subordinated the interest of individual parents in fashioning a curriculum to reflect their own values not only because satisfaction of all diverse desires would be administratively impossible, but also because satisfaction of the individualistic interest would be paradoxically counterproductive to preserving free expression."[56]

For example, a New York trial court denied a parental request for Dickens' *Oliver Twist* and Shakespeare's *The Merchant of Venice* to be barred from the high school curriculum for religious reasons.[57] Plaintiffs alleged that both books tended to engender anti-Semitic sentiments, and thus, their use violated the First Amendment. Rejecting this contention, the court concluded that the books were not written with the explicit purpose of fostering religious discrimination or ridicule, and therefore, their suppression would interfere with free inquiry in the school. The court declared:

> Except where a book has been maliciously written for the apparent purpose of promoting and fomenting a bigoted and intolerant hatred against a particular racial or religious group, public interest in a free and democratic society does not warrant or encourage the suppression of any book at the whim of any unduly sensitive person or group of persons, merely because a character described in such book as belonging to a particular race or religion is portrayed in a derogatory or offensive manner. The necessity for the suppression of such a book must clearly depend upon the intent and motive which has actuated the author in making such a portrayal.[58]

More recently, a Michigan parent brought suit to enjoin the use of Kurt Vonnegut's *Slaughterhouse Five* in the public school curriculum, claiming among other charges that the novel's religious references violated the First Amendment.[59] The trial court enjoined use of the book, but the Michigan appellate court reversed and upheld the school. Reasoning that the book was not derogatory or preferential toward any sect, the court cautioned that if curriculum grievances based on religious preferences were allowed to stifle intellectual freedom, children would be deprived of the opportunity to study great literary works:

> If plaintiff's contention was correct, then public school students could no longer marvel at Sir Galahad's saintly quest for the Holy Grail, nor be introduced to the dangers of Hitler's *Mein Kampf*, nor read the mellifluous poetry of John Milton or John Donne. Unhappily, Robin Hood would be forced to forage without Friar Tuck and Shakespeare would have to delete Shylock from *The Merchant of Venice*. . . . Our Constitution does not command ignorance; on the contrary, it assures the people that the state may not relegate them to such a status and guarantees to all the precious and unfettered freedom of pursuing one's own intellectual pleasures in one's own personal way.[60]

Even though the individual parent has not had much success in challenging a school board's curricular decisions, organized groups of parents have been influential in securing changes in board policies and in determining the outcomes of school board elections. Thus the "comprehensive authority of the States and of school officials . . . to prescribe and control conduct in the schools"[61] increasingly has been exercised to restrict the curriculum in conformance with community values.

Several courts have dismissed claims that teachers' academic freedom or students' rights to be exposed to conflicting points of view have been impaired by the exercise of school board authority in banning specific curricular and library materials and course offerings.[62] The Supreme Court has acknowledged that public schools are vitally important as vehicles for "inculcating fundamental values necessary to the maintenance of a democratic political system,"[63] and that local school boards must be permitted "to establish and apply their curriculum in such a way as to transmit community values."[64] Accordingly, some courts have endorsed the board's power to censor materials based on the social, political, and moral tastes of its members.

For example, in 1979 an Indiana federal district court rejected students' assertions that the censorship of instructional materials and the elimination of certain courses from the high school curriculum violated their protected right to learn by restricting the free exchange of ideas.[65] The court declared that "it is legitimate for school officials to develop an opinion about what types of citizens are good citizens, to determine what curriculum and materials will best develop good citizens, and to prohibit the use of texts, remove library books, and delete courses from the curriculum as a part of the effort to shape students into good citizens."[66] Although the Seventh Circuit Court of Appeals vacated the district court's ruling to allow the students to initiate an amended complaint, the appeals court emphasized that challenges by students to curricular decisions of the school board must "cross a relatively high threshold" before implicating constitutional rights.[67] The court concluded that in the absence of an attempt at "rigid and exclusive indoctrination," the judiciary should not interfere with a school board's broad discretion in determining the curriculum based on its members "social, political, and moral" beliefs.[68] Recognizing that board members represent the local citizenry, the court emphasized that "the community has a legitimate, even a vital and compelling interest in 'the choice [of] and adherence to a suitable curriculum for the benefit of our young citizens'."[69]

The Second Circuit Court of Appeals has ruled on two occasions that school board censorship actions in connection with library materials have not impaired students' rights to be exposed to ideas and to acquire new knowledge. In 1972 the court upheld a school board's decision to remove a book with "objectionable" language from all junior high school libraries.[70] The court reasoned that dissatisfaction with the board's determination "hardly elevate[s] this intramural strife to First Amendment constitutional proportions."[71] In 1980 the same court reiterated that a school board's decision to remove "vulgar" and "obscene" books and to screen future library acquisitions did not create a risk of suppressing ideas.[72]

In 1981 the Third Circuit Court of Appeals held that performances by the high school drama club were a part of the school program and, therefore, the school board had a legitimate interest in assuring that the group did not perform a play at variance with the goals of the school's educational offerings.[73] In this case, parents had challenged the planned performance of the musical, *Pippin*, asserting that it was sacrilegious. The school board eventually prohibited the performance, but based its action on the musical's explicit sexual scenes, which were considered inappropriate for high school students. Although the federal district court and Third Circuit Court of Appeals upheld the school board's authority to impose the ban, it seems unlikely that the board's action would have been endorsed if the official reason for the ban had been that the musical offended the religious views of some patrons.

The judiciary has attempted to uphold the right of school board members to apply social and moral values in determining curricular materials and offerings, but some courts have intervened if censorship activity clearly has been motivated by religious concerns or a desire to suppress ideas.[74] For example, in 1982 the Eighth Circuit Court of Appeals afforded constitutional protection to students' right to be exposed to controversial ideas when it struck down a Minnesota school board's attempt to ban certain films from the public school. Concluding that the board initiated the ban because the films' religious and ideological content offended some parents, the court held that there must be a "substantial" governmental interest before impairing "students' right to receive information."[75] The court noted that the board's suppression of ideas for impermissible reasons had an obvious "chilling effect" on teachers and students.[76]

In a case that has received national attention, *Pico* v. *Island Trees School District*, the U.S. Supreme Court rendered its first decision in a censorship controversy.[77] The splintered Court affirmed the Second Circuit Court of Appeal's ruling that a school board's censorship action may have compromised students' protected rights. Accordingly, the case was remanded to the federal district court for a trial.

The controversy in *Pico* involved a New York school board's decision to remove nine library books for being anti-Christian, anti-American, anti-Semitic, "and just plain filthy."[78] Although the Second Circuit Appellate Court had endorsed the authority of school boards to remove objectionable materials in other cases,[79] in this situation the court reasoned that there were substantial questions regarding the legitimacy of the board's motivation and procedures. Recognizing that board members should be encouraged to make "thoughtful applications" of personal standards of taste, morality, and political beliefs in carrying out their duties, the court declared:

> Where, however, as in this case, evidence that the decisions made were based on defendant's moral or political beliefs appears together with evidence of procedural and substantive irregularities sufficient to suggest an unwillingness on the part of school officials to subject their political and personal judgments to the same sort of scrutiny as that accorded other decisions relating to the education of their charges, an inference emerges that political views and personal taste are being asserted not in

the interests of the children's well-being, but rather for the purpose of establishing those views as the correct and orthodox ones for all purposes in the particular community.[80]

Affirming the appellate court's conclusion that the case should be remanded for a trial, the divided Supreme Court did not provide clear guidance for resolving future censorship controversies. Indeed, seven opinions were written in the case, conveying diverse points of view as to the governing legal principles. Although five members of the Court concluded that the case warranted a trial to determine if the students' rights had been abridged, only three of the justices endorsed the notion that students have a protected right to receive information.[81] Justice Brennan's opinion, which was supported by Justices Marshall and Stephens, stated that "our Constitution does not permit the official suppression of *ideas*,"[82] and "local school boards may not remove books from school library shelves simply because they dislike the ideas contained in those books and seek by their removal to 'prescribe what shall be orthodox in politics, nationalism, religion, or other matters of opinions'."[83] Yet, Chief Justice Burger's dissent, which was endorsed by three other justices, asserted that "there is not a hint in the First Amendment, or in any holding of this Court, of a 'right' to have the government provide continuing access to certain books."[84]

Even Justice Brennan cautioned that the Court's conclusion in *Pico* might have been different if the school board had "employed established, regular, and facially unbiased procedures for the review of controversial materials."[85] He further suggested that with proper procedures, a school board might be able to "allay suspicions" about its motivation for removing library books.[86] The plurality opinion also indicated "full agreement" with the notion that "there is a legitimate and substantial community interest in promoting respect for authority and traditional values be they social, moral, or political."[87] Thus, assuming that a school board has proper procedures for reviewing challenges to curricular materials, one might infer that decisions concerning which materials to remove could be based on the personal tastes of board members. Since there is often a fine line between moral and social values and religious beliefs, might such decisions also reflect religious preferences? The Supreme Court's *Pico* decision did not clarify what constitutes "proper motivation" for restricting student access to materials.

Judge Rosenn of the Third Circuit Court of Appeals has noted the "inherent tension" between the school board's two essential functions of "exposing young minds to the clash of ideologies in the free marketplace of ideas" and instilling basic community values in our youth.[88] However, it appears that in a growing number of school districts the former function is being subjugated to the latter. And with fundamentalist groups becoming increasingly successful in influencing school board policies, board action to purge schools of materials considered Godless or offensive to Christian values seems destined to continue. Until the Supreme Court clarifies the scope of students' rights to receive information and the school board's authority to base curricular decisions on its members' personal values, curriculum censorship controversies will undoubtedly generate a steady flow of litigation.

Alleged Establishment of the Religion of Secular Humanism

Assertions that public school instruction advances the notion that "man, rather than God, is the source of all knowledge and truth,"[89] have been the basis for many of the curricular challenges discussed in this chapter. Fundamentalist groups have claimed that the public school is unconstitutionally establishing the religion of secular humanism by teaching subjects such as sex education and evolution and by introducing students to anti-Christian materials. This sentiment has also nurtured the growth of private Christian academies and has been cited as a major impetus for the escalating home education movement.[90]

Those advocating that secular humanism is a religion and that public schools are advancing this faith rely heavily on statements from the following documents, which have appeared in publications of the American Humanist Association and American Ethical Union. *Humanist Manifesto I*, written in 1933, sought to make "religious humanism" better understood by explaining that it is an alternative to traditional theism, based on modern "man's larger understanding of the universe, his scientific achievements, and his deeper appreciation of brotherhood."[91] *Humanist Manifesto II*, which was signed by 114 individuals in 1973, asserted in its preface:

> As in 1933, humanists still believe that traditional theism, especially faith in the prayer-hearing God, . . . is an unproved and outmoded faith. . . . Humanism is an ethical process through which we can all move, above and beyond divisive particulars, heroic personalities, dogmatic creeds, and ritual customs of past religions or their mere negation.[92]

In 1980 a group of 58 scholars and scientists signed a third document, *A Secular Humanist Declaration*, warning that "the reappearance of 'dogmatic authoritarian religions' threatens intellectual freedom, human rights and scientific progress."[93] The Declaration explains that secular humanism places trust in human intelligence and the scientific method rather than in divine guidance.

Antihumanists have argued that the use of the word "faith," the disavowance of traditional theism, and the discussion of beliefs of "ultimate concern" in the above documents comprise the basic tenets of the religion of secular humanism. These groups claim that humanists view the self-sufficiency and centrality of "Man" in a similar way that theists worship God.[94] They further contend that since humanists view science as the ultimate guide to human progress, science itself takes on a religious character. Indeed, some have argued that secular humanism has developed a "scientific theology" that is being established by the state.[95] An example proffered is the teaching of evolutionary concepts, which rule out any possibility of supernatural intervention in the origin of the universe and humanity. John Whitehead and John Conlan have asserted that "for years Secular Humanists have used the public school system to teach generations of school children their doctrine and dogma."[96]

Science and health instruction and materials used in English classes have been the major targets of claims that public schools are establishing the religion of secular humanism, but many other facets of the public school curriculum have come under attack. There even have been efforts to secure federal legislation that would bar certain secular humanistic subjects and materials from public education. For example, in 1976 the following provision was introduced in Congress as an amendment to an education bill:

> No grant, contract, or support is authorized under the foreign studies and language development portions of Title II of the bill for any educational program, curriculum research or development, administrator-teacher orientation, or any project involving one or more students or teacher-administrators involving any aspect of the religion of secular humanism.[97]

Although the proposed amendment passed the House, it was not included in the final version of the act that was signed into law.

The fundamentalist/humanist controversy has become emotionally charged, with serious accusations emanating from both camps. Some humanists have asserted that the absolutist morality championed by conservative evangelicals poses a threat to reason, democracy, and freedom. They have assailed supernatural religion as an enemy "of the rational process that leads to progress" and have denounced efforts of the "Radical Religious Right" to purge public schools of all material "that encourages thinking or is inconsistent with majoritarian orthodoxy."[98] On the other hand, some fundamentalists have referred to humanism as "Satan's philosophy," which promises ultimate doom unless it is completely eradicated.[99] They have used the term "secular humanism" as a residual category encompassing everything taught in public education that does not reinforce Christian beliefs. Carrying this dichotomy to its logical extension, no instruction could be merely neutral or nonreligious. All subjects in public schools would either promote theism or secular humanism—both asserted to be in violation of the establishment clause! There is some sentiment that the "academic integrity" of public education is seriously jeopardized by those seeking to replace the *nonreligious* approach to the study of history, science, and literature with instruction "more responsive to their own particular moral and religious values."[100]

In only a few cases has the constitutional status of secular humanism been raised, and courts have not yet provided clear guidance as to whether or not it constitutes a religion. Instead, in the cases where the subject has been broached, courts usually have dismissed the specific allegation but have not elaborated on what constitutes secular humanism, if it is indeed a religion.[101] For example, among other claims in a Texas case involving a challenge to the teaching of evolution, plaintiffs asserted that instruction in evolution unconstitutionally advances "secularism." However, the federal district court concluded that the school board's approach to the teaching of evolution was connected to religion by "too tenuous a thread on which to base a First Amendment complaint."[102] The court declared that it was "cited to no case in which so nebulous an intrusion upon the principle of religious neutrality has been condemned by the Supreme Court."[103] The Washington, D.C. federal district court dismissed a similar challenge to a Smithsonian Institution display pertaining to man's evolution. The court reasoned that the exhibit "in no way treats evolution as part of a religion, secular humanism or otherwise."[104] It concluded that the primary effect of the evolution exhibit was "not to advance a religious theory or to inhibit plaintiffs in their religious beliefs," but to present a body of scientific knowledge.[105]

In several cases involving challenges to sex education programs, courts have rejected claims that such instruction is antagonistic to traditional religious beliefs or advances a "humanistic, amoral" faith.[106] Also, in the West Virginia censorship case discussed previously, the federal district court concluded that it would take "a complete loosening of the imagination" to find that placing the allegedly Godless, anti-Christian books and materials in public schools constitutes an establishment of the religion of secular humanism.[107]

More recently, in upholding the termination of a teacher for using prayer and Bible reading in a public school classroom, a Pennsylvania court rejected the assertion that the dismissal constituted hostility toward theism and established secular humanism.[108] However, the court suggested that secular humanism *is* a religion under establishment clause prohibitions, but it did not elaborate on what specific practices would advance this belief.[109] In an earlier case, a Michigan federal district court also indicated that secular humanism is a religion: "In light of the decided cases, the public schools, as between theistic and humanistic religions, must carefully avoid any program of indoctrination in ultimate values."[110]

Those asserting that advancement of a secular humanistic belief abridges the First Amendment rely heavily on dicta from two Supreme Court decisions. In 1961 the Court struck down a Maryland constitutional provision requiring a notary public to declare a belief in God.[111] The Court reasoned that such a condition violated the First Amendment by forcing a person to profess a religious belief, and thereby advancing theistic faiths. The Court observed in a footnote that "among religions in this country which do not teach what would generally be considered a belief in the existence of God are Buddhism, Taoism, Ethical Culture, Secular Humanism and others."[112] Two years later, when prayer was barred from public schools, the Supreme Court noted that "the state may not establish a 'religion of secularism' in the sense of affirmatively opposing or showing hostility to religion, thus preferring those who believe in no religion over those who do not believe."[113]

Although the Supreme Court has not clarified what constitutes governmental advancement of a secular faith that would be barred by the establishment clause, the Court has adopted a somewhat expansive definition of what constitutes a religious belief under the First Amendment. In cases dealing with conscientious objectors to military service, the Court has ruled that beliefs based on moral convictions are entitled to protection under the free exercise clause.[114] In 1965 the Court noted that beliefs occupying a "parallel position" to that of traditional theism are constitutionally protected.[115] Those contending that secular humanism is a religion claim that since beliefs based on conscience rather than God have received free exercise protection, they should also be subject to establishment clause prohibitions.[116]

In 1982 an Alabama federal judge suggested that courts will have to consider secular faiths in addition to Christianity in assessing the constitutionality of various public school activities:

> The religions of atheism, materialism, agnosticism, communism and socialism have escaped the scrutiny of the courts throughout the years, and make no mistake, these are to the believers religions; they are ardently adhered to and quantitatively advanced in the teachings and literature that is presented to the fertile minds of the students in the various school systems.[117]

The judge further asserted that it is "common knowledge" that miscellaneous antitheistic doctrines are being advanced in public education, and "it is time to recognize that the constitutional definition of religion encompasses more than Christianity and prohibits as well the establishment of a secular religion."[118]

It appears that any nonreligious subject might be attacked as exhibiting hostility toward theism and thus advancing a secular faith. One commentator has noted that if this line of reasoning is carried to its logical conclusion, it would "call for the abolition of the public schools as being themselves in violation of the First Amendment."[119] If the Supreme Court should ultimately conclude that public schools are unconstitutionally advancing the religion of secular humanism through their instructional program, the implications would indeed be significant.

Conclusion

Religious challenges to the public school program are becoming more numerous and complex. Unlike requests for specific exemptions which involve primarily free exercise rights, claims that public school offerings should be altered for religious reasons implicate the establishment and free exercise clauses. Such claims also raise questions about the state's plenary power to determine the public school curriculum, parental rights to direct the upbringing of their children, and students' rights to be exposed to new information.

The judiciary has attempted to uphold decisions of state legislatures and local school boards regarding educational offerings unless such decisions have clearly compromised constitutional rights. Parents usually have not prevailed in their religious challenges to the state's authority to include particular activities, subjects, and materials in the public school curriculum. However, more complicated issues are raised when religious groups secure legislative or school board support for their demands. While the Supreme Court has struck down blatant state efforts to restrict the curriculum for religious reasons (e.g., barring the teaching of evolution), the scope of the state's authority to tailor curricular offerings to the preferences of the dominant religion remains unclear.

One of the most troublesome issues facing the courts pertains to what constitutes a religious belief and, therefore, is subject to establishment clause prohibitions. What public school practices advance a humanistic faith in contravention of the First Amendment? Judicial guidance is needed to distinguish permissible *nonreligious* instruction from instruction that disavows traditional religion to the extent that it establishes an antitheistic creed. Providing such clarification may prove to be an awesome judicial task. But without such judicial guidance, almost all aspects of the public school curriculum appear vulnerable to First Amendment challenge.

Footnotes

1. Epperson v. Arkansas, 393 U.S. 97, 107 (1968), quoting from Joseph Burstyn, Inc. v. Wilson, 343 U.S. 495, 505 (1952).

2. McCollum v. Board of Educ., 333 U.S. 203, 235 (1948) (Jackson, J., concurring).

3. Bill Ebarb, "Sex Education—Who Needs It? Who Knows?" *Compact* 13 (Summer 1979):3, 19-22.

4. For a discussion of allegations that the public school is establishing the religion of secular humanism, *see* text with note 89.

5. Cornwell v. State Bd. of Educ., 314 F. Supp. 340 (D. Md. 1969).

6. Hopkins v. Hamden Bd. of Educ., 289 A.2d 914, 921 (Conn. C.P. 1971).

7. Although the health course including sex education was mandatory, the court noted that parents who objected to the curriculum could select an alternative to public education or seek an exemption from the class for their children. For a discussion of parents' rights to have their children excused from sex education instruction on religious grounds, *see* text with note 66, chapter 3.

8. 289 A.2d at 924.

9. *See* Citizens for Parental Rights v. San Mateo County Bd. of Educ., 124 Cal. Rptr. 68 (Cal. App. 1975); Hobolth v. Greenway, 218 N.W.2d 98 (Mich. 1974); Valent v. New Jersey State Bd. of Educ., 274 A.2d 832 (N.J. Super. 1971); Medeiros v. Kiyosaki, 478 P.2d 314 (Hawaii 1970).

10. For a discussion of this issue, *see* Annual Project, "Education and the Law: State Interests and Individual Rights," *Michigan Law Review* 74 (1976):1438-39.

11. Citizens for Parental Rights v. San Mateo County Bd. of Educ., 124 Cal. Rptr. 68, 90 (Cal. App. 1975), citing Griswold v. Connecticut, 381 U.S. 479, 482 (1965).

12. Smith v. Ricci, 446 A.2d 501 (N.J. 1982), *appeal dismissed sub nom.* Smith v. Brandt, 103 S. Ct. 286 (1982).

13. *See Education Daily*, 11 April 1980, pp. 1-2; *Education U.S.A.* 22, 7 July 1980, p. 335.

14. Malnak v. Yogi, 440 F. Supp. 1284 (D.N.J. 1977), *aff'd* 592 F.2d 197 (3d Cir. 1979).

15. *Id.*, 440 F. Supp. at 1287.

16. For a discussion of implications of this case, see Robert O'Neil, *Classrooms in the Crossfire* (Bloomington, Ind.: Indiana University Press, 1981), pp. 79-82.

17. *See* O'Neil, *ibid.*, pp. 175-79.

18. Meyer v. Nebraska, 262 U.S. 390 (1923).

19. Epperson v. Arkansas, 393 U.S. 97 (1968).

20. *Id.* at 106.

21. Mercer v. Michigan State Bd. of Educ., 379 F. Supp 580 (E.D. Mich. 1974), *aff'd mem.*, 419 U.S. 1081 (1974).

22. *Id.*, 379 F. Supp. at 586. There also have been a few First Amendment challenges to the authority of the state and its agents to alter extracurricular programs for religious reasons. While the free exercise clause has not been interpreted as requiring school authorities to make religious accommodations in extracurricular schedules, in a noteworthy 1981 decision the New Jersey Supreme Court ruled that the establishment clause permits such accommodations to be made. A school board's policy that required schools to avoid conflicts with traditional religious exercises "to the maximum extent possible" in scheduling student activities other than interscholastic athletic events was challenged under the establishment clause by student members of a drama group. A state trial court held that the rule as implemented served to advance religion, but the appeals court and subsequently the New Jersey Supreme Court upheld the policy, reasoning that the rule is designed to increase extracurricular participation rather than to advance religion. The appellate court also rejected the assertion that community opposition to the rule created excessive governmental entanglement with religion. Noting that the board's action may have the effect of accommodating religious beliefs by scheduling extracurricular activities at times that will not conflict with most religious services, the court found the policy's effect on the advancement of religion to be "merely incidental." However, the court did not address what constitutes a "traditional" religion under the rules. Also, the court did not address whether "nontraditional" religious sects

might have a valid equal protection claim if extracurricular activity schedules accommodate *only* well-established denominations. Student members of Playcrafters v. Board of Educ., 424 A.2d 1192 (N.J. Super. 1981), *aff'd per curiam*, 438 A.2d 543 (N.J. 1981).

23. *See* Gerald Caplan, "Evolution and the Biblical Account of Creation: Equal Time," in *School Law in Changing Times*, ed. M. A. McGhehey (Topeka, Kans.: National Organization on Legal Problems of Education, 1982), p. 67; Education Commission of the States, *Legislative Review* 12 (8 March 1982), p. 1. There have even been efforts to secure federal legislation to this effect. *See* text with note 97.

24. *See* Clifford Hooker, "Creation Science Has No Legitimate Educational Purpose," *West's Education Law Reporter* 1 (1982):1071-72, n. 9.

25. Scopes v. State, 289 S.W. 363 (Tenn. 1927).

26. *Id.* at 366.

27. 393 U.S. 97 (1968).

28. *Id.* at 106. *See also* Moore v. Gaston County Bd. of Educ., 357 F. Supp. 1037 (W.D.N.C. 1973), in which reinstatement was ordered of a student teacher who had been discharged for questioning the literal interpretation of the Bible and indicating approval of Darwin's theory.

29. Daniel v. Waters, 515 F.2d 485 (6th Cir. 1975). *See also* Steele v. Waters, 527 S.W.2d 72 (Tenn. 1975).

30. *See* Caplan, "Evolution and the Biblical Account of Creation: Equal Time," p. 67.

31. For a discussion of the tripartite test, *see* Lemon v. Kurtzman, 403 U.S. 602, 612-13 (1971); text with note 80, chapter 1; note 46, chapter 6.

32. McLean v. Arkansas Bd. of Educ., 529 F. Supp. 1255, 1264 (E.D. Ark. 1982). While basing its holding on the establishment clause violation, the judge did comment on other claims raised by plaintiffs and defendants, *id.*, at 1273-74.

33. *Id.* at 1274. In February 1982 Arkansas Attorney General Stephen Clark announced that the federal judge's ruling would not be appealed. *See Nolpe Notes* 17 (February 1982):1 *See also* McLean v. State, 663 F.2d 47 (8th Cir. 1981), in which several organizations and individuals attempted unsuccessfully to secure a court order stipulating that the Arkansas Attorney General could not adequately defend the "equal time" law.

34. Aguillard v. Treen, No. 81-4787 51 U.S.L.W. 2352 (E.D. La. 1982). *See Education Daily*, 24 November 1982, pp. 1-2.

35. *Ibid., Education Daily*, p. 2.

36. Keith v. Louisiana Depart. of Educ., 553 F. Supp. 295 (M.D. La. 1982). *See Education Daily*, 30 June 1982, p. 1.

37. Creationists have attempted to capitalize on the new "punctuated equilibrium" theory, suggesting that new species have emerged by splitting off randomly from existing ones, rather than through natural selection. However, paleontologist Stephen

Gould, one of the originators of the new theory, has asserted that his work is misrepresented when used to support creationism. He has stated that his argument is with Darwin's theory of natural selection, not with evolution which "is a fact." *Newsweek*, 29 March 1982, p. 46. For a discussion of the creation-science perspective, *see* George Hahn, "Creation-Science and Education," *Phi Delta Kappan* 63 (April 1982):553-55.

38. *See* text with note 33. *See also* Wright v. Houston Independent School Dist., 366 F. Supp. 1208 (S.D. Tex. 1972), in which the federal district court held that the teaching of evolution in a biology course did not hold Christian beliefs "up to contempt and scorn" or establish the religion of secular humanism; text with note 102.

39. Kim McDonald, "Forced Teaching of Creationism Threatens Integrity of Education, Science Group Says," *The Chronicle of Higher Education*, 13 January 1982, p. 1.

40. *See Education Daily*, 5 January 1982, p. 4.

41. "New York City Rejects Textbooks Uncritical of Creationism Theory," *Louisville Times*, 25 June 1982, p. B-4. In other school districts such as Lexington, Kentucky; Scarsdale, New York; and Huntsville, Alabama, school boards have taken a stand to keep creationism out of the classroom. *See Education Daily*, 5 January 1982, p. 4.

42. Segraves v. State of California, No. 278978 (Cal. Super., Sacramento, 1981). *See* Harvey Siegel, "Creationism, Evolution, and Education: The California Fiasco," *Phi Delta Kappan* 63 (October 1981):95-101.

43. *See Education Daily*, 11 March 1981, pp. 5-6.

44. Hendren v. Campbell, No. 5577-0139 (Ind. Super., Marion County, 1977).

45. *Id.*

46. Dale v. Board of Educ., Lemmon Independent School Dist., 316 N.W.2d 108 (S.D. 1982).

47. *Nolpe Notes* 17, (June 1982):3.

48. Because the judiciary has not been persuaded to accept the argument that creation-science is indeed science rather than religion, in future suits creationists will likely rely on free expression rights in asserting that students have a right to be exposed to the Genesis account. Since the Supreme Court has ruled that college students have a free speech right to assemble and express their views—including religious views—in state-supported facilities, Widmar v. Vincent, 102 S. Ct. 269 (1982), it might be argued that the expression of religious views should share similar protection in public elementary and secondary schools. *See* text with note 45, chapter 2.

49. "Censorship: The Rules Have Changed," *Education U.S.A.* 22 (24 March 1980):227. *See also* Stephen Arons, "The Crusade to Ban Books," *Counterpoint* (November, 1981):19; "Newsnotes," *Phi Delta Kappan* 61 (June 1980):722.

50. "Newsnotes," *ibid. See also* "Book Banning in America," *New York Times*, 20 December 1981, Book Review Section, p. 16.

51. This study was conducted by the Association of American Publishers, the American Library Association, and the Association for Supervision and Curriculum Development. *See Education Daily*, 3 August 1981, pp. 1-2.

52. For a general discussion of curriculum censorship litigation, *see* Martha McCarthy, "Curriculum Censorship: Actors and Interests Involved," in *Public Schools and the First Amendment*, (Bloomington, Ind.: Phi Delta Kappa, 1983); Nelda Cambron-McCabe, "School Board Censorship: Library Books and Curriculum Materials," in *School Law in Changing Times*, ed. M. A. McGhehey (Topeka, Kans.: National Organization on Legal Problems of Education, 1982), pp. 78-89.

53. Williams v. Board of Educ. of County of Kanawha, 388 F. Supp. 93 (S.D. W. Va. 1975). For a discussion of the West Virginia controversy, *see* O'Neil, *Classrooms in the Crossfire*, pp. 3-9; Ralph Fuller, "Textbook Selection: Burning Issue?" *Compact* 9 (June 1975):6-8; *Censoring Textbooks: Is West Virginia the Tip of the Iceberg?* (Washington, D.C.: Institute for Educational Leadership, 1974).

54. Right to Read Defense Committee of Chelsea v. School Committee of Chelsea, 454 F. Supp. 703, 713 (D. Mass. 1978), citing Keefe v. Geanakos, 418 F.2d 359, 361-62 (1st Cir. 1969).

55. James v. Board of Educ., 461 F.2d 566, 575 (2d Cir. 1972).

56. Annual Project, *Michigan Law Review*, p. 1441.

57. Rosenberg v. Board of Educ. of City of New York, 92 N.Y.S.2d 344 (Sup. Ct., Kings County, 1949).

58. *Id.* at 346.

59. Todd v. Rochester Community Schools, 200 N.W.2d 90 (Mich. App. 1972).

60. *Id.* at 93-94.

61. Tinker v. Des Moines Independent School Dist., 393 U.S. 503, 507 (1969).

62. *See* Zykan v. Warsaw Community School Corp., 631 F.2d 1300 (7th Cir. 1980); Cary v. Board of Educ. of the Adams-Arapahoe School Dist., 598 F.2d 535, 544 (10th Cir. 1979); Adams v. Campbell County School Dist., 511 F.2d 1242 (10th Cir. 1975); Presidents Council, Dist. 25 v. Community School Bd. No. 25, 457 F.2d 289 (2d Cir. 1972), *cert. denied*, 409 U.S. 998 (1972).

63. Ambach v. Norwick, 441 U.S. 68, 77 (1979).

64. Pico v. Island Trees School Dist., 102 S. Ct. 2799 (1982).

65. Zykan v. Warsaw Community School Corp., No. 579-68 (N.D. Ind. 1979), *vacated and remanded*, 631 F.2d 1300 (7th Cir. 1980).

66. *Id.* No. 579-68, slip opinion at 4.

67. *Id.*, 631 F.2d at 1306.

68. *Id.* at 1306-07.

69. *Id.* at 1304, citing Palmer v. Board of Educ., 603 F.2d 1271, 1274 (7th Cir. 1979).

70. Presidents Council, Dist. 25 v. Community School Bd. No. 25, 457 F.2d 289 (2d Cir. 1972).

71. *Id.* at 291-92.

72. Bicknell v. Vergennes Union High School Bd. of Directors, 638 F.2d 438 (2d Cir. 1980).

73. Seyfried v. Walton, 668 F.2d 214 (3d Cir. 1981).

74. *See* Sheck v. Baileyville School Committee, 530 F. Supp. 679 (D. Me. 1982); Salvail v. Nashua Bd. of Educ., 469 F. Supp. 1269 (D.N.H. 1979); Right to Read Defense Committee v. School Committee of the City of Chelsea, 454 F. Supp. 703 (D. Mass. 1978).

75. Pratt v. Independent School Dist., 670 F.2d 771, 777 (8th Cir. 1982).

76. *Id.* at 778.

77. 474 F. Supp. 387 (E.D.N.Y. 1979), *vacated and remanded*, 638 F.2d 404 (2d Cir. 1980), *aff'd* 102 S. Ct. 2799 (1982).

78. *Id.*, 474 F. Supp. at 390.

79. *See* Bicknell v. Vergennes Union High School Bd. of Directors, 638 F.2d 438 (2d Cir. 1980); Presidents Council, Dist. 25 v. Community School Bd. No. 25, 457 F.2d (2d Cir. 1972).

80. 638 F.2d at 417.

81. Justices White and Blackmun concurred that the case should be remanded for trial, but they did not endorse the plurality opinion's treatment of the First Amendment issue. However, Justice White did not voice disagreement with Justice Brennan's reasoning; he simply felt that any discussion of the First Amendment claim by the Supreme Court was inappropriate since the case was being remanded for a trial on the substantive issues. 102 S. Ct. at 2816-17 (White, J., concurring).

82. 102 S. Ct. at 2810.

83. *Id.*, citing West Virginia State Bd. of Educ. v. Barnette, 319 U.S. 624, 642 (1943).

84. *Id.* at 2819 (Burger, C. J., dissenting). Justices Powell, Rehnquist, and O'Conner joined in the Chief Justice's dissent and also wrote individual dissenting opinions.

85. *Id.* at 2811.

86. *Id.* at 2812.

87. *Id.* at 2806, citing Brief for Petitioners. Two months after the Supreme Court's decision, the Island Trees school board decided to place the nine controversial books back in the school library. However, the board resolution stipulated that the parents of a student who had checked out any of the nine books would receive a written notice that their child had material they might find objectionable. *See Nolpe Notes* 17 (August 1982):6. Subsequently, in January 1983, the board voted four-to-three to rescind the resolution, thus removing all restrictions on student access to the books. *See* "L. I. School Board Ends Its Battle to Ban Books," *The New York Times*, 31 January 1983, p. 15.

88. Seyfried v. Walton, 668 F.2d 214, 219 (3d Cir. 1981) (Rosenn, J., concurring).

89. *See* John Whitehead and John Conlan, "The Establishment of the Religion of Secular Humanism and Its First Amendment Implications," *Texas Tech Law Review* 10 (1978):30-31.

90. *See* Chester Nolte, "Home Instruction in Lieu of Public School Attendance," in *School Law in Changing Times*, ed. M. A. McGhehey (Topeka, Kans.: National Organization on Legal Problems of Education, 1982), pp. 2-3; Michael Baker, "Regulation of Fundamentalist Christian Schools: Free Exercise of Religion v. the State's Interest in Quality Education," *Kentucky Law Journal* 67 (1978-79):415. *See also* chapter 7 for a discussion of state regulatory activity in connection with parochial schools and home education programs.

91. *Humanist Manifesto I*, 1933. This document was signed by 34 people, including John Dewey. *See* Whitehead and Conlan, "Secular Humanism," pp. 31-33.

92. *Humanist Manifesto II*, 1973. Among signers of this document was B. F. Skinner. *See* Homer Duncan, A Critical Review of the New Secular Humanist Declaration (Lubbock, Tex.: Missionary Crusader, undated).

93. *See* Duncan, *ibid*; Kenneth Briggs, "Secular Humanists Attack a Rise in Fundamentalism," *The New York Times*, 15 October 1980, p. A-18.

94. *See* Whitehead and Conlan, "Secular Humanism," pp. 36-45.

95. *See* Rene Dubos, *A God Within* (New York: Charles Scribner and Sons, 1972), p. 44.

96. Whitehead and Conlan, "Secular Humanism," p. 56. They further contend that John Dewey has had a tremendous influence on the "evolutionary movement" in education, *ibid*, n. 266.

97. 122 *Cong. Rec.* H 4,317-4,319 (daily ed., 12 May 1976). This amendment was introduced by Representative Conlan from Arizona. *See Education Amendments Conference Report*, Rep. No. 1701, 94th Cong., 2d Sess. 211 (1976).

98. *See* "Mind Control in the Schools: The Censorship Battle," Special Report, People for the American Way, Washington, D.C., 1982; Briggs, "Secular Humanists Attack a Rise in Fundamentalism." A magazine, *Free Inquiry*, has recently been established by humanists to counteract "the growth of intolerant sectarian creeds" that allegedly are attempting to impose their moral values on the rest of society.

99. *See* Duncan, *A Critical Review of the New Secular Humanist Declaration*; Briggs, "Secular Humanists Attack a Rise in Fundamentalism."

100. J. Wood, "Secular Humanism and Public Schools: Myth or Reality," *Public Education Religion Studies Center Newsletter* 5 (Winter 1978):7. *See also* Robert Davidow, "'Secular Humanism' as an 'Established Religion': A Response to Whitehead and Conlan," *Texas Tech Law Review* 11 (1979):54-55. A few attempts to reconcile the extreme points of view have been made. *See* Jaroslav Pelikan, "From Reformation Theology to Christian Humanism," *Luther Magazine* (May 1982):1-4; text with note 43, chapter 8.

101. In rejecting a state tax relief measure for parents of nonpublic school students, the First Circuit Court of Appeals suggested that parents dissatisfied with the humanistic orientation in public schools should seek a prohibition against instruction that advances secular humanism, if it is a religion. Rhode Island Federation of Teachers, AFL-CIO v. Norberg, 630 F.2d 850, 854 (1st Cir. 1980).

102. Wright v. Houston Independent School Dist., 366 F. Supp. 1208, 1210 (S.D. Tex. 1972).

103. *Id.*

104. Crowley v. Smithsonian Institute, 462 F. Supp. 725, 727 (D.D.C. 1978).

105. *Id.*

106. *See* Smith v. Ricci, 446 A.2d 501 (N.J. 1982), *appeal dismissed sub nom.* Smith v. Brandt, 103 S. Ct. 286 (1982); Hopkins v. Hamden Bd. of Educ., 289 A.2d 914 (Conn. C.P. 1971); text with note 4.

107. Williams v. Board of Educ. of County of Kanawha, 388 F. Supp. 93, 96 (S.D. W. Va. 1975).

108. Fink v. Board of Educ. of the Warren County School Dist., 442 A.2d 837 (Pa. Commw. 1982).

109. *Id.* at 843.

110. Reed v. VanHoven, 237 F. Supp. 48, 53 (W.D. Mich. 1965).

111. Torcaso v. Watkins, 367 U.S. 488 (1961).

112. *Id* at 495, n. 11.

113. School Dist. of Abington Township v. Schempp, 374 U.S. 203, 225 (1963).

114. *See* United States v. Seeger, 380 U.S. 163, 175 (1965); United States v. Ballard, 322 U.S. 78, 86 (1944).

115. United States v. Seeger, *id.* at 166.

116. *See* Whitehead and Conlan, "Secular Humanism," p. 17.

117. Jaffree v. James, 544 F. Supp. 727, 732 (S.D. Ala. 1982).

118. *Id.*, n. 2.

119. Paul Freund, "Public Aid to Parochial Schools," *Harvard Law Review* 82 (1969):1685.

Chapter Five

Rental, Shared-Time, and Released-Time Arrangements

This chapter addresses the legality of various arrangements between churches and public schools whereby facilities and/or students are shared in some manner. Specifically, the chapter covers proprietary agreements, situations in which students are enrolled simultaneously in public and parochial schools, and released-time programs in which public school students are excused to receive religious instruction. The constitutionality of rental and shared-time programs hinges primarily on an interpretation of establishment clause prohibitions; released-time programs involve both free exercise and establishment clause considerations.

Proprietary Rental Arrangements

Several lawsuits have challenged the use of public educational facilities by religious groups during noninstructional hours as unconstitutionally advancing religion. Generally, such arrangements have been upheld as long as the public school district is functioning purely as a proprietor. For example, the New Jersey Supreme Court endorsed a church's rental of a public school building at a rate reflecting the costs associated with using the facility.[1] Noting that the church used the building for religious worship services at a time the public school was not in session, the court concluded that the school district was functioning as a proprietor and was not promoting religion. Similarly, the Arizona Supreme Court held that the Arizona Board of Regents was authorized to lease the football stadium at Arizona State University for a series of religious services.[2] The court held that the rental of state facilities at fair market value for occasional religious services does not constitute state aid to religion.

In some states, by statute, local boards of education are granted discretionary authority to permit school use for any legal assembly. Interpreting such a statutory provision, the Florida Supreme Court ruled that the school board did not abuse its authority by allowing several churches to hold Sunday meetings in public school buildings, pending completion of their own new worship facilities.[3] However, the Pennsylvania Supreme Court interpreted a similar state statute as not obligating a public school district to make school facilities available for religious meetings, even though nonsectarian groups were allowed to hold activities in the school.[4] Recognizing that Pennsylvania law authorizes local boards to adopt rules governing facility use, the court reasoned that the board was not required to treat sectarian and nonsectarian organizations similarly, as long as its policy was uniformly applied to all religious groups.

In several situations, public school districts have rented facilities for instructional use from churches. Some public school boards have leased or rented space from parochial schools as a solution to temporary overcrowding in the public school district. Such arrangements usually have been judicially condoned if they have not involved an exchange of students between the public and private school and have maintained the integrity of the public school program free from sectarian influences. For example, a federal district court upheld an arrangement in Rhode Island in which a public school system in need of additional classroom space leased a portion of a parochial school building after precautions had been taken to prevent the intermingling of the two school programs.[5] Similarly, a New York trial court upheld a public school district's rental of classroom space from both a Jewish synagogue and a Roman Catholic church, noting that there were no parochial school students being instructed in the facilities and that the arrangement was necessary because of the phenomenal growth in the public school population.[6] The Nebraska Supreme Court also endorsed a school district's authority to lease classroom space from a parochial school where the instruction provided in the leased classrooms was totally secular and under the control of the public school.[7] In one of the few federal court cases on this issue, the Seventh Circuit Court of Appeals upheld a lease arrangement whereby an old public high school was closed and students were moved into a more modern facility that had formerly been a parochial school and was leased from the Catholic Diocese.[8]

However, if a lease or rental agreement has resulted in religious influences in the public school program, such arrangements have been disallowed under the establishment clause. In an early Iowa case, a public school district rented the upper floor of a Catholic school for public school classes. The board's action was challenged, and the Iowa Supreme Court concluded that the two floors actually operated as one school with all students receiving sectarian instruction.[9] Reasoning that the effect of this arrangement was public support of a parochial school, the court enjoined the school district from continuing the rental agreement.

The Supreme Court of New Mexico also struck down an arrangement whereby public school pupils were taught in buildings owned by the Catholic Church, with members of the religious order providing the instruction.[10] Evidence established that religious emblems were displayed in the schools, religious literature was distributed, religious instruction was provided, and the religious order selected the teachers, who were accepted by the public school board without question. Concluding that a Catholic school system supported by public funds was operating within the public school system, the court enjoined the arrangement. The court further held that under the First Amendment, public school classes cannot be held in buildings owned by a church if such premises are also used in part for a private school. In essence, the court ruled that any rental property used for a public school must be under total control of public school authorities during school hours.

While most controversies over rental arrangements have focused on the legality of using public schools for devotional meetings or religious facilities for public school classes, future legal disputes may also involve the rental of public school space for parochial school classes. With declining public school enrollments, it might seem fiscally advantageous to rent portions of public school buildings for private school use. For example, in 1980 a Minneapolis Lutheran high school signed a five-year agreement to lease classrooms in a public high school with declining enrollment.[11] The Lutheran school operates a separate school within the public school facility but does not depend on the public school to provide courses, aside from industrial arts instruction provided on a contractual basis. As long as such arrangements are strictly proprietary and do not involve the exchange of pupils between the public and private schools, they probably will survive judicial challenges.

Shared-Time or Dual-Enrollment Programs

Some rental or lease arrangements between public and parochial schools have also entailed the sharing of students. The U.S. Senate Education Subcommittee defined shared-time programs in the following manner in 1973:

> As generally used in current literature in the field of education, the term 'shared time' means an arrangement for pupils enrolled in nonpublic elementary or secondary schools to attend public schools for instruction in certain subjects . . . regarded as being mainly or entirely secular, such as laboratory science and home economics.[12]

The instruction is provided by public school personnel, but the program might be housed in facilities leased or rented from a parochial school. In shared-time programs, students usually take more costly secular courses such as industrial arts from public school teachers, while subjects such as social studies and literature are generally reserved for the private school.[13] Under some arrangements parochial students receive remedial instruction and other auxiliary services from public school teachers.

The sharing of students between public and private schools has been defended on several grounds. One argument is that since the parochial school carries a substantial portion of the community's educational load, assistance to the school in the form of providing certain secular classes for parochial students serves the total educational effort of the community. In situations where parochial schools would be forced to close without the shared-time program, public school authorities often have supported shared-time arrangements to ward off a sudden influx of students in the public schools.

Shared-time or dual-enrollment programs also have been viewed as one way to comply with regulations of federal categorical funding laws. For example, Title I of the Elementary and Secondary Education Act of 1965 provides federal assistance to meet the needs of educationally and culturally disadvantaged students in private as well as public schools.[14] In numerous states, Title I guidelines are implemented by having public school personnel provide remedial instruction and other auxiliary services for nonpublic school students. Also, in some instances dual-enrollment arrangements have been used to comply with the provisions of the Education for All Handicapped Children Act of 1975, which requires that appropriate educational programs be provided for disabled pupils.[15]

The provision of auxiliary services for special need private school students has been defended as a general health and safety measure with an incidental relationship to the instructional program of parochial schools.[16] While courts in some states have concluded that the use of public funds to support these services violates state constitutional provisions,[17] the U.S. Supreme Court has ruled that state-supported remedial and therapeutic programs do not implicate the establishment clause as long as they are provided at religiously neutral sites, even if only parochial school students are served in particular programs.[18] Federally funded auxiliary services have been endorsed even where public school teachers have been assigned to parochial schools to provide the services.[19]

Shared-time programs in which parochial students receive part of their *regular* instruction from public school teachers have seemed less likely to withstand scrutiny under the First Amendment. Such arrangements have been challenged as unconstitutionally aiding sectarian schools by enabling them to offer a complete curriculum, partly at public expense. Although some state courts have upheld such programs, in recent federal court rulings the judiciary has tended to invalidate shared-time arrangements under the establishment clause. Illustrative state and federal cases are reviewed below.

State courts in Illinois and Michigan have upheld specific programs involving the dual enrollment of students in public and parochial schools. In 1966 an Illinois appeals court reasoned that the object of compulsory attendance mandates is to ensure that all children are educated, not that they are educated in one prescribed manner.[20] The court concluded that the school board has the power to create experimental programs as long as each child receives a complete education. The state requirement that a child attend school the "entire time it is in session" was interpreted as permitting dual-enrollment programs.[21]

Similarly, the Michigan Supreme Court concluded that certain types of shared-time arrangements do not violate the state constitutional amendment forbidding the use of public funds to aid directly or indirectly any nonpublic school.[22] The Michigan Attorney General had interpreted the amendment, which was proposed by the Council Against Parochiaid, as forbidding the use of public monies for shared-time programs. The court disagreed and concluded that shared-time or dual-enrollment programs do not violate either the Michigan or U.S. constitutions. The court declared that premises occupied by lease or other arrangements for public school instruction are to be considered public schools: "This is true even though the lessor or grantor is a nonpublic school and even though such premises are contiguous or adjacent to a nonpublic school."[23] The court noted that shared-time programs differ from the provision of unconstitutional public subsidies to parochial schools in that no funds are paid to a private agency, the selection and control of teachers remains with the public school, and the public school system prescribes the curriculum: "These differences in control are legally significant."[24]

Applying the rationale espoused by the state supreme court, a Michigan appeals court subsequently upheld the constitutionality of three other shared-time programs.[25] In all three situations public school teachers provided instruction in certain secular subjects to nonpublic school students in facilities leased from parochial schools. The court concluded that the programs did not advance religion but merely enabled "parents to take advantage of both the secular education offered by . . . public schools and the sectarian education offered by parochial schools."[26] The court reasoned that the incidental aid provided to nonpublic schools through shared-time programs does not implicate state or federal constitutional prohibitions.

Other courts, however, have invalidated shared-time programs as advancing the religious enterprise in violation of the establishment clause. For example, a Kentucky federal district court struck down a contractual arrangement involving a shared-time program between a public school district and parochial school.[27] Because of shortage of space in the public school, classrooms were rented from a Catholic school to provide special classes taught by public school teachers. Students who enrolled in the special classes attended the parochial school for the remainder of their instruction. Noting that the "demarcation of violative practices is ultimately one of degree," the court ruled that implementation of the contested contract entailed "an impermissible involvement with religion as contemplated by court decisions construing the Establishment Clause."[28] The court reasoned that the leased classrooms could not be considered an extension of the public school because only parochial students were served by public school personnel in these classrooms. The arrangement was found to provide a double benefit to the Catholic school—the rental fee and the salaries of the public school teachers who teach only parochial students.

A similar program was struck down by the New Hampshire federal district court.[29] In this case the agreement stipulated that the public school district

105

would lease rooms in a parochial school for instruction in secular subjects by public school teachers. The leased rooms were to be free of religious symbols, and parochial students were considered public enrollees for purposes of the special classes. Invalidating the arrangement, the court reasoned that such a partnership necessitates excessive governmental entanglement with religion and must be characterized as subsidizing the parochial school. The court declared that "creating mini-public schools within the bosom of parochial schools is merely a legalistic way of channeling direct financial aid to the latter on a broad front."[30]

An Oregon appeals court also struck down a shared-time program in which junior high school parochial school pupils attended public school academic classes in an annex of the parochial school where all religious symbols had been removed.[31] The students received instruction in music, art, physical education, and religion in the parochial school. Concluding that no bona fide public school had been established since only parochial school students were served by the arrangement, the court ruled that the school district was unconstitutionally aiding a religious school. The court stated: "Whatever other infirmities might exist . . ., the exclusion of all but parochial school students from consideration for enrollment, and the making of placement decisions as to these students on religious rather than the customary geographical criteria is, in itself, fatal to defendants' claims."[32]

Although shared-time programs in Michigan have been upheld under state law, the federal judiciary recently has struck down two such arrangements under the First Amendment. In 1980 a Michigan federal district court invalidated a dual-enrollment program that was initiated because the scheduled closing of a parochial high school would have caused overcrowding in the public school.[33] An agreement was made whereby the private school would remain open with its pupils attending some classes in an annex leased by the public school district. The lease enabled the private school to remain open with its students receiving a complete education in the parochial school partly at public expense. The court concluded that this arrangement constituted "the greatest benefit which the state could bestow upon a sectarian school: the financial ability to continue its educative religious functions without bearing all of the otherwise prohibitive costs of doing so."[34]

In August 1982 a federal district court invalidated an extensive shared-time program in the Grand Rapids, Michigan, school district.[35] This decision may have implications for approximately 100 other Michigan school systems that operate similar programs. The federal judge found that the arrangement in Grand Rapids advanced religion and created excessive governmental entanglement with sectarian affairs in violation of the establishment clause, since 40 of the 41 private schools involved in the program were religiously oriented. Under the program, the public school district rented space from parochial schools to offer a variety of courses to students enrolled in the private schools for the remainder of their instruction. The judge reasoned that nearly all of the

106

beneficiaries of the arrangement were parochial school students. He further noted the political divisiveness resulting from budget appropriation "battles" associated with the program.[36]

The school district plans to appeal the decision to the Sixth Circuit Court of Appeals and will argue that the shared-time classes have no direct relationship to the operation of the church schools. The school district's attorney has asserted that "we are just committed to providing services to as broad a segment of the community as possible."[37] If this case should eventually be reviewed by the U.S. Supreme Court, it might resolve the First Amendment issues associated with shared-time programs involving lease arrangements between public and private schools.

A 1982 Maryland case focused on a different type of shared-time controversy in that a rental or lease agreement was not involved in the dispute. A Maryland appeals court was called on to evaluate a claim that parochial school students have a constitutional right to enroll in selected portions of the public school program.[38] The controversy focused on a county board of education's 1980 policy limiting participation in its All-County Music Program to public school students. Academic credit is given for participation in the music program, which comprises bands, choral groups, and orchestras. Prior to 1980 private school students had been allowed to audition for positions in the All-County Band on an equal basis with public school pupils. Several parochial students who had participated in the band under the prior policy challenged the board's action as violating their constitutional rights. They asserted that having established the music program, the board was obligated to extend this benefit to private as well as public school students.

Rejecting the assertion that the board's policy interfered with free exercise rights, the appeals court reasoned that the right to attend a parochial school does not "establish a concomitant right for these children to remain eligible for participation in public school programs."[39] The court declared that the school board has a legitimate interest in confining public school programs to public school students. If such a policy were not allowed, the court observed that "there would be no device to preclude, for example, a private school having difficulty securing a qualified chemistry teacher from unilaterally deciding to transport the entire student body to a nearby public school for their chemistry education."[40] While recognizing that the board could elect to permit private school student participation in the band, the court concluded that it was not required to do so in light of the broader implications with obvious potential for administrative disruption. The court also rejected plaintiffs' claims that equal protection and state statutory rights were impaired by the board's action.

Both public and parochial schools are facing increasing budgetary problems, exacerbated by inflation, rising energy costs, and declining enrollments. Therefore, it seems likely that local communities will continue to consider various types of shared-time or dual-enrollment programs to meet the educational needs of both public and parochial school students. The legality of such arrangements will depend on judicial interpretations of applicable state statutory and constitutional provisions and on an assessment of whether the programs provide impermissible aid to religious institutions under the establishment clause.

Although courts will review challenged shared-time programs on a case-by-case basis, some of the arrangements seem particularly vulnerable to legal attack. If only former full-time parochial students are taught by public teachers in the shared-time program operated in classrooms leased from the parochial school, the arrangement is not likely to withstand judicial scrutiny. However, the judiciary has seemed less inclined to find an establishment clause violation in connection with shared-time programs involving the provision of auxiliary services for special need students, especially in connection with federally funded programs.

Released Time for Religious Instruction

Leo Pfeffer has defined a released-timed program as "a system of religious education in connection with the public school under which those children desiring to participate in religious instruction are excused from the secular studies for a specified period weekly, while those children not participating in religious instruction remain under the jurisdiction and supervision of the public school for the usual period of secular instruction."[41] Released-time programs have been challenged as advancing religion in violation of the establish-ment clause. Such programs have been defended as a permissible accommodation to the free exercise of beliefs. On two occasions the U.S. Supreme Court has addressed these competing assertions in connection with releasing public school students for religious instruction.

In *McCollum* v. *Board of Education* the Supreme Court struck down a released-time program in which religious educators came into the public school to provide sectarian instruction.[42] In this 1948 case, the Court concluded that the program violated the establishment clause because tax-supported schools were being used to aid religious groups in their efforts to spread their faith. Also, the Court noted that the cooperation required between church and school authorities in implementing the program constituted impermissible governmental involvement with sectarian concerns.

Four years later, however, the Supreme Court upheld a released-time program in *Zorach* v. *Clauson*.[43] In this case the religious instruction was provided off school grounds and was not administered cooperatively by public schools and churches. The Court observed:

> We are a religious people whose institutions presuppose a Supreme Being. We guarantee the freedom to worship as one chooses. We make room for as wide a variety of beliefs and creeds as the spiritual needs of man deem necessary. We sponsor an attitude on the part of government that shows no partiality to any one group and that lets each flourish according

to the zeal of its adherents and the appeal of its dogma. When the state encourages religious instruction or cooperates with religious authorities by adjusting the schedule of public events to sectarian needs, it follows the best of our traditions. For it then respects the religious nature of our people and accommodates the public service to their spiritual needs.[44]

Noting that it is unconstitutional for public schools to advance sectarian concerns, the Court found "no constitutional requirement which makes it necessary for government to be hostile to religion and to throw its weight against efforts to widen the effective scope of religious influence."[45] Accordingly, the Court held that public school schedule accommodations to allow students to receive religious instruction elsewhere do not implicate establishment clause prohibitions.

Most states responded to the *Zorach* ruling by enacting statutes permitting students to be released from public schools for a designated amount of time to receive religious instruction off school grounds. Indiana law, for example, provides that upon request of a parent or guardian, children can be excused from school for not more than 120 minutes of religious instruction per week.[46] It was reported that over 30% of the nation's students were participating in some type of released time program within eight years after the *Zorach* decision was rendered.[47] Several of these programs have generated legal challenges.

In 1976 the Supreme Court declined to review a Fourth Circuit Appellate Court decision sanctioning a program of Week-Day Religious Education (WRE) in which students received religious instruction in a mobile unit parked next to school property.[48] A federal district court had invalidated the WRE, reasoning that it required cooperation between church and school that abridged First Amendment guarantees. The appellate court disagreed and relied on *Zorach* in ruling that the program was constitutional since the public schools merely adjusted schedules to accommodate religious instruction and did not use public facilities or funds for such purposes. The appeals court reiterated that not all programs providing "indirect or incidental benefits" to religious institutions violate the First Amendment.[49]

Also, the Wisconsin Supreme Court upheld a released-time program challenged on both federal and state constitutional grounds.[50] Although the contested program was similar to the one upheld by the Supreme Court in *Zorach*, plaintiffs asserted that it created excessive governmental entanglement with religion, noting that this criteria was introduced in establishment clause cases after the *Zorach* decision.[51] However, the court reasoned that the program of voluntary religious instruction held off school grounds necessitated only minimal schedule accommodations rather than excessive entanglement. The court also found unpersuasive the plaintiffs' allegation that "students who remain in class are denied the right to a free and public education supported by everyone's taxes without disruption of their schedules, classes, or programs."[52] The court was not convinced that classroom activities come to a halt during the released-time period, thus creating a disadvantage for nonparticipants. The court further rejected the assertion that students released from class to attend the religious instruction were singled out for special benefits. Instead, the court concluded that the released-time program constituted an appropriate accommodation to the exercise of religious beliefs.

Only a few courts have invalidated released-time programs held off school grounds. A New York trial court struck down a school district's released-time program as violating state law requiring public school children to attend school during the entire time that the public school is in session.[53] The court further held that state aid was unconstitutionally provided for religious institutions because report cards for the religious instruction were printed during school hours on school presses.

In an Oregon case a state appeals court struck down a released-time program in which elementary public school students who were housed in a parochial school building were released for religious instruction held in another room in the building.[54] The court concluded that this arrangement was not a bona fide released-time program and in effect constituted a parochial school with some publicly supported teachers. The court noted that the public school district paid no rent for using the annex of the parochial school and that the Catholic school officials determined which students could be enrolled in the public school annex.

While endorsing a released-time program in Utah, the Tenth Circuit Court of Appeals enjoined the school's practice of awarding elective course credit for the secular aspects of instruction received at a Mormon seminary.[55] The program included an hour of instruction each day oriented toward the tenets of the Church of the Latter Day Saints to which approximately two-thirds of the school's students belonged. The court reasoned that the award of credit for portions of the released-time instruction would entangle school officials with the church. However, the court suggested that under certain circumstances, released-time classes might be used to satisfy graduation requirements:

> If the school officials desire to recognize released-time classes general-ly as satisfying some elective hours, they are at liberty to do so if their policy is neutrally stated and administered. Recognizing attendance at church-sponsored released-time courses as satisfying graduation re-quirements advances religion no more than recognizing attendance at released-time courses or full-time church-sponsored schools as satisfying state compulsory attendance laws. If the extent of state supervision is only to insure, just as is permitted in the case of church-sponsored full-time private schools, that certain courses are taught for the requisite hours and that teachers meet minimum qualification standards, nothing in either the establishment or free exercise clauses would prohibit recognizing *all* released-time classes or *none*, whether religious in content or not, in satisfaction of graduation requirements. It is when, as here, the program is structured in such a way as to require state officials to monitor and judge what is religious and what is not religious in a private religious in-

stitution that the entanglement exceeds permissible accommodations and begins to offend the establishment clause.[56]

The appeals court also reasoned that the period spent by students in the released-time program could be counted in measuring the school's eligibility for state funds.

While specific released-time arrangements are likely to generate additional legal challenges, the law seems clear that students can be released from public school classes to receive religious instruction held away from public school grounds. However, judicial endorsement of such arrangements is somewhat difficult to reconcile with judicial invalidation of released-time programs where the instruction is conducted on public school premises. The central distinction between the *McCollum* and *Zorach* cases was the location of the religion classes. In both cases it was admitted that released-time programs have a religious purpose and serve to advance sectarian beliefs. Yet, as long as such programs are held off school grounds, even in mobile units parked next to school property, they have been judicially condoned.

If a majority of the students are excused without penalty from the regular academic program to attend religious instruction, one might argue that the machinery of the state is being used to advance sectarian concerns. Choper has asserted that compelling children to attend school and then releasing them "from their legal duty upon the condition that they attend religious classes" is "beyond all question a utilization of the tax-established and tax-supported public school system to aid religious groups to spread their faith."[57]

It might also be argued that the suggestion of state endorsement of religious activities is greater in connection with excusing students from the *regular* school program for religious instruction than in allowing a few students to hold a prayer meeting in a public school classroom *before* school. In 1980 when the Second Circuit Court of Appeals barred such prayer meetings from a public high school, the court noted that students have access to community facilities for devotional meetings when school is not in session.[58] It would seem that similar access is available during nonschool hours for religious instruction. Perhaps the overemphasis on "locale" in assessing the legality of released-time programs has obscured the more crucial issue of the state's stamp of approval being placed on sectarian activities.

Furthermore, since most students take part in released-time programs where established, it might be asserted that there is indirect coercion for all students to participate. It has been reported that at least 90% of the students participate in most of the released-time programs which are in operation.[59] Often children of minority faiths have enrolled in the religious classes of the majority because they have not wanted "to be marked."[60] The following statement was made by a nonparticipating student in an affidavit submitted in the *Zorach* case:

> When the released-time students departed . . . I felt left behind. The released children made remarks about my being Jewish and I was made

very much aware of the fact that I did not participate with them in the released-time program. I endured a great deal of anguish as a result of this and decided that I would like to go along with the other children to the church center rather than continue to expose myself to such harassment. I asked by mother for permission to participate in the released-time program and to accompany my Catholic classmates to their religious center, but she forbade it.[61]

It appears that dismissed-time programs would be constitutionally more defensible than released-time programs. Under a dismissed-time arrangement, school would periodically be dismissed early or start late so children could attend religious instruction or engage in other activities such as music lessons or drama groups.[62] In such a program, the indirect pressure to attend religious classes would be removed. Moreover, children would have several options as to how to spend the "dismissed" time, rather than being confined to a choice between religious instruction or staying at the public school.

Conclusion

Various legal arrangements between public schools and religious institutions have generated a substantial body of litigation. Purely proprietary agreements, whereby churches rent public schools for after-school use or church facilities are rented by public school districts in need of additional instructional space, generally have received judicial endorsement. However, programs in which students are shared between public and parochial schools have been more controversial. While a few shared-time programs have been upheld, the judiciary has struck down arrangements that have been viewed as a ploy to provide state aid to parochial schools.

Released-time programs for public school pupils to receive religious instruction off public school grounds have been condoned by the Supreme Court as constituting a permissible accommodation to the free exercise of religious beliefs. However, establishment clause questions continue to be raised in connection with such programs. Also, it seems likely that future suits will include allegations that released-time arrangements violate the state educational rights of nonparticipating students, who are compelled to attend school but allegedly do not receive any educational benefits during the time that most of their classmates are released for religious instruction.

Footnotes

1. Resnick v. East Brunswick Township Bd. of Educ., 343 A.2d 127 (N.J. Super. 1975), rev'd 389 A.2d 944 (N.J. 1978). The lower court had enjoined the school district from renting its facilities for religious services at rentals defraying only the cost of janitorial services rather than all costs associated with facility use.

2. Pratt v. Arizona Bd. of Regents, 520 P.2d 514 (Ariz. 1974).

3. Southside Estates Baptist Church v. Board of Trustees, 115 So. 2d 697 (Fla. 1959).

4. McKnight v. Board of Public Educ., 76 A.2d 207 (Pa. 1950).

5. Thomas v. Schmidt, 397 F. Supp. 203 (D.R.I. 1975).

6. Brown v. Heller, 273 N.Y.S.2d 713 (Sup. Ct., Westchester County, 1966).

7. State *ex rel.* School Dist. of Hartington v. Nebraska State Bd. of Educ., 195 N.W.2d 161 (Neb. 1972).

8. Buford v. Southeast DuBois County School Corp., 472 F.2d 890 (7th Cir. 1972), *cert. denied*, 411 U.S. 967 (1973).

9. Knowlton v. Baumhover, 166 N.W. 202 (Iowa 1918).

10. Zellers v. Huff, 236 P.2d 949, 956, 965 (N.M. 1951).

11. *Education U.S.A.* 22 (4 August 1980); 360.

12. Staff of Senate Committee on Labor and Public Welfare, 88th Congress, 1st Session, *Proposed Federal Promotion of "Shared Time Education"* (Comm. Print 1963), p. 1.

13. *See* David Tavel, *Church-State Issues in Education*, Fastback #123 (Bloomington, Ind.: Phi Delta Kappa, 1979), p. 20.

14. 20 U.S.C. § 241a *et seq. See* 45 C.F.R. 116, 116a, 121a (1980). *See also* text with note 63, chapter 6.

15. 20 U.S.C. § 1401 *et seq.* Dual-enrollment programs involving handicapped children are unique in that some disabled public school pupils are enrolled in private schools through contractual arrangements because appropriate programs to address their needs are not available in the public school district. *See* Commonwealth v. School Committee of Springfield, 417 N.E.2d 408 (Mass. 1981); North v. District of Columbia Bd. of Educ., 471 F. Supp. 136 (D.D.C. 1979); Elliot v. Board of Educ. of City of Chicago, 380 N.E.2d 1137 (Ill. App. 1978).

16. *See* Traverse City School Dist. v. Attorney General, 185 N.W.2d 9, 21 (Mich. 1971). For a more detailed discussion of litigation pertaining to public support of diagnostic, therapeutic, and remedial services for parochial school students, *see* text with note 64, chapter 6.

17. *See* People *ex rel.* Klinger v. Howlett, 305 N.E.2d 129 (Ill. 1973); Special Dist. for Educ. and Training of Handicapped Children v. Wheeler, 408 S.W.2d 60 (Mo. 1966).

18. Wolman V. Walter, 433 U.S. 229, 247 (1977).

19. National Coalition for Public Educ. and Religious Liberty v. Harris, 489 F. Supp. 1248 (S.D.N.Y. 1980), *appeal dismissed sub nom.* National Coalition for Public Educ. and Religious Liberty v. Hufstedler, 449 U.S. 808 (1980). *See also* State *ex rel.* School Dist. of Hartington v. Nebraska State Bd. of Educ., 195 N.W.2d 161 (Neb. 1972).

20. Morton v. Board of Educ. of City of Chicago, 216 N.E.2d 305 (Ill. App. 1966).

21. *Id.* at 308.

22. Traverse City School Dist. v. Attorney General, 185 N.W.2d 9 (Mich. 1971).

23. *Id.* at 20.

24. *Id.* at 19.

25. Citizens to Advance Public Education v. Porter, 237 N.W.2d 232 (Mich. App. 1976).

26. *Id.* at 238.

27. Americans United for Separation of Church and State v. Board of Educ., 369 F. Supp. 1059 (E.D. Ky. 1974).

28. *Id.* at 1062.

29. Americans United for Separation of Church and State v. Paire, 359 F. Supp. 505 (D.N.H. 1973).

30. *Id.* at 511.

31. Fisher v. Clackamas County School Dist. 12, 507 P.2d 839 (Ore. App. 1973).

32. *Id.* at 844.

33. Americans United for Separation of Church and State v. Porter, 485 F. Supp. 432 (W.D. Mich. 1980).

34. *Id.* at 437.

35. Americans United for Separation of Church and State v. School Dist. of City of Grand Rapids, 546 F. Supp. 1071 (W.D. Mich. 1982). In September 1982 Supreme Court Justice O'Connor refused to reinstate the Grand Rapids shared-time program pending appellate review. *See Education Daily*, 17 September 1982, p. 5.

36. *Id.*, 546 F. Supp. at 585.

37. *Education Daily*, 25 August 1982, p. 4, quoting attorney William Farr.

38. Thomas v. Allegany County Bd. of Educ., 443 A.2d 622 (Md. App. 1982).

39. *Id.* at 625.

40. *Id.* at 626.

41. Leo Pfeffer, *Church, State, and Freedom* (Boston: Beacon Press, 1967), p. 370.

42. 333 U.S. 203 (1948).

43. 343 U.S. 306 (1952).

44. *Id.* at 313-14.

45. *Id.* at 314.

46. Ind. Code Ann. 20-8.1-3-22 (Burns).

47. R. B. Dierenfield, "The Extent of Religious Influence in American Public Schools," *Religious Education* 56 (1961):177.

48. Smith v. Smith, 391 F. Supp. 443 (W.D. Va. 1975), *rev'd* 523 F.2d 121 (4th Cir. 1975), *cert. denied*, 423 U.S. 1073 (1976).

49. *Id.*, 523 F.2d at 125, quoting from Meek v. Pittenger, 421 U.S. 349, 359 (1975).

50. Holt v. Thompson, 225 N.W.2d 678 (Wis. 1975).

51. The excessive entanglement criterion was first used in an education case in Lemon v. Kurtzman, 403 U.S. 602 (1971). *See* text with note 46, chapter 6.

52. 225 N.W.2d at 687.

53. Stein v. Brown, 211 N.Y.S. 822 (Sup. Ct., Westchester County, 1925).

54. Fisher v. Clackamas County School Dist. 12, 507 P.2d 839 (Ore. App. 1973). This case also involved a challenge to a shared-time program. *See* text with note 31.

55. Lanner v. Wimmer, 463 F. Supp. 867 (D. Utah 1978), *aff'd in part, rev'd in part*, 662 F.2d 1349 (10th Cir. 1981).

56. *Id.*, 662 F.2d at 1361.

57. Jesse Choper, "Religion in the Public Schools: A Proposed Constitutional Standard," *Minnesota Law Review* 47 (1963):393.

58. Brandon v. Board of Educ. of Guilderland Central School Dist., 635 F.2d 971 (2d Cir. 1980), *cert. denied*, 102 S. Ct. 970 (1981). *See* text with note 41, chapter 2.

59. Choper, "Religion in the Public Schools," pp. 396-97.

60. *Ibid.*, p. 388, citing Pfeffer and Baum, *Public School Sectarianism and the Jewish Child*, p. 19.

61. Affidavit quoted in Pfeffer, *Church, State and Freedom*, p. 357.

62. *See* Robert Cushman, "Public Support of Religious Education in American Constitutional Law," *Illinois Law Review* 45 (1950):354-56; Russell Sullivan, "Religious Education in the Schools," *Law and Contemporary Problems* 14 (Winter 1949):93.

Chapter Six

State Aid to Parochical Schools

State legislative bodies have enacted a variety of measures providing financial benefits to nonpublic schools, their students, and parents of private school pupils. Such provisions have been challenged as advancing religion because about 85% of all nonpublic schools in the nation are church-affiliated.[1] Legislative efforts to aid private schools have been particularly prevalent in states such as New York, Maryland, and Pennsylvania, which have a large concentration of parochial school students. In litigation involving the use of public funds for sectarian education, courts have been called upon to address sensitive questions regarding the appropriate relationship between the state and parochial schools. Legal activity in this arena also has significant fiscal implications for public education.

In the first major decision involving a challenged state law providing aid to nonpublic school students, the Supreme Court observed that "in the words of Jefferson, the clause against establishment of religion by law was intended to erect a 'wall of separation between Church and State'."[2] However, as noted in chapter 1, this wall of separation has been subject to multiple interpretations. While it might appear that any form of state aid to parochial schools (parochiaid) would violate the establishment clause, several types of assistance that benefit primarily the *students* rather than the religious *institutions* have been judicially endorsed under the First Amendment. The Supreme Court has not provided clear guidance in parochiaid cases; indeed, recent decisions have provided more questions than answers as to the scope of permissible aid to sectarian schools. Moreover, some types of parochiaid considered lawful under the U.S. Constitution[3] have been invalidated under a specific state's constitutional provisions. As a result, the legality of public assistance to nonpublic education differs across states. The following sections focus on judicial interpretations of the validity of various forms of parochiaid under the establishment clause and applicable state constitutional mandates.

Transportation Aid

In 1947 the Supreme Court delivered a landmark decision in which it upheld a New Jersey law allowing the use of public funds to provide transportation services for nonpublic school students. The five-to-four decision in *Everson* v. *Board of Education* resulted from a challenge to a New Jersey statute authorizing local school districts to transport children to private (primarily parochial) as well as public schools.[4] Acknowledging that the transportation aid might encourage some parents to send their children to sectarian schools, the Court nonetheless held that the legislation served a public welfare purpose in assisting all pupils to get to school safely and expeditiously. Concluding that the law benefited students rather than religious institutions, the Court noted that "State power is no more to be used so as to handicap religions, than it is to favor them."[5] The Court equated the provision of school transportation to the provision of other public services such as police and fire protection.

The majority opinion in *Everson* included strong statements regarding establishment clause prohibitions against aid to religious schools. Justice Black, writing for the majority stated:

> [T]he "establishment of religion" clause of the First Amendment means at least this: Neither a state nor the Federal Government can set up a church. Neither can pass laws which aid one religion, aid all religions, or prefer one religion over another. . . . No tax in any amount, large or small, can be levied to support any religious activities or institutions, whatever they may be called, or whatever form they may adopt to teach or practice religion. Neither a state nor the Federal Government can, openly or secretly, participate in the affairs of any religious organizations or groups and vice versa.[6]

In fact, from the tenor of the language until the end of the opinion, it appeared that the majority was going to invalidate the New Jersey statute. Justice Jackson, dissenting in *Everson*, commented on this incongruence in the majority opinion:

> [T]he undertones of the opinion, advocating complete and uncompromising separation of Church from State, seem utterly discordant with its conclusion yielding support to their commingling in educational matters. The case which irresistibly comes to mind as the most fitting precedent is that of Julia who, according to Byron's reports, "whispering 'I will ne'er consent,'—consented."[7]

While the *Everson* case established that state aid to transport nonpublic school students does not violate the First Amendment, it did not clarify the scope of the state's authority in this arena. Must states provide such services to nonpublic school students? Can states provide greater transportation assistance for nonpublic school students than is made available for public school pupils? In addressing these questions, courts have looked to state law as well as the First Amendment of the U.S. Constitution.

A federal district court invalidated an Iowa statute providing transportation aid for private school students outside the school district of their residence because the law assisted a special class composed mainly of sectarian school students.[8] Other courts have concluded that expenditure of state funds to transport parochial school students violates state law. Two years after the *Everson* decision, the Washington Supreme Court rejected the child benefit rationale, concluding that transportation aid for nonpublic school students abridged the state constitutional ban against using public funds to support religious institutions.[9] The supreme courts of some other states such as Missouri, Alaska, and Oklahoma also have concluded that aid to transport nonpublic school students violates state constitutional and statutory prohibitions.[10] Several courts also have rejected the assertion that equal protection rights of nonpublic school students are impaired if they are denied state-supported transportation to school.[11]

However, it should be noted that the West Virginia Supreme Court reached a contrary conclusion as to a school district's obligation to provide transportation for nonpublic school pupils under a state law authorizing county boards of education to support transportation for all students.[12] A particular school board interpreted the law as permitting, but not requiring, local boards to transport nonpublic school pupils. But the court reasoned that since the school board had exercised its discretion affirmatively by providing bus transportation for public school pupils, it could not arbitrarily discriminate among children of school age.

Several other state courts have interpreted state constitutional provisions as permitting the use of public funds to transport pupils to sectarian schools and, accordingly, have upheld statutes to this effect.[13] Indeed, some states have specifically amended their constitutions to authorize legislative appropriations for this purpose. For example, in 1938 New York's constitution was amended to allow the expenditure of public funds for private school transportation,[14] and New Jersey's constitutional revision of 1947 contains a similar provision.[15]

Some courts have even upheld transportation aid provisions that include special accommodations for nonpublic school pupils. For example, a Wisconsin appeals court interpreted state law as requiring school districts to transport nonpublic school students on days the public school was closed for vacation.[16] Also, the Connecticut federal district court upheld a statute allowing regional or local boards of education to transport pupils to schools in contiguous districts and providing state reimbursement for half the costs up to an aggregate and per-pupil dollar limit.[17] Although primarily parochial school students benefited from this statute, the court found no constitutional violation.

In 1979 the U.S. Supreme Court dismissed an appeal of a Pennsylvania high court decision upholding a state law that requires school districts to provide free transportation to students attending schools up to 10 miles beyond the boundaries of the public school district of their residence.[18] Under the law, transportation of nonpublic school students is required if the busing of public school children is authorized, even if no public school pupils are bused outside district lines. Despite several challenges to the law, state and federal courts have not been persuaded that it violates the establishment clause.[19]

Relying on the fact that the Supreme Court declined to invalidate the Pennsylvania law, in 1983 the First Circuit Court of Appeals upheld a Rhode Island statute providing for the transportation of students beyond the public school district of their residence within specified geographic regions.[20] Since primarily parochial students are eligible for the interdistrict busing, the lower court ruled that the law inescapably aids sectarian schools and excessively entangles the government with religion.[21] Disagreeing, the appeals court found that the law satisfies the establishment clause as long as public and parochial students are eligible for transportation to *their schools* on the same terms and the relative cost per student for sectarian and public school transportation remains "roughly proportional."[22] However, the appeals court did invalidate the section of the statute requiring certain governmental inquiries regarding comparisons of sectarian schools in instances where private school students are seeking special permission to be bused to a school outside the region.

It appears that although states are not obligated to transport nonpublic school students, in the absence of state constitutional prohibitions they may enact legislation to that effect, even if such laws result in greater benefits for private than for public school pupils. With rising energy costs associated with pupil transportation, it seems likely that nonpublic schools and their patrons will continue to press for legislation authorizing or requiring state assistance in this domain. It also seems probable that measures providing transportation aid to nonpublic school pupils will continue to be challenged, given the financial crises existing in many public school districts. Since the Supreme Court has ruled that such aid is permissible under the First Amendment, the legality of specific practices will hinge primarily on interpretations of applicable state constitutional and statutory provisions.

Loan of Textbooks

In 1930 the U.S. Supreme Court first addressed the legality of using public funds to provide textbooks for private school students. In this case the court upheld the constitutionality of a Louisiana statute authorizing state aid to purchase textbooks that were loaned to nonpublic as well as to public school students.[23] The statute was challenged under the Fourteenth Amendment as unconstitutionally appropriating public funds for private purposes. The establishment clause was not used because at the time of this case the Supreme Court had not interpreted the First Amendment as applying to state as well as federal action.[24] Rejecting the Fourteenth Amendment claim, the Supreme Court concluded that the contested statute had a public purpose in that it benefited all children and not religious institutions: "The school children and the state alone are beneficiaries."[25] The Court reasoned that the state's interest "is education broadly; its method, comprehensive. Individual interests are aided only as the common interest is safeguarded."[26]

Subsequently, in *Board of Education* v. *Allen*, the Supreme Court directly addressed the constitutionality of loaning secular textbooks to nonpublic school students under the establishment clause.[27] In a six-to-three decision, the Court upheld a New York law requiring local school boards to loan textbooks free of charge to private school students in grades seven through twelve. The books loaned to nonpublic school students did not have to be the same as used in public schools, but they had to be approved by local boards of education or other public school authorities. Noting that parochial schools perform a valuable public function in providing secular education in addition to religious training, the Court majority reasoned that the statute served a public purpose by benefiting all students. The majority conceded that books "are critical to the teaching process, and in a sectarian school that process is employed to teach religion,"[28] but nonetheless concluded that the secular and sectarian functions of religious schools could be separated.

Justice Black, who wrote the majority opinion in *Everson*, issued a strong dissent in *Allen*, distinguishing state aid to transport nonpublic school students from the use of public funds to supply their books.[29] He asserted that books are "the most essential tool of education" and "the heart of any school," while transportation is a convenient public welfare service:

> I still subscribe to the belief that tax-raised funds cannot constitutionally be used to support religious schools, buy their school books, erect their buildings, pay their teachers, or pay any other of their maintenance expenses, even to the extent of one penny. The First Amendment's prohibition against governmental establishment of religion was written on the assumption that state aid to religion and religious schools generates discord, disharmony, hatred, and strife among our people, and that any government that supplies such aids is to that extent a tyranny. And I still believe that the only way to protect minority religious groups from majority groups in this country is to keep the wall of separation between church and state high and impregnable as the First and Fourteenth Amendments provide. The Court's affirmance here bodes nothing but evil to religious peace in this country.[30]

Noting that the New York law "does not as yet formally adopt or establish a state religion," he declared that "it takes a great stride in that direction and coming events cast their shadows before them."[31]

In a separate dissenting opinion, Justice Fortas took issue with the majority's conclusion that the New York aid program "merely makes available to all children the benefits of a general program to lend school books free of charge."[32] Because the books given to parochial school students are selected by the sectarian authorities, he asserted that the program is "hand-tailored to satisfy the specific needs of sectarian schools."[33] According to Fortas, this loan of "special" books constitutes the use of public funds to aid religious institutions. Justice Douglas, also dissenting, questioned how the Court could endorse such aid, given that a textbook is "the chief . . . instrumentality for propagating a particular religious creed or faith."[34]

Despite the strong dissents in *Allen*, the majority opinion has remained the governing precedent on this issue. The Supreme Court majority has subsequently reiterated in several cases that the use of public funds to buy secular textbooks and loan them to nonpublic school students does not violate the First Amendment. For example, in the mid-1970s the majority upheld Pennsylvania and Ohio statutory provisions allowing the loan of books "acceptable for use in public schools" to nonpublic school students.[35] However, in 1973 the Court did rule that states cannot loan textbooks to students attending racially exclusive private schools because such use of public funds would unconstitutionally aid racial discrimination.[36] The Court noted that the establishment clause permits a greater degree of state aid to nondiscriminatory than to discriminatory religious schools.

In two cases, measures providing state aid for textbooks used by private school students have been invalidated by lower courts because of the manner in which the aid was provided. In a New Jersey arrangement, public school students were loaned textbooks, but parents of private school students were reimbursed for the costs of such books.[37] The three judge federal district court disallowed the reimbursements made directly and exclusively to parents of nonpublic—primarily sectarian—school students as unconstitutionally advancing religion. Also, the Illinois Supreme Court invalidated a plan whereby books furnished to public school students were purchased with local funds, while books for nonpublic school students were purchased with state monies.[38] The Court concluded that the program afforded a special economic benefit to nonpublic school students.

As with transportation aid, the permissibility under the First Amendment of using public funds to provide textbooks for parochial students does not mean that this practice will withstand scrutiny under state law.[39] In 1961 the Oregon Supreme Court ruled that the distribution of free textbooks to parochial school children violated the state constitutional prohibition against public support of religious institutions.[40] Similarly, the supreme courts of Michigan, Nebraska, Missouri, and Massachusetts have rejected the child benefit theory in barring the loan of textbooks to private school students under state constitutional provisions that prohibit the use of public funds for religious purposes.[41]

In the most recent state court decision on this issue, the California Supreme Court struck down a state law that provided for the loan of textbooks to nonpublic school pupils, calling the child benefit doctrine "logically indefensible."[42] The court concluded that "the nonpublic school, not its pupils, is the motivating force behind the textbook loan."[43] The court reasoned that the benefits to the pupil and to the school cannot be separated; "it is an undeniable fact that books are a critical element in enabling the school to carry out its essential mission to teach the students."[44] Thus, the court ruled that the parochiaid measure violated the state constitution's prohibition against the appropriation of public funds to aid sectarian schools.

Since the constitutional provisions of California, Nebraska, Oregon, Missouri, Massachusetts, and Michigan are quite similar to those of many other states, additional challenges to state legislation authorizing the loan of textbooks to private school pupils seem imminent.[45] However, in states where parochial school forces have attained considerable political influence, it does not appear that state courts will reject the child benefit rationale in reviewing challenged parochiaid measures. Thus, in the absence of a change in sentiment on the part of the federal judiciary, substantial diversity across states as to the legality of providing textbooks for nonpublic schools students seems destined to persist.

Other Types of Parochiaid

State legislatures, particularly those in states with a large concentration of private school students, have not confined their parochiaid efforts to textbooks and transportation. Various other types of aid have been proposed and challenged under the establishment clause. Indeed, there has been at least one parochiaid controversy on the Supreme Court's docket almost every term since 1970.

In a signficant 1971 decision, *Lemon* v. *Kurtzman*, the Court first applied the "excessive entanglement" standard in a parochiaid case, and in so doing, struck down statutory provisions in Pennsylvania and Rhode Island.[46] The Pennsylvania law provided financial support to nonpublic elementary and secondary schools in the form of reimbursement for the costs of teachers' salaries, textbooks, and instructional materials in specified secular subjects. The Rhode Island legislation provided for a salary supplement paid directly by the states to nonpublic school teachers. The Supreme Court accepted the asserted secular purposes of the laws and did not find it necessary to assess whether their primary effect advanced religion, because evidence of excessive governmental entanglement with religion was sufficient to invalidate the statutes under the establishment clause.[47] The Court reasoned that comprehensive and continuing state surveillance would be required to ensure that the aid was not used for sectarian purposes. The Court further concluded that these programs would foster entanglement in terms of political divisiveness, noting that "political division along religious lines was one of the principal evils against which the First Amendment was intended to protect."[48]

During the next few years, the Supreme Court invalidated several parochiaid statutes under the three-pronged test, finding particular potency in the "excessive entanglement" criterion.[49] It struck down a New York law providing grants for the maintenance and repair of school facilities, tuition reimbursements to low-income parents of nonpublic school pupils, and state tax benefits to all parents of nonpublic school students as having the primary effect of advancing religion.[50] It also invalidated a New York law providing state aid for tests (a majority of which were teacher-prepared) and record keeping associated with subjects required by the state.[51] The Court noted that "we cannot ignore the substantial risk that these examinations, prepared by teachers under the authority of religious institutions, will be drafted with an eye, unconsciously or otherwise, to inculcate students in the religious precepts of the sponsoring church."[52] Subsequently, the Court invalidated Pennsylvania provisions allowing tuition reimbursement to parents of nonpublic school students,[53] the direct loan of instructional materials and equipment to nonpublic schools, and the provision of auxiliary programs such as guidance counseling, speech and hearing services, and remedial instruction provided by public school personnel on the premises of nonpublic schools.[54] The Court majority concluded that since the very purpose of church-related schools "is to provide an integrated secular and religious education," aid for neutral, secular instructional materials and equipment "inescapably results in the direct and substantial advancement of religious activity."[55]

While it appeared that the Supreme Court was embarking on a course disallowing most types of parochiaid from 1971 until 1976, recent rulings may portend a reversal of this trend. Since the latter 1970s, Supreme Court decisions in this arena have been characterized by a severely divided bench and have not provided clear criteria for distinguishing permissible from prohibited types of aid. Illustrative is *Wolman* v. *Walter*, a 1977 case involving the constitutionality of an Ohio parochiaid law.[56]

Seven different opinions were written in *Wolman*. Never before had the Supreme Court justices differed so much in their reasoning in a church-state case. At least five of the justices endorsed the purchase of secular books, reusable workbooks, or manuals used in public schools for loan to nonpublic school students; provision of the same standardized tests and scoring services available in public schools; provision of speech, hearing, and psychological diagnostic services in nonpublic schools; and provision of special therapeutic services performed in a public school, a public center, or a mobile unit located off the nonpublic school premises.

A majority of the Court, however, drew the line at using public funds for instructional materials, audiovisual equipment, and field trip transportation. Five justices concluded that the loan of neutral or secular instructional materials to pupils and parents instead of to the nonpublic schools themselves did not make the plan substantively different from one invalidated previously by the Supreme Court.[57] In disallowing assistance for field trips, the Court majority reasoned that such trips are part of the curriculum and therefore distinct from transportation to and from school. The majority again concluded that excessive entanglement between church and state would result from the monitoring that would be required.

Subsequently, the Supreme Court refused to order Ohio officials to recover instructional equipment and materials loaned by public school districts to private schools under the invalidated statute.[58] The Court affirmed, without an opinion, an Ohio federal district court ruling in which the lower court concluded that the nonpublic schools could retain the materials and equipment already in the schools. The district court reasoned that if the judiciary became involved in the return of equipment, it would risk unconstitutional government entanglement with religion. It further noted that the increasing obsolescence of the equipment lessened the likelihood of a constitutional violation in any case.

The ambiguous *Wolman* decision has provided fodder for private school lobbyists who are pressing for more extensive types of parochiaid. One legal commentator has observed that under *Wolman*, "the dividing line between church and state has become a porous sieve through which government dollars can flow with relative ease into the pockets of sectarian schools."[59] The Minnesota legislature has interpreted *Wolman* as barring the loan of instructional materials for classroom use, such as wall maps, but permitting the loan of secular materials designed primarily for individual pupils such as photographs, pamphlets, prepared slides, filmstrips, video programs, desk charts and maps, and learning kits.[60] If this interpretation ultimately receives judicial endorsement, there would seem to be few First Amendment constraints on legislative discretion in supplying secular instructional materials to parochial schools because most teaching aids are designed for individual pupil use.[61] As noted in Justice Stevens' *Wolman* opinion, the economic reality is not reduced by subtle distinctions "between direct and indirect subsidies, or between instructional materials like globes and maps on the one hand and instructional materials like textbooks on the other."[62]

Diagnostic, Therapeutic, and Remedial Services

In some states, statutes specify that various types of diagnostic, therapeutic, and remedial services will be provided for private as well as public school children. In addition, under several federal categorical funding programs, regulations stipulate that nonpublic school children must be provided certain services that are "comparable in quality, scope and opportunity for participation" to those provided for children in public schools. As noted in chapter 5, Title I of the Elementary and Secondary Education Act of 1965, which is targeted toward educationally deprived children in areas with a high concentration of low-income families, is the largest federal program with a private school component.[63] Such federal programs as well as state-funded auxiliary services for parochial students have generated legal challenges.

Courts have addressed the legality of state-supported services provided by public school personnel to nonpublic school students under the First Amendment and state constitutional and statutory provisions. In 1973 the Illinois Supreme Court concluded that state grants to fund auxiliary services in private, primarily parochial, schools violated the establishment clause.[64] Similarly, the Missouri Supreme Court held that public school teachers could not provide auxiliary services in a private school, nor could private school students be released to receive such services at the public school. The court reasoned that the former practice violated the establishment clause, whereas the latter abridged state compulsory attendance mandates requiring all children to attend a public or private school for the full time it is in session.[65]

In contrast, the Michigan Supreme Court ruled that state-funded auxiliary services such as health, speech, diagnostic, counseling, drivers' training, and remedial programs could be provided by public school personnel at nonpublic school sites without abridging federal or state constitutional provisions.[66] The court reasoned that such health and safety measures have only "an incidental relation" to the regular instruction of private school children and do not entail "the passage of pubic funds into private school hands for purposes of running the private school operation."[67]

In 1975 the U.S. Supreme Court addressed the constitutionality of a portion of a Pennsylvania statute authorizing remedial and accelerated instruction, guidance counseling, and testing, speech, and hearing services provided on nonpublic school premises. Striking down the measure, the Court concluded that the public employee delivering such services might depart from the required religious neutrality when performing important educational services in "an atmosphere dedicated to the advancement of religious belief."[68] The measure was invalidated primarily on entanglement grounds because the state would be required to engage in continual surveillance to assure that the publicly funded auxiliary teachers remained neutral. The Court did note, however, that speech and hearing remediation seems to fall within permissible "general welfare services;" the provision of such services was invalidated because it could not be severed from the unconstitutional portions of the statute.

In 1977 the Supreme Court again addressed the constitutionality of providing auxiliary services for nonpublic school students in *Wolman*.[69] As noted previously, the Court endorsed the provision of diagnostic speech, hearing and psychological services on nonpublic school premises and the provision of therapeutic, guidance, and remedial services for private school students at public locations. A majority of the Court reasoned that diagnostic services provided on nonpublic school premises are general health services and not closely associated with the educational mission of the nonpublic school. Recognizing the limited contact between the diagnostician and pupil, the Court majority concluded that this relationship "does not provide the same opportunity for the transmission of sectarian views as attends the relationship between teacher and student or that between counselor and student."[70] Regarding therapeutic and remedial services, the majority held that as long as they are provided "at truly religiously neutral locations," the dangers associated with offering the services in a "pervasively sectarian atmosphere" can be avoided.[71] The Court majority was not troubled by the fact that only sectarian pupils might be served at a particular neutral site; dangers arise "from the nature of the institution, not from the nature of the pupils."[72]

Federally funded auxiliary programs for private school students have also been challenged under the establishment clause as well as state constitutional provisions. The Michigan Supreme Court has ruled that the state constitution does not preclude the use of federal Title I funds to provide special educational services for pupils in nonpublic schools. The court reasoned that such funds do not become public monies of the state under the control of local school boards, but rather are considered "a trust and must be used by state agencies in accordance with Federal guidelines and for the purposes for which the funds were granted."[73]

In 1974 the U.S. Supreme Court addressed a controversy regarding Missouri's obligation to provide "comparable services" for nonpublic school pupils under Title I.[74] Plaintiffs alleged that nonpublic school students were being deprived of comparable services because the state refused to assign public school teachers to provide services on the premises of nonpublic schools. The state contended that its constitution and laws bar such an arrangement. The Supreme Court declined to address whether the assignment of publicly employed teachers to provide remedial services in parochial schools contravenes the First Amendment. Instead, the Court concluded that the Title mandate of "comparable services" does not necessitate on-the-premises instruction in private schools. The Court noted that while states have several options for providing comparable services to eligible private school pupils, the provision of inferior programs for nonpublic school pupils does not satisfy federal requirements. Acknowledging that the formulation of comparable services consistent with state law might prove challenging for both private and public school authorities, the court concluded that this "difficult," but "not impossible," task could be accomplished.[75] The Court observed, however, that if education officials could not formulate an acceptable plan to meet Title I guidelines while respecting state constitutional and statutory provisions, Missouri was not obligated to participate in the Title I funding program. In essence, federal funding programs are not intended to preempt state law.

Although the Supreme Court has not endorsed the provision of *state-supported* remedial services on private school premises, in 1980 the court declined to overturn a decision in which a New York federal district court upheld the use of *federal funds* to pay public school teachers assigned to sectarian schools to provide Title I remedial services.[76] The district court ruled that neither the federal law nor New York's program to implement the law violate the establishment clause because the religious schools have no control over the remedial programs, and funds do not flow directly to the private schools. It concluded that the program is clearly a student aid program, carefully designed to avoid excessive government entanglement.[77]

It appears from litigation to date that therapeutic and remedial services funded by the *state* may be vulnerable to legal challenge if provided on non-public school premises,[78] while similar *federally funded* programs in private schools are likely to be condoned under the establishment clause. Thus, it seems that establishment clause prohibitions are being applied differently, depending on the source of the public funds. Whether the Supreme Court intends such a double standard remains to be clarified in subsequent litigation.

State-Prescribed Tests and Record Keeping Services

The state's authority to assist nonpublic schools with state-required testing and record keeping activities also has generated litigation under the establishment clause. In *Wolman* the Supreme Court majority found no constitutional violation in providing for nonpublic school students state-prescribed tests and scoring services as used in public schools in secular subjects.[79] The Court noted that nonpublic school personnel were not involved in either drafting or scoring the examinations and that state aid was not provided for the administration of the tests by private school employees.

Subsequently, in a significant 1980 case, *Committee for Public Education and Religious Liberty* v. *Regan*, the Supreme Court endorsed the state of New York's distribution of up to $20 million to private schools for the cost of record keeping and testing services mandated by the state.[80] Seven years earlier, the Court had invalidated a New York law providing nonpublic schools reimbursement for the administration, grading, compiling, and reporting of teacher-prepared tests in addition to state-required examinations.[81] As a result of the 1973 ruling, state legislation was revised to provide payments to cover only the costs associated with state-prepared examinations. Initially, the trial court invalidated the revised law, but on appeal the Supreme Court remanded the case for reconsideration in light of *Wolman*.[82] The trial court subsequently upheld the law, and the Supreme Court affirmed the lower court's ruling in a five-to-four decision.

Justice White, writing for the majority in *Regan* declared that aid for state-required examinations and record keeping was shown to "serve the state's legitimate secular ends without any appreciable risk of being used to transmit or teach religious views."[83] However, White emphasized that this was a close decision and did not provide a "litmus-paper test to distinguish permissible from impermissible aid to religiously oriented schools."[84] Noting that the serious split on the Court might reflect conflicting viewpoints among Americans on church-state separation, White cautioned that the decision "sacrifices clarity and predictability for flexibility."[85]

Justice Blackmun, in a strong dissent, called the *Regan* ruling "a long step backwards in the inevitable controversy that emerges when a state legislature continues to insist on providing public aid to parochial schools."[86] He claimed that the law clearly has the primary effect of advancing religion since it calls for millions of public dollars to be paid annually to New York parochial schools. Justice Stevens, also dissenting, asserted that this 1980 decision builds on "a long line of cases making largely ad hoc decisions about what payments may or may not be constitutionally made to nonpublic schools."[87] He called for a resurrection of the "high and impregnable wall between church and state constructed by the framers of the First Amendment."[88]

The *Regan* decision, similar to other rulings upholding parochiaid measures, has significant fiscal implications. Several states currently require nonpublic school students to participate in standardized testing programs, and other states are considering such requirements as an alternative to prescriptive programmatic standards for private schools.[89] Also, many states have instituted some type of student competency testing requirement to assure that pupils who receive high school diplomas demonstrate mastery of minimum skills considered necessary for success in adult roles.[90] Relying on the *Regan* precedent, it seems likely that private schools included in various statewide testing programs will seek public aid to cover the costs associated with administering the tests.

Tax Relief for Parents of Nonpublic School Students

One of the most volatile church-state controversies involves the constitutionality of state and federal tax relief for parents of nonpublic school students. In 1973 the Supreme Court struck down a New York statute that allowed state income tax credits for parents of nonpublic school pupils.[91] Under the provision, parents could subtract from their adjusted gross income for state income tax purposes a designated amount for each dependent for whom they had paid at least $50 in nonpublic school tuition. Noting that over 85% of New York's private schools were sectarian, the Court concluded that the measure aided religion. The Court reasoned that the program rewarded parents for sending their children to parochial schools and, therefore, had the primary effect of advancing religion.

More recently, other tax relief measures have been judicially struck down. The Supreme Court affirmed by summary action a decision in which the Third Circuit Court of Appeals invalidated a New Jersey law providing state taxpayers a personal deduction of up to $1,000 against gross income for any dependent child attending a nonpublic elementary school full-time.[92] Finding no constitutional distinction between this measure and the earlier New York provision, the appeals court ruled that the deduction had the primary effect of advancing religion.[93] The First Circuit Court of Appeals also struck down a Rhode Island statute allowing state tax deductions from personal gross income for costs associated with tuition, textbooks, and transportation in public or private elementary and secondary schools.[94] The court found that the measure primarily benefitted parents of sectarian school pupils and created excessive governmental entanglement with religion.[95]

In contrast to the prevailing judicial posture, in 1982 the Eighth Circuit Court of Appeals affirmed a federal district court's conclusion that a Minnesota tax benefit program, almost identical to the Rhode Island plan, does not abridge the First Amendment.[96] The contested Minnesota law allows parents with children enrolled in either public or private schools to claim as a deduction on their state income tax returns up to $500 of the annual expenses for elementary pupils and $700 for secondary students. The federal district court considered the key determination to be whether the law primarily benefits religious organizations, which would be unconstitutional, or whether it is more akin to a tax exemption for religious property, which has been condoned by the Supreme Court.[97] The court concluded that the latter precedent is controlling in connection with the contested tax deduction provision. The court reasoned that the deduction is available to all taxpayers who incur school-related expenses for their children and thus satisfies the constitutional test of governmental neutrality toward religion. Affirming the lower court's decision, the appellate court concluded that substantial benefits flow to the public under the Minnesota provision; public school patrons can deduct bus fare, equipment rental, summer school tuition, and costs of special sports attire associated with public school attendance. The court distinguished the Minnesota law from the impermissible New York tax credit program that bestowed benefits *only* on parents of private school students.[98] However, the appeals court could not distinguish the Minnesota and Rhode Island provisions, and admittedly differed from the First Circuit Court of Appeals in interpreting the applicable legal principles.[99]

Faced with opposing appellate rulings on comparable state provisions, the U.S. Supreme Court agreed to review the Minnesota case, and in June 1983 the sharply divided Court upheld the contested law. The five member majority in *Mueller* v. *Allen* found the Minnesota law "vitally different" from the earlier New York provision, declaring that "a state's decision to defray the cost of educational expenses incurred by parents—regardless of the type of schools their children attend—evidences a purpose that is both secular and understandable.[100] The majority reasoned that such state assistance to a "broad spectrum" of citizens does not have the primary effect of advancing religion. Noting that most recent decisions in which the Court has invalidated state aid to parochial schools have involved the direct transmission of public funds to such schools, the majority concluded that the establishment clause does not prohibit "the sort of attenuated financial benefit, ultimately controlled by the private choices of individual parents, that eventually flows to parochial schools from the neutrally available tax benefit at issue in this case."[101]

The four dissenting justices found no difference between tax credits and deductions, contending that both have the substantive effect of advancing religion in that they benefit primarily parochial school patrons and ultimately sectarian schools. They claimed that in *Mueller*, for the first time, the Supreme Court has upheld state aid for religious schools without any assurances that the support will be restricted to secular functions in those schools.[102] While the full impact of this decision cannot yet be assessed, it will undoubtedly provide an impetus for other states to enact measures similar to the Minnesota law.

State tax benefit programs have not been the only source of controversy. There also has been considerable activity at the federal level to secure federal tuition tax credits for parents of nonpublic school pupils. A widely publicized measure, introduced in Congress in 1977, would have provided credits to be deducted from income taxes owed for 50% of the tuition up to $500 paid for each student in elementary or secondary school or college or a cash refund if the taxpayer owed less in taxes than the amount of the credit.[103] Although this bill did not receive congressional support, the parochial school aid lobby has continued to press for similar tax relief measures.[104] Advocates of such measures contend that First Amendment rights are not implicated because the proposed tax relief covers all forms of education and not just religious schools.[105]

However, opponents of such tax relief programs assert that they undermine public education and may result in an educational caste system, whereby only lower-class and difficult to educate children will remain in public schools. Some have argued that such programs will increase school segregation as well as provide unconstitutional aid to sectarian education.[106] Several groups representing private schools also have voiced fears that such tax relief measures will foster nonpublic school "harassment" by the Internal Revenue Service.[107]

In April 1982 President Reagan revealed his proposal for federal income tax credits up to 50% of each child's tuition costs, starting with a maximum credit of $100 in 1983 and rising to $500 in 1985.[108] The administration has claimed that such a program would benefit low- and middle-income families, since only families earning $50,000 or less could receive the full credit. In announcing his plan, President Reagan noted that "private education is not a divisive threat to our system of education. . . . Alternatives to public education tend to strengthen public education."[109] The administration has called the plan a measure to seek equity for working parents who face a double burden of paying taxes to support public education and paying tuition for their children's private education. Unlike the Packwood-Moynihan bill, taxpayers who owe less in taxes than the amount of the credit would not receive a refund under the Reagan proposal.

This proposal has generated substantial criticism because of its fiscal implications and its potential effect on public schools. Senator Hollings from South Carolina has asserted that Reagan's proposal is "not just unconstitutional, uneconomical and unfair, but at this point is unconscionable" because of the drive to curb federal spending.[110] Officials of major education associations also have assailed the proposal as undermining public education and leading toward a pauper public school system.[111]

In September 1982 the Senate Finance Committee approved a tuition tax credit provision with more restricted eligibility and stronger anti-discrimination protections than included in the original Reagan proposal. Although this provision did not reach the Senate floor in 1982, a bill incorporating many of the Finance Committee's modifications has been placed before the 98th Congress. If this or a similar measure is enacted into law, a First Amendment challenge will likely follow. Advocates of such tax relief provisions are optimistic that the Supreme Court will uphold their constitutionality. However, in light of the recent *Mueller* decision, eligibility under a federal law may have to be broadened to include public as well as private school patrons, and the measure may have to provide tax deductions for educational expenses instead of tuition tax credits.

Conclusion

The financial crisis facing parochial education coupled with increasing national interest in providing viable alternatives to public education suggest that legislative attempts to assist nonpublic schools and their constituencies will continue. The results of a national survey, released in the fall of 1982, indicated that state-aid programs for religious schools have expanded substantially in recent years, particularly in states with large parochial school populations.[112] The study also reported that over half of the states administer at least one program that is "arguably unconstitutional."

The judiciary has recognized that the establishment clause requires governmental neutrality toward religion, but the Supreme Court has noted that this "principle is more easily stated than applied."[113] While courts have condoned the use of public funds to support various secular aspects of nonpublic education, they have not been blind to the fact that when the state assists a religious institution in performing a secular task, the institution's resources are freed for religious purposes.[114] Whether measures such as state aid for auxiliary services and instructional materials will be considered beyond the "verge" of permissable aid under the establishment clause remains to be clarified in future litigation.[115]

At present, clear guidelines do not exist, and the contours of permissible parochiaid vary from one jurisdiction to the next. Jesse Choper has referred to parochiaid decisions as "ad hoc judgments which are incapable of being reconciled on any principled basis."[116] The Supreme Court has noted that resolution of establishment clause cases is "not easy" and is plagued by dissension among the justices on the bench.[117] Sidney Buchanan has observed that with the 1947 *Everson* case, the Supreme Court started "down a conceptual road of uncertain destination."[118] Recent decisions certainly support this conclusion.

There is some dissatisfaction with the child benefit doctrine as a rationale to justify public expenditures to supply textbooks, transportation, and other services to assist parochial schools in maintaining a complete educational program. Since practically all school expenditures are designed to aid children, if the child benefit theory is carried to its logical conclusion, it would justify the use of public funds for almost any private school program with the exception of religious instruction. Several legal scholars have questioned whether the child benefit notion can be defended as a constitutional doctrine.[119]

Yet, with the division on the Supreme Court over parochiaid questions, it seems unlikely that the current Court will renounce the child benefit rationale or take a restrictive stance toward parochiaid.[120] The recent *Mueller* decision may signal greater leniency in the Court's application of the establishment clause to measures providing indirect aid to parochial education. The *Mueller* majority suggested that parochial school patrons—and indirectly the schools themselves—are entitled to some return for their significant societal contributions in providing high quality instruction and alternatives to public education.[121] Assuming that additional parochiaid measures can withstand first amendment scrutiny, challenges to such measures may increasingly be initiated on the basis of state law. While some state courts have invalidated various types of public aid for private schools under state constitutional mandates, such judicial action has not taken place in the states providing the most substantial aid to nonpublic education.

It is somewhat ironic that efforts to obtain various types of public financial assistance for parochial education have been accompanied by efforts to secure less governmental regulation of religious schools. Legal activity pertaining to the government's role in monitoring church-related schools is addressed in the next chapter.

Footnotes

1. This figure is based on a survey conducted by the National Center for Educational Statistics in 1981. *See Education Daily*, 14 July 1982, p. 1; text with note 22, chapter 7.

2. Everson v. Board of Educ., 330 U.S. 1, 16 (1947), citing Reynolds v. United States, 98 U.S. 145, 164 (1878).

3. For a discussion of the judicial criteria applied in establishment clause cases, *see* Lemon v. Kurtzman, 403 U.S. 602, 612-13 (1971); text with note 46. *See also* text with note 73, chapter 1.

4. 330 U.S. 1 (1947).

5. *Id.* at 18.

6. *Id.* at 15-16.

7. *Id.* at 19 (Jackson, J., dissenting).

8. Americans United for Separation of Church and State v. Benton, 413 F. Supp. 955, 960 (S.D. Iowa 1975).

9. Visser v. Nooksack Valley School Dist. No. 506, 207 P.2d 198 (Wash. 1949). *See also* Mitchell v. Consolidated School Dist. No. 201, 135 P.2d 79 (Wash. 1943).

10. Matthews v. Quinton, 362 P.2d 932, 939 (Alaska 1961); McVey v. Hawkins, 258 S.W.2d 927 (Mo. 1953); Gurney v. Ferguson, 122 P.2d 1002 (Okla. 1941). A Delaware superior court also ruled that a statute providing free transportation for sectarian school students violated the state constitution, State *ex rel.* Traub v. Brown, 172 A. 835 (Del. Super. 1934).

11. *See* Leutkemeyer v. Kaufmann, 364 F.Supp. 376 (W.D. Mo. 1973), *aff'd* 419 U.S. 888 (1974); Frame v. South Bend Community School Corp., No. 581-0344 (N.D. Ind. 1981); Epeldi v. Engelking, 488 P.2d 860 (Idaho 1971), *cert. denied*, 406 U.S. 957 (1972).

12. State *ex rel.* Hughes v. Board of Educ., 174 S.E.2d 711 (W. Va. 1970), *cert. denied.* 403 U.S. 944 (1971).

13. *See* Attorney General v. School Committee of Essex, 439 N.E.2d 770 (Mass. 1982); State *ex rel.* Bouc v. School Dist. of City of Lincoln, 320 N.W.2d 472 (Neb. 1982); School Dist. of Pittsburgh v. Commonwealth Depart. of Educ., 382 A.2d 772 (Pa. Commw. 1978); West Morris Regional Bd. of Educ. v. Sills, 279 A.2d 609 (N.J. 1971). Among states with statutes specifically authorizing the use of public funds to transport private school students are California, Connecticut, Illinois, Indiana, Kansas, Kentucky, Louisiana, Maine, Maryland, Massachusetts, Michigan, Nebraska, New Hampshire, New Jersey, New York, New Mexico, North Dakota, Ohio, Oregon, Pennsylvania, and Rhode Island. *See* Kern Alexander, *School Law* (St. Paul, Minn.: West Pub. Co., 1980), p. 186.

14. N.Y. Const., Art. 11, § 4. The constitutional amendment followed court action invalidating a statute that provided state aid for private school transportation. *See* Judd v. Board of Educ. of Union Free School Dist. No. 2, 15 N.E.2d 576 (N.Y. 1938).

15. N.J. Const., Art. VIII, § 4.

16. Hahner v. Board of Educ., 278 N.W.2d 474 (Wis. App. 1979).

17. Cromwell Property Owners Ass'n, Inc. v. Toffolon, 495 F. Supp. 915 (D. Conn. 1979).

18. School Dist. of Pittsburgh v. Depart. of Educ. of Pennsylvania, 443 U.S. 901 (1979).

19. *See* McKeesport Area School Dist. v. Pennsylvania Dept. of Educ., 392 A.2d 912 (Pa. 1978), *appeal dismissed*, 446 U.S. 970 (1980); School Dist. of Pittsburgh v. Dept. of Educ. of Pennsylvania, 443 U.S. 901 (1979); Bennett v. Kline, 486 F. Supp. 36 (E.D. Pa. 1980). Aid to nonpublic schools for transportation associated with educational field trips also has generated litigation. In 1977 the Supreme Court majority struck down the portion of an Ohio law providing public funds for such assistance in Wolman v. Walter, 433 U.S. 229, 253-54, *see* text with note 56. However, the Pennsylvania statute provides for field trip transportation for non-public school students as well as for aid in transporting such students to and from school, and the field trip provision has not yet been contested. *See* McKeesport, 446 U.S. at 978 (Blackmun, J., concurring) and at 972-76 (White, J., concurring), where differing opinions were voiced as to how the Supreme Court should rule on the Pennsylvania field trip provision if called upon to assess its constitutionality.

20. Members of Jamestown School Committee v. Schmidt, 525 F.Supp. 1045 (D.R.I. 1981), *aff'd in part, rev'd in part*, 699 F.2d 1 (1st Cir. 1983.)

21. 525 F.Supp. 1045. *See also* Members of Jamestown School Committee v. Schmidt, 427 F.Supp. 1338, 1348-49 (D.R.I. 1977).

22. 699 F.2d at 9.

23. Cochran v. Louisiana State Bd. of Educ., 281 U.S. 370 (1930).

24. *See* Cantwell v. Connecticut, 310 U.S. 296 (1940), in which the Supreme Court interpreted the Fourteenth Amendment as protecting individuals from state as well as federal action interfering with their First Amendment religious freedoms. *See also* text with note 63, chapter 1.

25. Cochran v. Louisiana State Board of Educ., 281 U.S. 370, 375 (1930).

26. *Id.* at 375.

27. 392 U.S. 236 (1968).

28. *Id.* at 245.

29. *Id.* at 251-54 (Black, J., dissenting).

30. *Id.* at 253-54.

31. *Id.* at 251.

32. *Id.* at 270 (Fortas, J., dissenting).

33. *Id.* at 271.

34. *Id.* at 257 (Douglas, J., dissenting).

35. Wolman v. Walter, 433 U.S. 229 (1977) (Ohio provision); Meek v. Pittenger, 421 U.S. 349 (1975) (Pennsylvania provision).

36. Norwood v. Harrison, 413 U.S. 455 (1973). In this case the schools did not assert that their discriminatory practices were based on religious tenets. Thus the court did not have to balance a free exercise claim against antidiscrimination protections.

37. Public Funds for Public Schools of New Jersey v. Marburger, 358 F. Supp. 29 (D.N.J. 1973), *aff'd mem.*, 417 U.S. 961 (1974).

38. People *ex rel.* Klinger v. Howlett, 305 N.E.2d 129 (Ill. 1973). The court also struck down the provision of auxiliary services for nonpublic school students and yearly grants made to parents of private school students as partial payment for their educational expenses.

39. Among states with specific statutes that permit the use of public funds for textbooks distributed to nonpublic school pupils are Iowa, Louisiana, Mississippi, New Mexico, New York, and Rhode Island. *See* Alexander, *School Law*, p. 193.

40. Dickman v. School Dist. No. 62 C, 366 P.2d 533 (Ore. 1961), *cert. denied sub nom.* Carlson v. Dickman, 371 U.S. 823 (1962).

41. Bloom v. School Committee of Springfield, 379 N.E.2d 578 (Mass. 1978); *In re* Advisory Opinion, 228 N.W.2d 772 (Mich. 1975); Paster v. Tussey, 512 S.W.2d 97 (Mo. 1974), *cert. denied*, 419 U.S. 1111 (1975); Gaffney v. State Department, 220 N.W.2d 550 (Neb. 1974). *See also* Haas v. Independent School Dist. No. 1, 9 N.W.2d 707 (S.D. 1943), in which the South Dakota Supreme Court interpreted a state law, providing that textbooks would be supplied to pupils, as excluding students in private schools.

42. California Teachers' Association v. Riles, 632 P.2d 953, 962 (Cal. 1981).

43. *Id.*, citing Meek v. Pittenger, 421 U.S. 349, 379-80 (1975).

44. *Id.* at 963.

45. The child benefit doctrine has been criticized by several legal commentators. *See* text with note 119.

46. 403 U.S. 602 (1971). This standard was first introduced in Walz v. Tax Commission, 397 U.S. 664, 674 (1970). *See* text with note 80, chapter 1.

47. 402 U.S. at 612-13.

48. *Id.* at 622. Choper has noted that there always will be political divisiveness related to religion because religious groups increasingly are taking positions on political issues. He has argued that the constitutionality of legislation should be assessed on the basis of whether or not it advances or impedes religion, not on the basis of potential political divisiveness. Jesse Choper, "The Religion Clauses of the First Amendment: Reconciling the Conflict," *University of Pittsburgh Law Review* 41 (1980):684.

49. It should be noted that the Supreme Court has been less inclined to find an establishment clause violation in connection with state aid to private institutions of higher education. Several differences between colleges and elementary and secondary school students (e.g., age, maturity, and vulnerability to indoctrination) have been offered as partial justification for this double standard. Also, students are compelled by law in all states to attend elementary and at least part of secondary school, whereas postsecondary education is totally voluntary. The Supreme Court has been more willing to accept the assertion that the religious and secular functions can be separated in sectarian institutions of higher education (where an atmosphere of academic freedom is maintained) than in parochial elementary and secondary schools (where religious indoctrination permeates the instructional program). The double standard applied seems to be based primarily on the *character* of the institutions and their clientele, rather than on the *form* of the aid. *See* Roemer v. Board of Public Works, 426 U.S. 736 (1976) (upholding annual noncategorical state grants to private colleges and universities); Hunt v. McNair, 413 U.S. 734 (1973) (upholding the issuance of state revenue bonds to finance construction in a church-related college); Tilton v. Richardson, 403 U.S. 672 (1971) (upholding federal grants for private college and university construction under the Higher Education Facilities Act). Possibly this double standard eventually will be eliminated as the current Supreme Court seems less inclined to find an establishment clause violation in connection with aid to parochial elementary and secondary schools than was true from 1971 to 1976. *See* text with notes 56, 80.

50. Committee for Public Educ. and Religious Liberty v. Nyquist, 413 U.S. 756 (1973).

51. Levitt v. Committee for Public Educ. and Religious Liberty, 413 U.S. 472 (1973).

52. *Id.* at 480.

53. Sloan v. Lemon, 413 U.S. 825 (1973).

54. Meek v. Pittenger, 421 U.S. 349 (1975).

55. *Id.* at 366. Various types of parochiaid have also been struck down by state and lower federal courts. *See*, for example, Decker v. O'Donnell, 661 F.2d 598 (7th Cir. 1980) (assignment of employees paid under the Federal Comprehensive Employment and Training Act to work in church-operated schools); Americans United for Separation of Church and State v. Oakey, 339 F. Supp. 545 (D. Vt. 1972) (statute

allowing school districts partial reimbursement for assisting religious schools with current operating expenses including teachers' salaries); Swart v. South Burlington Town School Dist., 167 A.2d 514 (Vt. 1961) (public school district's payment of tuition for students to attend sectarian high schools); Almond v. Day, 89 S.E.2d 851 (Va. 1955) (statute providing state funds for the education of military orphans in public or private schools approved by the state superintendent of instruction).

56. 433 U.S. 229 (1977). At the time of this case it was estimated that 96% of Ohio's private school students attended sectarian schools.

57. Meek v. Pittenger, 421 U.S. 349, 366 (1975).

58. Wolman v. Walter, 444 U.S. 801 (1979). *See also* Wolman v. Essex, 544 F. Supp. 491 (S.D. Ohio 1982).

59. Sidney Buchanan, "Governmental Aid to Sectarian Schools: A Study in Corrosive Precedents," *Houston Law Review.* 15 (1978):816.

60. *Education Daily*, 13 May 1980, pp. 5-6.

61. The significant financial impact of *Wolman* is reflected by the fact that the biennial appropriation by the Ohio legislature to implement the challenged law was $88,800,000. *See* 433 U.S. at 233.

62. 433 U.S. at 265 (Stevens, J., concurring in part, dissenting in part).

63. 20 U.S.C. § 241a *et seq.* (1976). *See* text with note 14, chapter 5.

64. People *ex rel.* Klinger v. Howlett, 305 N.E.2d 129 (Ill. 1973).

65. Special Dist. for Educ. and Training of Handicapped Children v. Wheeler, 408 S.W.2d 60 (Mo. 1966).

66. Traverse City School Dist. v. Attorney General, 185 N.W.2d 9 (Mich. 1971).

67. *Id.* at 22.

68. Meek v. Pittenger, 421 U.S. 349, 371 (1975).

69. 433 U.S. 229 (1977).

70. *Id.* at 244.

71. *Id.* at 247.

72. *Id.* at 248.

73. Traverse City School Dist. v. Attorney General, 185 N.W.2d 9, 23 (Mich. 1971). *See also* State *ex rel.* School Dist. of Hartington v. Nebraska State Bd. of Educ., 195 N.W.2d 161 (Neb. 1972).

74. Wheeler v. Barrera, 417 U.S. 402 (1974).

75. *Id.* at 424.

76. National Coalition for Public Educ. and Religious Liberty v. Harris, 489 F. Supp. 1248 (S.D.N.Y. 1980), *appeal dismissed sub nom.* National Coalition for Public

Educ. and Religious Liberty v. Hufstedler, 449 U.S. 808 (1980). However, the Seventh Circuit Court of Appeals ruled that federal employees hired under the Comprehensive Employment Training Act could not be assigned to religious schools because they would be under the daily supervision of religious institutions and in effect no longer be governmental employees. Decker v. O'Donnell, 661 F.2d 598 (7th Cir. 1980).

77. Courts also have endorsed the use of public funds to support educational services for handicapped pupils who have been placed in private facilities because appropriate programs are not available in the public school district. *See* Martha McCarthy, *Judicial Interpretations of What Constitutes Appropriate Programs and Services for Handicapped Children* (Bloomington, Ind.: Council for Administrators of Special Education, 1981). *See also* note 15, chapter 5.

78. The Michigan Supreme Court, however, reached a contrary conclusion. *See* text with note 66. *See also* Thomas Griffin, "Public Aid to Private Schools: A Shift in Direction?" *West's Education Law Reporter* 1 (1982):757.

79. 433 U.S. 229, 238-40 (1977).

80. 444 U.S. 646 (1980).

81. Levitt v. Committee for Public Educ. and Religious Liberty, 413 U.S. 472 (1973). *See* text with note 51.

82. Levitt v. Committee for Public Educ. and Religious Liberty, 433 U.S. 902 (1977).

83. Committee for Public Educ. and Religious Liberty v. Regan, 444 U.S. 646, 662 (1980).

84. *Id.*

85. *Id.*

86. *Id.* (Blackmun, J., dissenting).

87. *Id.* at 671 (Stevens, J., dissenting).

88. *Id.*

89. *See* note 35, chapter 7.

90. *See* Diana Pullin, "Minimum Competency Testing and the Demand for Accountability," *Phi Delta Kappan* 63 (September 1981):20-22; *Viewpoints in Teaching and Learning* 56, no. 3 (1980) (entire issue).

91. Committee for Public Educ. and Religious Liberty v. Nyquist, 413 U.S. 756 (1973).

92. Public Funds for Public Schools v. Byrne, 590 F.2d 514 (3d Cir. 1979), *aff'd* 442 U.S. 907 (1979).

93. *Id.*, 590 F.2d at 518-20 (3d Cir. 1979).

94. Rhode Island Federation of Teachers AFL/CIO v. Norberg, 479 F. Supp. 1364 (D.R.I. 1979), *aff'd* 630 F.2d 855 (1st Cir. 1980).

95. *Id.*, 630 F.2d at 862.

96. Mueller v. Allen, 514 F. Supp. 998 (D. Minn. 1981), *aff'd* 676 F.2d 1195 (8th Cir. 1982), *aff'd* 51 U.S.L.W. 5050 (June 29, 1983). *See also* Minnesota Civil Liberties Union v. Roemer, 452 F. Supp. 1316 (D. Minn. 1978).

97. The court cited Walz v. Tax Commissioners, 397 U.S. 664 (1970), in which the Supreme Court held that tax exemptions for nonprofit educational, charitable, and religious institutions cover property solely used for religious purposes.

98. 676 F.2d at 1199-1200, distinguishing Committee for Public Educ. and Religious Liberty v. Nyquist, 413 U.S. 756 (1973).

99. *Id.* at 1200-1201. *See* Rhode Island Federation of Teachers AFL/CIO v. Norberg, 630 F.2d 855 (1st Cir. 1980).

100. 51 U.S.L.W. at 5052.

101. *Id.* at 5053. However, given the Supreme Court's recent decision that racially discriminatory religious schools are not entitled to tax exempt status, it follows that tax deductions could not be claimed for educational expenses paid to such schools operating in violation of established national policy. *See* Bob Jones University v. United States, Goldsboro Christian Schools v. United States, 51 U.S.L.W. 4593 (May 24, 1983); text with note 108, chapter 7.

102. *Id.* at 5058 (Marshall, J., dissenting).

103. For a discussion of this bill, *see Education Daily*, 3 August 1978, p. 1; *Education Daily*, 20 January 1978, p. 3.

104. The bill placed before Congress in 1981 resembled the 1977 provision except for limiting the allowable credit or refund to $250 for the first year of its implementation. *See* "Packwood-Moynihan Parochiaid Bill Introduced," *Church and State* (4 April 1981):3. *See also Education Daily*, 19 July 1982, pp. 1-2.

105. *See Education Daily*, 16 April 1982, p. 1.

106. *See* Leslie Gerstman, "Constitutionality of Tuition Tax Relief Upheld," *West's Education Law Reporter* 2 (1982):5. In November 1981 Washington, D.C., voters overwhelmingly rejected a tuition tax credit proposal, *Education Times* 2 (9 November 1981):1.

107. *Education Daily*, 28 April 1982, p. 3.

108. *Education Daily*, 16 April 1982, p. 1. It has been estimated that the tax credit program would cost the federal government $100 million in 1983, rising to about $1.5 billion by 1987. *Education Daily*, 23 June 1982, p. 1. A report released in August 1982 by the National Coalition for Public Education indicated that, under the Reagan proposal, federal spending per private school pupil would increase from $43 in 1980-81 to $329 in 1984-85, while federal expenditures would decrease per public school pupil from $207 to $105 during the same period. *See Education Daily*, 19 August 1982, pp. 1-2.

109. *Education Daily*, 16 April 1982, p. 2.

110. "Reagan Offers Private School Tax Break," *Louisville Times*, 15 April, 1982, p. A-1.

111. *Education Daily*, 7 July 1982, p. 3.

112. The study was commissioned by Americans United for Separation of Church and State and conducted by Albert Papa, research associate at the University of Virginia. *See Education Daily*, 3 November 1982, p. 5.

113. Roemer v. Board of Public Works, 426 U.S. 736, 747 (1976).

114. *Id.*

115. In Everson v. Board of Educ., 330 U.S. 1, 16 (1947), the Supreme Court majority noted that its decision extended to the "verge of forbidden territory under the Religion Clauses."

116. Choper, "The Religion Clauses of the First Amendment," p. 680.

117. Committee for Public Educ. and Religious Liberty v. Regan, 446 U.S. 646, 662 (1980).

118. Buchanan, "Governmental Aid to Sectarian Schools," p. 793.

119. *See* Buchanan, *ibid.*, pp. 794-835; Leo Pfeffer, *Church, State and Freedom* (Boston, Mass.: Beacon Press, 1967), pp. 558-71; Griffin, "Public Aid to Private Schools," pp. 757-59.

120. For a discussion of the posture of Supreme Court Justices toward church-state issues, *see* Charles Faber, "The Warren Court and the Burger Court: Some Comparisons of Education-related Decisions," *Nolpe School Law Reporter* 10 (1981):31-35; Walfred H. Peterson, *Thy Liberty in Law* (Nashville, Tenn.: Broadman Press, 1978), pp. 157-58.

121. Mueller v. Allen, 51 U.S.L.W. 5050, 5052, 5054 (June 29, 1983).

Chapter Seven

Governmental Regulation of Parochial Schools

This chapter covers several discrete, but related, issues pertaining to governmental relations with religious schools. Discussed first are the legal conflicts between the state's *parens patriae* role to assure an educated citizenry and parental rights to direct the education of their children according to their religious values. Specifically, this analysis focuses on the state's authority and duty to regulate parochial elementary and secondary schools and home education programs. The remainder of the chapter deals with the application of selected federal laws to parochial schools and the tax exempt status of sectarian schools with racially discriminatory policies.

The State's Regulatory Authority

It is well established that parents have some control over where, but not whether, their children are educated. In 1925, when the Supreme Court upheld the right of parents to select private education as an alternative to public schooling, the Court also noted that the state has a general welfare interest in mandating school attendance for all children within its jurisdiction.[1] Historically the state's interest in providing for universal education has focused on the collective welfare of the state rather than on the individual interests of the child.[2] As discussed in chapter 1, parents have been charged with the duty to ensure that their children receive an education so as not to burden society with illiterate citizens. Furthermore, an enlightened citizenry has been recognized as essential to safeguard our democratic form of government.

The judiciary also has acknowledged that the state can override parental rights in directing the upbringing of their offspring if the welfare of the children is at stake. The doctrine of *parens patriae* came to America from the English court of chancery where the chancellors of the king were held accountable to protect all infants in the kingdom from parental abuse, neglect, or other types of mistreatment.[3] In the United States the state has replaced the crown in the area of child welfare.

In a significant 1944 case, the Supreme Court upheld the state's *parens patriae* authority when pitted against a free exercise claim.[4] In this case a child's guardian, who was a Jehovah's Witness, gave the child religious magazines to sell on the street. The guardian was convicted of violating the Massachusetts child labor law by permitting a child under 12 years of age to sell the material. Recognizing the importance of the individual's right to exercise religious beliefs, the Court nonetheless ruled that the state's interest in protecting the welfare of the child was controlling: "It is the interest of youth itself, and of the whole community, that children be both safeguarded from abuses and given opportunities for growth into free and independent well-developed men and citizens."[5] The Court further elaborated on the relationship between parental rights and the state's *parens patriae* role.

> . . . neither rights of religion nor rights of parenthood are beyond limitation. Acting to guard the general interest in youth's well-being, the state as *parens patriae* may restrict the parent's control by requiring school attendance, regulating or prohibiting the child's labor, and in many other ways. Its authority is not nullified merely because the parent grounds his claim to control the child's course of conduct on religion or conscience.[6]

In subsequent cases the Supreme Court has reiterated that the state has broader power to regulate conduct of children than conduct of adults. In 1962 the Court emphasized that the state has an obligation to protect children from parental abuse: "Unfortunately, experience has shown that the question of custody, so vital to a child's happiness and well-being, frequently cannot be left to the discretion of parents."[7] The power of the parent, even when "linked to a free exercise claim," may be limited by the state if it appears that parental decisions will jeopardize the health, safety, or future well-being of the child.[8] In 1982 the Court recognized the state's authority to terminate parental custody to protect the physical and emotional needs of children, when there is evidence of parental incapacity, even in the absence of misconduct or "a threat of serious harm to the children."[9]

Based on the compelling governmental interests in protecting the welfare of children and the general society, courts traditionally have upheld the state's *parens patriae* authority to monitor and regulate private schools. In an illustrative case, the Washington Supreme Court commented: "Under the compulsory school attendance law, the legislature delegated to the district or county superintendent the authority to determine the minimum standards for a private school, in order that, in the exercise of his discretion, attendance at a qualified private school may be approved."[10] Other courts have also noted that the control of schools, public or private, resides with the state legislature.[11] In 1968 the U.S. Supreme Court declared that "if the State must satisfy its interest in secular education through the instrument of private schools, it has a proper interest in the manner in which those schools perform their secular educational function."[12]

However, the state's *parens patriae* authority has not always prevailed when in conflict with parental interests in directing the upbringing and education of their children.[13] If the state interferes with parents' childrearing decisions, it must show that such intervention is required to protect the child or the state. In 1923 the Supreme Court ruled that a Nebraska law requiring all instruction in public or private grammar schools to be in English abridged Fourteenth Amendment liberty rights.[14] Among the law's defects, the Court found that it unconstitutionally interfered with parental rights to have their children taught in German in a private school. Two years later the Court invalidated an Oregon statute that required all children to attend public schools, reasoning that private schools have a right to exist and parents have a right to choose private education for their children. The court declared that "the child is not the mere creature of the State; those who nurture him and direct his destiny have the right, coupled with the high duty, to recognize and prepare him for additional obligations."[15]

In the same decade the Supreme Court invalidated a Hawaii statute that was intended to promote the "Americanism" of students enrolled in private Japanese schools.[16] The statute, empowering the territorial government to regulate most details of the schools, was held to "deprive parents of fair opportunity to procure for their children instruction which they think important and we cannot say is harmful."[17] The Court noted that the statute in effect makes foreign language schools public schools, under complete control of the Department of Education, even though they receive no public support. Accepting the state's authority reasonably to regulate private schools, the Court declared that the state cannot totally strip a parent of "all control and direction of the education of his child."[18]

More recently the Supreme Court has recognized a "private realm of family life which the state cannot enter" without compelling justification.[19] In 1972 the Supreme Court noted that when the interests of parenthood are combined with a legitimate free exercise claim, a substantial state interest is required to sustain the validity of its regulations.[20] The Court declared that "a State's interest in universal education, however highly we rank it, is not totally free from a balancing process when it impinges on fundamental rights and interests."[21] Accordingly, the state must pursue the least restrictive means to attain its objectives if free exercise rights are at stake.

With increasing frequency, courts have been called upon to balance these public and private interests in connection with First Amendment challenges to the state's power to regulate alternatives to public education. This legal activity has raised significant issues regarding the extent of the state's authority to monitor private schools and home education programs when free exercise rights are implicated.

State Regulation of Religious Schools

The National Center for Educational Statistics has reported an increase in the number of nonpublic schools since 1975, attributed primarily to the recent growth in fundamentalist Christian academies.[22] Nationwide, approximately five million students attended nonpublic schools in 1980-81, and 84% of these pupils attended religiously affiliated schools.[23] States vary considerably in their efforts to regulate nonpublic education. In some states private schools do not have to register with state authorities or comply with personnel or programmatic requirements. At the other end of the continuum, some states require private schools to employ state-certified teachers and satisfy detailed curriculum standards in secular subjects.[24]

Accompaying the recent growth in private religious academies have been attempts to maintain the autonomy of these schools so they can conduct religious training without state interference. The schools and their patrons have sought deregulation through legislation as well as through judicial invalidation of restrictive state standards applied to nonpublic schools. Some of these religious schools, which stress the Bible and moral absolutes, have asserted a free exercise right to determine the content as well as the methods of all instruction provided to their students. These schools have claimed that they should be considered an integral part of the church and thus subject only to state regulations applied to religious institutions.[25] Parents of pupils enrolled in the schools also have contended that they have a right to select an education for their children that reinforces their value system.

In states with extensive programmatic, personnel, and safety requirements for private schools, state authorities have justified the regulations as necessary to fulfill the government's obligation to assure an educated citizenry and to protect the welfare of children. They have argued that compulsory schooling mandates are meaningless unless the state retains the authority to monitor the quality of education provided outside the public domain.[26] To date courts have rendered conflicting opinions regarding the scope of the state's authority and duty to prescribe the *means* by which all children receive an education.

The Ohio Supreme Court has struck down comprehensive state regulations governing practically all aspects of the educational process in private schools. In 1976 the court applied the three-pronged balancing test to evaluate a claim that the state requirements impaired free exercise rights of religious schools.[27] The court concluded from the evidence that the plaintiffs satisfied their initial burden of demonstrating that their claim was based on sincerely held religious beliefs. Turning to the second criteria, the court found that the state regulations, prescribing almost to the minute how instructional time must be used, burdened the free exercise of beliefs. By requiring nonpublic school activities to "conform" to such prescriptive regulations, the court reasoned that the state would be interfering with the religious mission of some private schools. Finding that the regulations burdened the free exercise of sincerely held religious beliefs, the court then assessed whether there was a substantial state interest to justify the burden imposed. While acknowledging that the state is empowered to establish minimum regulations to assure that each child obtains a "high quality" general education, the court concluded that the "comprehensive regimentation" included in Ohio's standards as applied to nonpublic schools overstepped "the boundary of *reasonable* regulation."[28] The court declared that the minimum standards were "so pervasive and all-encompassing that total compliance with each and every standard by a nonpublic school would effectively eradicate the distinction between public and nonpublic education, and thereby deprive these appellants of their traditional interest as parents to direct the upbringing and education of their children."[29] The court further held that the expansive regulations impaired free exercise rights by prohibiting the plaintiffs from instilling sectarian beliefs without unreasonable governmental interference.

Four years later, the same court reversed a parent's conviction under the compulsory attendance law for sending his child to a school that did not conform to state standards. The court noted that the state board of education had not complied with the 1976 opinion by adopting new regulations for nonpublic schools that would "assure the provision of a 'general education of high quality'," but "not simultaneously suffocate 'independent thought and educational policy'."[30] The court declared that until the state adopts minimum standards that "go no further than necessary" to assure the state's legitimate interests in the education in private schools, "the balance is weighted, . . . in favor of a First Amendment claim to religious freedom."[31]

One commentator has suggested that the Ohio Supreme Court has approached a legal theory imposing a "strong presumption" that the state must seek alternative means to accomplish its objective "once it is demonstrated that the individual is being compelled to act contrary to his or her conscience."[32] If this analysis is correct and other courts should adopt similar logic, the free exercise clause will become a far more powerful tool for use in challenging state regulation of religious schools.

In a noteworthy 1979 case, the Kentucky Supreme Court also struck down the application of certain state regulations to private schools. The court concluded that such schools could not be required to meet state accreditation standards, employ certified teachers, or use prescribed textbooks.[33] The court reasoned that these stipulations applied to private schools violated the state constitution's guarantee that parents cannot be compelled to send their children to a school to which they may be conscientiously opposed. Although acknowledging that the state could require school attendance to ensure an educated citizenry, the court held that specified branches of study could not be required in church-related schools. The court also rejected the assertion that the state has a compelling interest in requiring all teachers to be certified, noting the inconclusive research relating teacher training to student academic achievement.[34] The court suggested that the state should monitor the quality of secular education provided in private schools by requiring the students to take an examination. If deficiencies should be noted among students attending a given school, then state action to close the school might be justified.[35] In 1980 the U.S. Supreme Court declined to review the case, thus leaving the Kentucky high court decision intact.

145

However, courts have not spoken in unison as to the autonomy of sectarian schools. In some states, challenged state requirements applied to nonpublic schools have been upheld. For example, North Dakota parents contested their convictions under compulsory attendance laws for sending their children to an unaccredited private school. Accepting that the parents were motivated by a sincere religious belief, the state supreme court nonetheless concluded that the minimum requirements for private schools pertaining to teacher certification, prescribed courses, and health and safety standards do not conflict with any espoused religious dogma.[36] Even assuming that the requirements might place some burden on the free exercise of religion, the court held that the state's overriding compelling interest in assuring a sufficient education for all resident children justifies minimum educational standards.

Similarly, in 1981 the Nebraska Supreme Court ruled that nonpublic schools do not have a right to be completely "unfettered by reasonable government regulations as to the quality of education furnished."[37] Officials of a sectarian school had refused to comply with Nebraska's education laws, asserting that such standards burdened the free exercise of religion without a compelling governmental interest. The Nebraska high court, however, rejected this claim and concluded that the state has the authority to require nonpublic schools and teaching personnel to meet minimum standards. The court distinguished the Nebraska minimum requirements pertaining to teacher qualifications, pupil records, and course approval from the more prescriptive Ohio regulations. The court concluded that the Nebraska religious school was attempting to thwart the state's legitimate and reasonable interest in carrying out its educational obligations. In 1981 the U.S. Supreme Court dismissed an appeal of this decision. Thus the high court has left standing two rulings in which the Kentucky and Nebraska supreme courts reached somewhat different conclusions.

The Nebraska controversy, however, did not end with the Supreme Court's action. In 1982 parents of children who had attended the fundamentalist school unsuccessfully attempted to secure an injunction to keep the school open.[38] The parents claimed that the school afforded the only viable educational alternative consistent with their religious beliefs. They challenged the state regulations as interfering with parental rights and separating education *from* religion, which runs counter to their philosophy that education *is* religion. Finding these assertions unpersuasive, the judge concluded that the plaintiffs' "alleged injury seems precipitated more by obstinance than by the caprice of the state."[39]

The activity to secure autonomy for religious academies has not been confined to judicial forums. Indeed, some of the major efforts have focused on securing legislative endorsement of deregulation. For example, after a North Carolina trial court upheld state regulations applied to private schools,[40] fundamentalist religious groups focused their efforts on changing the state statutes. Following an intensive lobbying effort, the legislature removed many of the requirements previously applied to nonpublic schools.[41] Thus the appeal of the trial court decision, which was pending before the state supreme court at the time of the legislative action, became moot.

It was reported that 32 new schools were established in North Carolina within six months following the deregulation.[42] These schools no longer have to satisfy programmatic or teacher qualification standards. They must only maintain attendance and immunization records; comply with fire, safety, and health laws; operate on a regular schedule for nine months (excluding reasonable holidays); and administer annual standardized achievement tests, the results of which must be available for state inspection. The deregulation has been criticized by public school authorities; one education official has asserted that under the revised standards, "you can have some children play poker at night for nine months and then give them a diploma."[43]

While some of the most volatile controversies have focused on programmatic and personnel requirements applied to religious schools, other state regulations also have come under attack. For example, in 1981 the Eighth Circuit Court of Appeals addressed a First Amendment challenge to the application of regulations of the Arkansas Activities Association to private schools.[44] The contested provision requires schools participating in interscholastic athletic activities sponsored by the association to obtain state accreditation. A noncertified Christian academy challenged its exclusion from interscholastic athletics as impairing its free exercise rights. The school asserted "that, as a Christian school owing its entire allegiance to God, it could not be forced to serve two masters" by submitting to the accreditation standards.[45] Upholding the requirement, the court reasoned that the state is empowered to enforce reasonable regulations designed to advance legitimate health, safety, and welfare interests. The court declared that the questioned regulation falls clearly within "the permissible exercise of state power over nonpublic religious schools. The state's requirements are both neutral and secular."[46] The court did not find that the accreditation standards pose any undue burden on the free exercise of religious beliefs; therefore, the state acted within its authority to condition participation in certain interscholastic athletic activities on compliance with the standards.

Fundamentalist academies increasingly are asserting a free exercise right to be exempt from state and local health, safety, and zoning regulations except for those applied to the parent church. The primary concern is not that the schools cannot satisfy the requirements; instead, the religious academies contend that they are part of the church's ministry and should not be singled out for special treatment.[47] In essence, it is being argued that sectarian educational programs should be considered "churches" rather than "schools" for state regulatory purposes.

In 1982 the Washington Supreme Court ruled that a church school may be entitled to an exemption from the city's fire and zoning codes.[48] The trial court had upheld enforcement of the city's fire, health, and zoning regulations in connection with prohibiting the operation of a Christian academy that did not meet the standards. Reversing the trial court's decision, the state high court reasoned that the city's interest in the safety of children must be balanced against the church's interest in maintaining a school to instill its religious tenets. Noting that the evenhanded enforcement of the city regulations may not "*directly* adversely impact religious beliefs," the court concluded that the "*indirect* effect . . . of the governmental regulation in this instance will profoundly impact the church and its members."[49] The court concluded that although the church did not have a fundamental tenet against compliance with building or zoning ordinances, the practical effect of enforcing such ordinances was to close down the church-operated school. The court remanded the case for a trial to determine if there are less restrictive means to achieve the state's objectives without unduly burdening the parents' constitutional right to provide their child an education oriented toward their religious faith.[50]

In contrast to the above decision, in 1982 the U.S. Supreme Court declined to review a case in which a Florida appeals court concluded that a church-related school was obligated to obtain a zoning permit for its educational program. The church, which has its own permit, asserted that the school is an "integral and inseparable ministry" of the church and that separate zoning permits would indicate an artificial bifurcation.[51] Church authorities conceded that the school would probably have no problem obtaining the controversial permit, but they nonetheless challenged the requirement. They argued that the government unduly burdened religious practice by subjecting the church's educational function to special regulations. Rejecting these assertions, the appellate court reasoned that church-related schools are subject to the same zoning requirements as other educational institutions.

Thus far the Supreme Court has declined to render an opinion in recent controversies over the state's authority to regulate nonpublic education. Therefore, standards vary from one jurisdiction to the next, and the scope of the state's *parens patriae* power in this arena remains somewhat ambiguous. Should the state's monitoring role be limited to assessing the output of sectarian schools in terms of student academic achievement, or does the state have a legitimate interest in regulating the personnel and program offerings in private schools? Does the free exercise clause entitle sectarian schools to special exemptions from state regulations applied to other nonpublic schools? Litigation in this arena has far-reaching implications because the state's duty to assure that all children receive a minimally adequate education is being seriously questioned. In some jurisdictions limitations are being judicially imposed on the state's traditionally recognized authority to override parental interests—including the exercise of religious beliefs—to protect the welfare of children and the state.

Moreover, fundamentalist religious groups are gaining political strength in their efforts to secure legislation that protects the autonomy of sectarian schools. Several states recently have removed certain programmatic and personnel specifications applied to nonpublic schools, and bills to this effect are pending in numerous other states.[52] One commentator has asserted that by deregulating religious schools, state legislatures are conferring a governmental function on religious organizations.[53] Assuming that the state has a constitutional duty to assure an educated citizenry, one might infer an "affirmative state obligation" to monitor and regulate public as well as private education.[54] While the issue of "reverse entanglement" (i.e., religious institutions assuming governmental functions) has not yet been litigated, "the ceding to religious organizations of a state's constitutional authority—and perhaps obligation—to ensure minimal educational advantages to all children raises legal and policy considerations and may forecast a future trend in establishment clause analysis."[55]

State Regulation of Home Education Programs

Related to state regulation of private schools is the state's authority to regulate home education programs. It was reported in 1980 that 39 states, by statute or administrative regulation, allow compulsory attendance mandates to be satisfied by home instruction or other alternatives to private or public schooling as long as such instruction is considered equivalent to public school offerings.[56] Of these states, 32 place initial approval responsibility on local school officials.

Dissatisfaction with the values taught in public education has caused an increasing number of parents to select home instruction instead of formal schooling. Chester Nolte has observed that parents are disenchanted with what they believe to be inexcusable "humanistic trends in the public schools, unnecessary compulsion amounting in effect to unconstitutional invasion of parental privacy, and exposure of their children in public schools to wordly influences, dirty language, drugs, crime and sex."[57] It was estimated in 1981 that between 10,000 and 30,000 families chose home instruction in lieu of formal public or private schooling.[58]

In some states home education programs do not have to register with state authorities or the local school board. Therefore, parents opting for home instruction often have maintained a low profile to avoid charges that they are violating compulsory attendance laws. As a result, an accurate estimate is not available regarding the number of children being educated at home or in a neighbor's home. Only a few home education programs have generated lawsuits to date, but such litigation is increasing. Cases usually are initiated by state authorities asserting that parents are violating compulsory attendance mandates because a given home education program allegedly is not equivalent to public school offerings.

Recently, conflicting opinions have been rendered on the issue of where the burden of proof resides in proving or disproving the equivalency of home instruction. On two occasions Missouri appellate courts have placed the burden on state officials to substantiate that home instruction (authorized by state law) is not comparable to the public school program. The courts reasoned that parents could not be convicted of neglecting to educate their children without "clear and convincing evidence" that "substantially equivalent" instruction was not being provided at home.[59] The courts concluded that if the inequivalency of home instruction is part of the charge against parents, the burden of supporting this charge resides with the state.

In contrast to the Missouri decisions, in 1981 the Iowa Supreme Court placed the burden of persuasion on parents to produce evidence that their children were entitled to be exempt from school attendance because they were receiving home instruction equivalent to the public school program.[60] The court reasoned that the use of the terms "certified teacher" and "equivalent instruction" in the compulsory education law are not unconstitutionally vague; "certified" is defined as holding a valid teaching license, and the statute provides criteria for assessing whether instruction is equal in kind and amount to that provided in public schools. The parents were found in violation of the law because they did not substantiate that the conditions for an exception to school attendance were satisfied. The court further noted that the parents did not present any evidence to show that the law burdens their free exercise of religious beliefs.

State licensing requirements for home tutors have been challenged in several cases. A Michigan federal district court upheld a state statute requiring parents who educate their children at home to comply with teacher certification standards. Accepting the state's legitimate "interest in insuring the minimum competency of those entrusted to teach," the court found it reasonable to use certification as the threshold standard of competency for home tutors.[61] In 1982 an Alabama criminal appeals court similarly ruled that the state requirement that private tutors must hold a teaching license does not violate parents' constitutional right to "liberty, privacy, and family integrity."[62]

In Florida home tutors are required to possess specific qualifications, but nonpublic schools are virtually unregulated in the state. In a recent case, parents, who were providing home instruction for their two children, asserted that they had established a private school rather than a home education program. However, a Florida appeals court concluded that the two minors, who were instructed by their mother (and occasionally by their elder sister) in their home where no other students would be permitted to "enroll," were not attending a private school.[63] Thus the court held that the students would be considered truant under the compulsory attendance law until enrolled in a private school or home program with a tutor meeting state requirements.

In some situations parents have asserted that free exercise rights excuse them from adhering to state-prescribed guidelines for approval of home education programs. While recognizing that state authority is subject to a balancing process when it impinges on free exercise rights, several courts have ruled that parents cannot totally disregard state law because of religious opposition to the public school curriculum. For example, the Massachusetts high court noted in 1955 that religious reasons did not constitute a valid defense for Buddhist parents to fail to secure approval from local public school authorities for their home education program.[64] Similarly, courts in Washington and Virginia have rejected assertions that religious beliefs justify noncompliance with state procedures for the approval of home instruction.[65]

In a significant 1981 case, two West Virginia parents were convicted of violating the compulsory attendance law by educating their children at home without seeking approval from the local board of education.[66] The law authorizes home education if the local board attests that the persons providing the instruction are qualified (even though not certified) in subjects required to be taught in the public schools. The parents asserted that they deserved an exemption from the statutory approval requirements for home instruction because free exercise rights were at stake. Disagreeing with this contention, the West Virginia high court distinguished the situation from the *Yoder* case where Amish youth were excused from compulsory attendance mandates after completing eighth grade. The court noted that *Yoder* involved an "ancient religious community which the record demonstrated had its own system of vocational and technical training designed to prepare its children for life in a pastoral, relatively self-contained society."[67] Furthermore, Amish youth attended public schools through eighth grade to assure acquisition of basic academic skills in the event that some children might choose to move outside the religious community. In contrast, the court observed that the children in the West Virginia case were not being prepared for a cloistered religious community, and at least one of the children had not completed eighth grade. The court reasoned that while in *Yoder* the balance of interests "tipped slightly in the direction of free exercise, in the case before us the balance is decidedly the other way."[68] Noting that the parents could have applied to the local school board for approval of their home instructional program, the court declared that religious beliefs cannot justify disregarding statutory procedures: "The *Yoder* case emphatically does not imply that the free exercise clause is an absolute bar to any intrusion whatsoever by the State."[69]

The West Virginia high court also addressed what is meant by "qualified instructors" under the state compulsory attendance law. The court interpreted such qualifications as extending beyond the basic skills to "an instructor's ability to afford students diverse forms of cultural enrichment ranging from organized athletics, art, music, and literature, to an understanding of the multiple possibilities for careers which this society offers."[70] The court noted that the state constitution entitles all children to a "thorough and efficient" education, which has been interpreted as a program that develops "the minds, bodies and social morality of its charges to prepare them for useful and happy occupations, recreation and citizenship . . ."[71] The court indicated that it would be difficult for parents choosing to instruct their children at home to demonstrate that they could provide such a program.

In an earlier case, a New Jersey court espoused somewhat similar reasoning in concluding that children need to have contact with peers in order for their education to be considered adequate under compulsory schooling mandates. The court declared: "In a cosmopolitan area such as we live in, with all the complexities of life, and our reliance upon others to carry out the functions of education, it is almost impossible for a child to be adequately taught in his home."[72] The court reasoned that the state has a legitimate interest in the method as well as result of educational programs.

However, a Massachusetts appeals court held that parents need not be certified teachers to instruct their children at home, nor must children be provided the same social group experiences as found in the public school.[73] The court suggested that, in evaluating home education petitions, the local school committee should consider whether the number of hours of instruction is the same as required in public schools, whether the tutors are competent instructors, whether the materials and programs are adequate, and whether the child will be tested periodically to measure educational progress and ensure that minimum standards are being maintained.

In 1982 a North Carolina federal district court considered the fact that the state did not have standards for assessing the quality of alternatives to public education when it ruled that a parent could not be convicted under the compulsory school attendance law for educating his children at home.[74] The court reasoned that by substantially deregulating private schools in 1979, the state had relinquished its interest in the quality of nonpublic education. In the absence of minimal educational standards, the court found that the state's compulsory school attendance mandate was "little more than empty coercion." Accordingly, the court ruled that the parent could not be prosecuted for violating the compulsory attendance statute.

If the home education movement continues to grow, courts increasingly may be called upon to assess the legality of specific programs. Currently, considerable diversity exists among states regarding regulations applied to home instruction; and in many states there is very little monitoring of such alternatives to formal schooling. Indeed, records are often incomplete regarding the number of children being educated at home. The judiciary has not clarified the scope of parents' free exercise rights to dictate the *manner* and *content* of their children's education. Does the parent or the state bear the burden of proving or disproving that a given home education program is equivalent to public school offerings?[75] Should equivalency be judged by program input or outcome standards or by some other criteria? Is the state's regulatory power reduced when home instruction is allegedly dictated by religious beliefs? Should the judiciary assume that the parents' interests are the same as the child's?[76] These are simply a few of the unresolved legal questions pertaining to the state's authority over home education programs when free exercise rights are involved.

Application of Federal Policies
to Religious Schools

State authority to regulate religious schools and home education programs has not been the only source of recent controversy regarding the appropriate governmental relationship to sectarian education. Federal laws and policies also have generated significant First Amendment litigation. In this section litigation is reviewed in which courts have addressed sensitive questions regarding the application of selected federal laws to religious schools and the obligation of such schools to conform to established national policy.

National Labor Relations Act

In 1979 the U.S. Supreme Court rendered a decision in which it held that the National Labor Relations Board (NLRB) did not have jurisdiction over lay faculty in religious schools.[77] The NLRB had asserted such jurisdiction under the National Labor Relations Act. After two Catholic dioceses refused to recognize employee organizations for bargaining purposes, representation was sought only for lay teachers. The schools still refused to recognize the unions and to bargain, so the unions subsequently filed charges of unfair labor practices with the NLRB. After reviewing the complaints, the NLRB ordered the schools to bargain collectively with the unions.

The Seventh Circuit Court of Appeals and subsequently the Supreme Court concluded that the NLRB had misinterpreted its scope of authority as extending to religiously affiliated schools. The appellate court noted that the NLRB's initial act of certifying a union as the bargaining agent for lay teachers would impinge upon the discretion of church authorities to direct teaching in accord with religious tenets. Concluding that religious schools are an integral part of the church, the court declared that governmental interference with management prerogatives, condoned in an ordinary commercial setting, is not acceptable in a zone protected by the First Amendment.[78]

Affirming the appellate decision, the Supreme Court noted that the NLRB's actions in connection with religious schools would go far beyond the resolution of factual issues into issues involving the school's religious mission. Such activities would "open the door to conflicts between clergy-administrators and the Board or conflicts with negotiators for unions."[79] Finding no clear expression of congressional intent to cover teachers in church-related schools under the act, the court held that Congress did "not contemplate that the Board would require church-operated schools to grant recognition to unions as bargaining agents for their teachers."[80]

Federal Unemployment Tax Act

Governmental regulation of sectarian schools has also generated controversy in connection with the application of federal unemployment tax programs

153

to employees of such schools. In 1981 the Supreme Court issued a unanimous opinion, holding that unincorporated church schools are exempt under the Federal Unemployment Tax Act (FUTA).[81] This law, originally part of the 1935 Social Security Act, establishes a cooperative federal-state program of benefits for unemployed workers. The controversy that led to the Supreme Court ruling involved two Lutheran schools that challenged FUTA's application to them as impairing free exercise rights. The dispute focused on amendments to FUTA which extended its coverage to most nonprofit institutions, but still exempted churches and organizations directly controlled by churches. In 1978 the U.S. Secretary of Labor interpreted the amended act as requiring church-run schools, even though not separate entities from the churches that operate them, to pay unemployment taxes.[82] The South Dakota Supreme Court endorsed this interpretation and ruled that the two unincorporated Lutheran schools were covered by FUTA.

The U.S. Supreme Court disagreed, interpreting the language of FUTA as exempting unincorporated religious schools.[83] The Court concluded that where the church hires, trains, and funds the school employees and governs school operations, such schools have no legal existence apart from the church. Noting that FUTA provides an exemption for "service performed . . . in the employ of . . . a church or convention or association of churches," the Court ruled that the statute clearly exempts schools whose primary purpose is to propagate a religious faith through integrated religious and educational training.[84] The Court rejected the argument that the exemption was limited to work actually performed in a church, reasoning that the nature of the employer, not the terms of the work performed, governs exempt status. Distinguishing these schools from incorporated religious schools, the Court ruled that the latter could qualify for an exemption under FUTA only with evidence that they are operated, controlled, or primarily supported by a church or group of churches.

Because the Supreme Court interpreted FUTA as exempting employees in unincorporated sectarian schools, it was not forced to address the free exercise claim raised by the Lutheran schools. In prior decisions both the Fifth Circuit Court of Appeals and an Illinois appellate court had also avoided the free exercise issue by similarly interpreting FUTA and comparable state provisions.[85] The Fifth Circuit Appellate Court suggested that if the judiciary is misinterpreting congressional intent by excluding church-operated schools from FUTA, Congress can act to clarify the law's intended coverage.[86]

In June 1982 the Supreme Court issued a second decision involving the application of unemployment tax programs to employees in church-related schools and again skirted the First Amendment issue.[87] In this case a California federal district court judge had addressed both free exercise and establishment clause considerations in connection with the application of FUTA and its state counterpart to sectarian schools. Supporting the notion that religious schools operated and controlled by churches are exempt from FUTA, the judge ruled that free exercise rights are impaired by the government tax program only in connection with such unincorporated schools. However, the judge's conclusion regarding the establishment clause issue was more controversial and sparked the appeal to the Supreme Court. The judge held that the application of the federal-state unemployment tax program to any religious schools (whether incorporated or not) unconstitutionally entangles the state with religion, since it would lead to governmental investigations of dismissals based on religious grounds to determine eligibility for unemployment benefits.

On appeal, state officials and the U.S. Justice Department asserted that the entanglement feared by the district court judge is "purely hypothetical" in connection with the application of FUTA and similar state provisions to sectarian schools with a legal identity apart from the parent church.[88] The Justice Department's brief to the Supreme Court stated that governmental contact with the schools involves "innocuous matters," such as requiring schools to keep records of former employees' wages, hours, and length of employment, and that such routine record keeping does not significantly entangle church and state.[89] The Justice Department contended that the government would not be involved in doctrinal disputes in determining benefits for fired parochial school employees and that the schools would still be free to establish conditions of employment dictated by their faith.

The Supreme Court declined to address the First Amendment issue and disposed of the case on jurisdictional grounds. Concluding that the case should never have been heard by the federal judiciary in the first place, the Court vacated the lower court's order, relying on the Tax Injunction Act, which prohibits federal court intervention in halting state tax collection where there are "plain, speedy and efficient" state remedies available.[90] The Court reasoned that if it addressed the First Amendment issues raised in the case, it would violate the longstanding policy that limits federal court interference in the administration of state taxes. Thus the Court did not resolve the constitutionality of applying government unemployment tax programs to religious schools that have no formal church ties. Justice Stevens, however, issued a strong dissent, claiming that the Court should have addressed the merits of the free exercise and establishment clause claims because a federal law is involved in the joint federal-state tax program.[91]

Civil Rights Act of 1870

The Civil Rights Act of 1870, Section 1981, stipulates that all individuals, irrespective of race, have the right to make and enforce contracts.[92] It is unclear, however, whether this law prohibits commercially operated religious schools from discriminating on the basis of race. In 1976 the Supreme Court ruled that the Act applies to private as well as public commercial operations, and therefore private schools that advertise for applicants cannot condition admission on racial considerations.[93] But the Court did not address the status of sectarian schools, leaving ambiguity as to whether religious schools are subject to the law's antidiscrimination provision.

The following year the Fifth Circuit Court of Appeals concluded that Section 1981 applied to a sectarian school, but the appeals court also sidestepped the First Amendment issue.[94] Noting the absence of references to school segregation in the church's written literature, the court reasoned that the school's policy of denying admission to minority students was not based on religious beliefs. Finding no free exercise violation, the court avoided the issue of·whether a racial discrimination policy grounded in sincerely held religious beliefs would exempt a school from Section 1981 coverage. The court did note, however, that "a school or church which holds racial segregation as a religious tenet should not be barred from asserting a free exercise defense to a Section 1981 claim . . ."[95]

The Fourth Circuit Court of Appeals applied similar reasoning in using Section 1981 to invalidate the expulsion of a white student for associating with black students in a commercially operated sectarian school.[96] The court held that the church school did not carry its burden of substantiating that "racial purity" was grounded in the religious tenets of the church. Concluding that the discriminatory practice was based on the personal preference of school authorities rather than on a sincere religious belief, the court did not have to balance free exercise rights against a Section 1981 claim of racial discrimination. Thus, while some racially discriminatory practices in sectarian commercially operated schools have been invalidated under Section 1981, the judiciary has not yet clarified whether legitimate religious beliefs can be used to justify noncompliance with this act.

Civil Rights Act of 1871

Section 1983 of the Civil Rights Act of 1871 provides that any person acting on behalf of the state who deprives another individual of rights secured by the U.S. Constitution or Federal laws is subject to personal liability.[97] This law, which rarely appeared in litigation until the 1960s, has recently become an important tool for individuals to use in vindicating abridgements of their federal rights. The Supreme Court has broadly interpreted "person" under this act as embracing political subdivisions of the state including school districts.[98] Teachers, and to a lesser extent students, in public schools have used Section 1983 in obtaining damages from school boards and school authorities for a variety of civil rights violations.[99] However, parochial school students and teachers have not shared similar success.

The crucial issue in determining the application of Section 1983 to sectarian schools is whether such schools are acting under color of state law. In a significant 1982 decision, the U.S. Supreme Court concluded that a private school, although regulated by the state, was not *dominated* by the state and, therefore, was not subject to liability under Section 1983.[100] In this case former teachers and a counselor attempted to secure damages from a private school for their dismissals that allegedly violated First, Fifth, and Fourteenth Amendment rights. Rejecting these claims, the Supreme Court reasoned that there was no "symbiotic relationship" between the private school and the state.[101] Although the school received some public funds and had to comply with a variety of state and federal regulations, the Court held that the private school was not fundamentally different from other "private contractors performing services for the government."[102] Finding that the school was not functioning under the color of state law, the Court ruled that the former employees could not rely on Section 1983 in challenging their dismissals.

In several cases the judiciary similarly has concluded that private school students cannot use Section 1983 to challenge disciplinary measures. In 1971 the Seventh Circuit Court of Appeals held that the expulsion of two students from a private school did not involve state action, even though the school was required to satisfy certain state educational standards.[103] Similarly, a Pennsylvania federal district court ruled that a private school student's expulsion was not subject to review under Section 1983 because the school had no significant relationship to the state.[104] Also, the Connecticut federal district court espoused comparable reasoning in ruling that a private school was not serving a public function, despite the school's receipt of minimal public support and its adherence to state accreditation standards and other education regulations.[105]

In order to invoke Section 1983 protections in challenging a private school's practices, it must be shown that the school's action is "fairly attributable to the state."[106] Courts to date have demanded proof of strong governmental attachments before concluding that a private school is functioning under color of state law.[107] Evidence that a parochial school enjoys tax-exempt status, receives some public financial support, and is governed by state education regulations has not been sufficient to establish the necessary nexus between the school and the state. Thus, while public schools have become increasingly vulnerable to Section 1983 liability in connection with the deprivation of employees' and students' federally protected rights, most private schools have successfully argued that they function outside the scope of Section 1983 coverage.

Tax-Exempt Status of Religious Schools
Engaging in Racially Discriminatory Practices

Religious schools have been granted an exemption under certain federal tax programs, but the tax-exempt status of religious institutions that operate under racially discriminatory policies has generated substantial controversy. The administrative, legislative, and judicial branches of the federal government have been involved in this volatile dispute, which may have broad implications for federal relations with religious schools. Legal developments in this arena made national newspaper headlines in 1982 and 1983, and only recently has the U.S. Supreme Court rendered an opinion on the legality of allowing tax exemptions for sectarian schools with discriminatory operating policies.[108]

The controversy actually started in 1970 when Mississippi parents and students obtained a preliminary court injunction prohibiting the Internal Revenue Service (IRS) from affording tax-exempt status to private schools in the state that discriminated on the basis of race.[109] The IRS subsequently announced that it would discontinue tax-exempt status or the allowance of charitable contributions and deductions in connection with racially discriminatory schools. In 1971 the preliminary court injunction was made permanent, and this decision was affirmed without an opinion by the U.S. Supreme Court.[110] Regulations issued by IRS in 1975 stipulated that private schools must substantiate that they are operating in a nondiscriminatory manner to maintain their tax-exempt status. Since 1975 more than 100 private schools have had their tax-exempt status discontinued because of discriminatory policies.

One such institution is Bob Jones University, a fundamentalist religious college located in Greenville, South Carolina. In 1976 the college received notice of revocation of tax-exempt status because of its racially restrictive admissions policy and policy prohibiting interracial dating and marriage among its students. The institution challenged the IRS action and received a favorable ruling from the federal district court.[111] The court held that Congress intended to treat religious educational institutions differently from nonreligious institutions, reasoning that there is no clear federal policy proscribing racial discrimination by religious organizations. The court also found no compelling evidence that social harm would result from allowing a tax exemption for a religious institution that prohibits interracial dating and marriage.

The Fourth Circuit Court of Appeals disagreed and reversed the lower court's decision. Concluding that the prohibition of racial discrimination—"governmental or private, absolute or conditional, contractual or associational"—is "clearly defined public policy," the appellate court ruled that a government subsidy in the form of a tax exemption cannot be awarded to organizations violating public policy.[112] The court declared that neither the free exercise or establishment clauses prohibit the government from applying the "most fundamental constitutional and societal values by means of a uniform policy, neutrally applied."[113]

The Fourth Circuit Court of Appeals also denied tax-exempt status to the Goldsboro (North Carolina) Christian Schools. These schools, which offer classes from kindergarten through grade twelve, refuse to admit black students because the mixing of races conflicts with their interpretation of the Bible. The schools have never received recognition as a tax-exempt entity, and they challenged the IRS position as impairing their First Amendment rights. The federal district court and subsequently Fourth Circuit Court of Appeals endorsed the IRS action because of the governmental policy against subsidizing public or private racial discrimination.[114]

158

These two cases, combined on appeal before the U.S. Supreme Court, raised sensitive questions about the interpretation of First Amendment religious guarantees as well as the authority of federal administrative agencies. The private schools asserted that their free exercise rights were impaired by conditioning tax-exempt status on denouncement of practices grounded in their faith. They also contended that the IRS acted without sufficient constitutional or statutory authority when it created the 1970 policy revoking the tax-exempt status of racially discriminatory schools.

Public interest in this case was particularly keen because of the involvement of the Reagan administration and Congress in the controversy. In January 1982 the Justice Department announced that it would revoke the rules used to deny tax-exempt status to Bob Jones University and the Goldsboro Christian Schools and refund the disputed social security and unemployment taxes the institutions had paid. The Reagan administration also asked the Supreme Court to declare the pending appeal moot in light of the IRS policy revocation. Two weeks later, reacting to massive protest from civil rights leaders, President Reagan announced that he would seek legislation to ban tax exemptions for racially discriminatory schools.[115] He indicated that the IRS policy was revoked because the agency is not empowered to form and enforce social law, whereas Congress does have such authority and would be encouraged to use it. Subsequently, the Washington, D.C., Court of Appeals enjoined the Reagan administration from granting tax exemptions to any school that discriminates on the basis of race.[116] Shortly after this decision, the Justice Department also changed its position on the mootness of the appellate decisions and asked the Supreme Court to hear the consolidated appeal.

The Supreme Court was faced with complex issues regarding the hierarchy of public policy considerations and the status of free exercise rights relative to other rights. More troublesome issues are involved in interpreting the application of federal policy to religious institutions than to those that lack religious ties. Does denial of tax-exempt status to religious schools because the practice of their faith conflicts with other constitutional rights represent hostility toward religion or suggest that elimination of racial bias is more important than free exercise of religious beliefs? Or is it simply a reaffirmation of the dichotomy between freedom to believe, which is absolute, and freedom to act, which is subject to reasonable governmental restrictions?[117]

In May 1983 the Supreme Court affirmed the appellate court's ruling. Recognizing that "determinations of public benefit and public policy are sensitive matters with serious implications for the affected institutions,"[118] the eight-member majority concluded that the government's overriding, fundamental interest in eradicating racial discrimination outweighs any burden that the denial of tax-exempt status places on the petitioners' free exercise rights. The Court declared that it would be "wholly incompatible with the concepts underlying tax exemption to grant tax-exempt status to racially discriminatory private educational entities."[119]

Justice Powell, who wrote a separate concurring opinion, was troubled by the "element of conformity" in the majority's reasoning.[120] He questioned whether many organizations currently enjoying tax-exempt status could demonstrate that they are operating in harmony with the public interest. Powell asserted that the Court's justification for charitable exemptions (because the exempt entity provides a clear public benefit) "ignores the important role played by tax exemptions in encouraging diverse, indeed often sharply conflicting, activities and viewpoints."[121]

There is some concern that since tax-exempt status can be conditioned on compliance with public policy prohibiting racial discrimination, religious schools might be required to conform to other national policies, such as prohibitions against sex discrimination, even if such mandates interfere with the religious mission of the schools. Might student disciplinary procedures and personnel practices also be scrutinized as a condition of receiving tax-exempt status? Ralph Mawdsley and Stephen Permuth have questioned whether "public policy" has become "merely a synonym for constitutional rights, and, if so, has tax exemption then really become a form of state action for purposes of applying such rights to religious institutions?"[122]

Conclusion

Legal disputes over the application of state and federal regulations to religious schools are controversial and complex. Sectarian schools with no separate identity from the church have been treated differently from other private schools in the application of certain federal laws such as the National Labor Relations Act and the Federal Unemployment Tax Act. However, the extent to which such schools must conform to "established national policy" remains unclear. The Supreme Court recently held that the free exercise clause does not entitle racially discriminatory sectarian schools to tax-exempt status, but the Court did not clarify what types of "settled" or "fundamental" public policy could be used as a condition of receiving tax-exempt status. Also, there is ambiguity regarding the application of civil rights laws to religious schools that do not receive governmental benefits. Do free exercise rights prevail over protections against racial discrimination in making and enforcing contracts? What constitutes the necessary state action to make sectarian schools vulnerable to suits seeking redress for the impairment of federally protected rights?

Many questions also remain unanswered in connection with the state's regulatory authority over religious schools. Courts have not yet clarified whether governmental interests in monitoring the adequacy of private education should override parents' interests in directing the religious upbringing of their children. Some courts have questioned the need for prescriptive state regulations placing the burden on state agencies to prove that private schools or home education programs are not providing secular instruction that is equivalent to the public school program. The efforts to deregulate private — primarily sectarian — education are placing the state's *parens patriae* role to ensure an educated citizenry under increasing attack.

Footnotes

1. Pierce v. Society of Sisters, 268 U.S. 510 (1925).

2. *See* Chester Nolte, "Home Instruction in Lieu of Public School Attendance," in *School Law in Changing Times*, ed. M. A. McGhehey (Topeka, Kans.: National Organization on Legal Problems of Education, 1982), p. 6; E.A.L. Beshoner, "Home Education in America: Parental Rights Reasserted," University of *Missouri-Kansas City Law Review* 49 (Winter 1981):191.

3. *See* Margaret Rosenheim, *Justice for the Child* (New York: Free Press of Glencoe, 1962), pp. 22-23.

4. Prince v. Massachusetts, 321 U.S. 158 (1944).

5. *Id.* at 165.

6. *Id.* at 166.

7. Ford v. Ford, 371 U.S. 187, 193 (1962).

8. *See* Wisconsin v. Yoder, 406 U.S. 205, 233-34 (1972).

9. Lehman v. Lycoming County Children's Services Agency, 102 S. Ct. 3231, 3234 (1982).

10. Shoreline School Dist. v. Superior Court for King County, 346 P.2d 999, 1003 (Wash. 1959).

11. *See* Scoma v. Chicago Bd. of Educ., 391 F. Supp. 452 (N.D. Ill. 1974); Board of Educ. of Aberdeen-Huntington Local School Dist. v. State Bd. of Educ., 189 N.E.2d 81 (Ohio App. 1962).

12. Board of Educ. of Central School Dist. No. 1 v. Allen, 392 U.S. 236, 247 (1968).

13. In an early Massachusetts case the state high court set aside the lower court's conviction of parents for violating compulsory attendance mandates by enrolling their children in a private school that had not been approved by the local school committee. The court stated that compulsory attendance mandates are designed to assure that all children are educated, "not that they shall be educated in any particular way." Commonwealth v. Roberts, 34 N.E. 402, 403 (Mass. 1893).

14. Meyer v. Nebraska, 262 U.S. 390 (1923). *See* text with note 18, chapter 4.

15. Pierce v. Society of Sisters, 268 U.S. 510, 535 (1925).

16. Farrington v. Tokushige, 273 U.S. 284 (1927).

17. *Id.* at 298.

18. *Id.* at 288.

19. *See* Stanley v. Illinois, 405 U.S. 645 (1972); Prince v. Massachusetts, 321 U.S. 158, 166 (1944). For a discussion of this topic, *see* "Developments in the Law—The Constitution and the Family," *Harvard Law Review* 93 (1980):1236-39, 1350-57.

20. Wisconsin v. Yoder, 406 U.S. 205, 233 (1972).

21. *Id.* at 214.

22. *Education Daily*, 14 July 1982, p. 1.

23. *Ibid.* The percentages of private school students enrolled in religiously affiliated schools ranged from 98% in Iowa to 40% in Mississippi.

24. *See* Joseph Blankenbeker, "An Analysis of Equivalent Instruction Statutes, Regulations and Court Decisions in the United States," (Ed.D. diss., Indiana University, 1977).

25. *See* text with notes 47 and 51.

26. *See* Cynthia West, "The State and Sectarian Education: Regulation to Deregulation," *Duke Law Journal*, no. 4 (1980):801-46. In a recent case, Attorney General v. Bailey, 436 N.E.2d 139 (Mass. 1982), *cert. denied sub nom.* Bailey v. Bellotti, 103 S. Ct. 301 (1982), the Massachusetts high court upheld a statute requiring private schools to provide names, ages, and addresses of their students. The court reasoned that the collection of these data to facilitate enforcement of the compulsory school attendance law does not violate the free exercise or establishment clauses.

27. State v. Whisner, 351 N.E.2d 750 (Ohio 1976).

28. *Id.* at 764. The lower court had upheld the state standards applied to public and private schools, reasoning that without such standards nonpublic school students would be deprived of their right to equal educational opportunities. For a discussion of the lower court's ruling, *see* 351 N.E.2d at 758.

29. *Id.* at 768. The court also recognized that a valid free exercise claim does not have to be based on beliefs of well-established religious sects. The court observed that to protect only beliefs of traditional sects would defeat the purpose of the free exercise clause, which is to safeguard religious minorities.

30. State *ex rel.* Nagle v. Olin, 415 N.E.2d 279, 287 (Ohio 1980).

31. *Id.* at 288. In 1981 the New Jersey federal district court enjoined the state board of higher education from applying its licensing regulations to a religious college. The injunction prohibited enforcement of a state court order that barred the college from awarding degrees and required notice on application materials to this effect. The court applied the *Yoder* balancing test and concluded that the state licensing requirement clearly interfered with the purpose of the fundamentalist religious college, which was to inculcate religious values and beliefs and train clergy and lay religious leaders. New Jersey-Philadelphia Presbytery v. New Jersey State Bd. of Higher Educ., 514 F. Supp. 506 (D.N.J. 1981). However, the following year the New Jersey Supreme Court found no First Amendment violation in connection with the application of statutes prohibiting unlicensed institutions from conferring baccalaureate degrees. The court reasoned that the state's substantial interest in regulating the bachelor's degree prevailed over the interests of a sectarian college whose religious doctrine precluded state licensure. New Jersey State Bd. of Higher Educ. v. Shelton College, 448 A.2d 988 (N.J. 1982). *See also* State *ex rel.* McLemore v. Clarksville School of Theology, 636 S.W.2d 706 (Tenn. 1982).

32. Richard Daley, "Public Regulation of Private Religious Schools," *Ohio State Law Journal* 37 (Fall 1976):923.

33. Kentucky State Bd. for Elementary and Secondary Educ. v. Rudasill, 589 S.W.2d 877 (Ky. 1979), *cert denied.* 446 U.S. 938 (1980).

34. *See* West, "The State and Sectarian Education," p. 825. A Michigan circuit court judge recently espoused somewhat similar reasoning in holding that private religious schools do not have to conform to state programmatic standards and teacher certification requirements. Noting that the private schools' students achieve well on standardized tests, the judge concluded that the state regulations do not ensure a minimum degree of educational quality. He further declared that certification requirements may even be harmful because they emphasize pedagogy at the expense of teacher competence in content areas, Sheridan Road Baptist Church v. State of Michigan, No. 80-26205AZ (Ingham County Cir. Ct. 1982).

35. 589 S.W.2d at 884. As a result of pressure to deregulate private schools, some state legislatures have replaced restrictive programmatic specifications with pupil examination requirements. For example, South Dakota and North Carolina have enacted legislation to this effect.

36. North Dakota v. Shaver, 294 N.W.2d 883 (N.D. 1980). In 1982 the North Dakota Supreme Court reiterated that religious academies can be required to satisfy teacher certification and state curriculum regulations, State v. Rivinius, 328 N.W.2d 220 (N.D. 1982). *See also* State v. Andrews, 651 P.2d 473 (Hawaii 1982), in which the Hawaii Supreme Court found that a statute requiring private schools to be licensed by the state did not impair First Amendment religious freedoms.

37. Nebraska v. Faith Baptist Church, 301 N.W.2d 571, 579 (Neb. 1981) *appeal dismissed sub nom.* Faith Baptist Church v. Douglas, 454 U.S. 803 (1981).

38. Prettyman v. State of Nebraska, 537 F. Supp. 712 (D. Neb. 1982).

39. *Id.* at 715.

40. State v. Columbus Christian Academy, No. 78 CVS 1678 (N.C. Super., Wake County 1978), *vacated as moot and dismissed* (N.C. 1979).

41. N.C. Gen. State. § 115-257.6 to .13, § 115-257.19 to .26 (Supp. 1979). *See* text with note 74.

42. West, "The State and Sectarian Education," p. 834.

43. "Private Schools Held Free of N.C. Standards," *Durham Morning Herald*, 5 October 1979, p. A-1.

44. Windsor Park Baptist Church v. Arkansas Activities Association, 658 F.2d 618 (8th Cir. 1981). Interscholastic athletics also generated First Amendment litigation in Delaware. The federal district court concluded that an unincorporated voluntary association of public high schools did not impair free exercise rights of parochial schools, which were excluded from the conference. Falencia v. Blue Hen Conference, 476 F. Supp. 809 (D. Del. 1979).

45. Windsor Park, *id.* at 620.

46. *Id.* at 621. Two years earlier, the First Circuit Court of Appeals struck down a different type of state regulatory activity, concluding that the Puerto Rico Department of Consumer Affairs violated both the free exercise and establishment clauses by investigating the costs of Catholic education. The court noted that the state regulatory

163

process would entail some determination of "necessary" and "reasonable" costs in running a private school that might entail value judgments at odds with the religious leaders of the school. The court also reasoned that the continuing governmental surveillance required to make such investigations would lead to unconstitutional entanglement with religion. Finding a burden on the free exercise of beliefs and a threat of entanglement between religious and governmental affairs, the court held that the state must justify its action by evidence of a compelling interest to be served. Concluding that mere concern over the inflationary spiral in the costs of private education was not sufficiently compelling, the court held that the department failed to show that it had pursued its secular objectives in the manner least intrusive of First Amendment freedoms. Surinach v. Pesquera de Busquets, 604 F.2d 73 (1st Cir. 1979).

47. In 1978 the Supreme Court dismissed an appeal of a decision in which a Texas civil appeals court upheld the state's authority to require religious child-care programs to meet minimum health and safety standards. The court rejected the assertion that such regulations interfered with the mission of evangelistic institutions. Roloff Evangelistic Enterprises v. State, 556 S.W.2d 856 (Tex. Civ. App. 1977), *appeal dismissed*, 439 U.S. 803 (1978).

48. City of Sumner v. First Baptist Church of Sumner, Washington, 639 P.2d 1358 (Wash. 1982).

49. *Id.* at 1361.

50. The court further held that on remand the trial court needs to review additional evidence regarding whether the church school qualifies for the "grandfather" exemption under the ordinance. The church was operating prior to enactment of the ordinance, but the record is incomplete as to whether the church's educational activities were sufficient at that time to conclude that the school (which was established after the ordinance was in effect) was merely a continuation of activities that would entitle the school to the grandfather exemption.

51. Faith Baptist Church of Boca Raton, Inc. v. City of Boca Raton, Florida, 402 So. 2d 1381 (Fla. App. 1981), *cert. denied*, 102 S. Ct. 1010 (1982).

52. *See Nolpe Notes* 17 (May 1982):7; West, "The State and Sectarian Education," pp. 801-3.

53. West, *ibid.*, p. 841.

54. *Ibid.*, p. 842.

55. *Ibid.*, p. 845.

56. The survey was conducted by the New Hampshire State Department of Education. *See Education U.S.A.* 22 (11 August 1980):366.

57. Nolte, "Home Instruction in Lieu of Public School Attendance," pp. 2-3.

58. John Holt, cited in *Education Daily*, 13 April 1981, p. 3. Estimates are usually based on reports from public school personnel regarding the number of students known to be instructed at home.

59. In re Monning, 638 S.W.2d 782, 788 (Mo. App. 1982); State v. Davis, 598 S.W.2d 189 (Mo. App. 1980). In an earlier case the Vermont Supreme court dismissed criminal proceedings against parents for violating compulsory attendance mandates because the state education department had made no determination of the "equivalency" of the instructional program the students were receiving at home. State v. LaBarge, 357 A.2d 121 (Vt. 1976).

60. State v. Moorhead, 308 N.W.2d 60 (Iowa 1981).

61. Hanson v. Cushman, 490 F. Supp. 109, 115 (W.D. Mich. 1980).

62. Jernigan v. State, 412 So. 2d 1242, 1246 (Ala. Crim. App. 1982).

63. State v. M. M. and S.E., 407 So. 2d 987 (Fla. App. 1981). In December 1982 the Virginia Supreme Court reached a similar conclusion in Grigg v. Commonwealth, 297 S.E.2d 799 (Va. 1982).

64. Commonwealth v. Renfrew, 126 N.E.2d 109 (Mass. 1955).

65. *See* Shoreline School Dist. v. Superior Court for King County, 346 P.2d 999 (Wash. 1960); Rice v. Commonwealth, 49 S.E.2d 342 (Va. 1948). *See also* Hill v. State, 410 So. 2d 431 (Ala. Crim. App. 1981).

66. State v. Riddle, 285 S.E.2d 359 (W. Va. 1981). *See also* Jernigan v. State, 412 So. 2d 1242 (Ala. Crim. App. 1982); State v. Bowman, 653 P.2d 254 (Ore. App. 1982).

67. *Id.* 285 S.E.2d at 361, discussing Wisconsin v. Yoder, 406 U.S. 205 (1972).

68. *Id.* at 362.

69. *Id.* at 364.

70. *Id.* at 366.

71. *Id.* at 364, citing Pauley v. Kelly, 255 S.E.2d 859, 877 (W. Va. 1979).

72. Stephens v. Bongart, 189 A. 131, 137 (N.J. Juvenile & Domes. Rela. Ct. 1937).

73. Perchemlides v. Frizzle, No. 16441 (Mass. Super., Hampshire County, 1978).

74. Duro v. District Attorney, No. 81-13-CIV-2 (E.D.N.C. 1982). This decision has been appealed to the Fourth Circuit Court of Appeals, and, if upheld, could have significant implications for the vitality of compulsory school attendance laws. For a discussion of the deregulation of private education in North Carolina, *see* text with note 41.

75. If other courts should adopt the reasoning of Missouri appellate courts and place the burden on the state to substantiate that specific home instructional programs are not equivalent to public school offerings, it may become increasingly difficult for state authorities successfully to challenge such programs. *See* In re Monning, 638 S.W.2d 782 (Mo. App. 1982); State v. Davis, 598 S.W.2d 189 (Mo. App. 1980); text with note 59.

76. Supreme Court Justice Douglas has argued that such an assumption should not be made. *See* Wisconsin v. Yoder, 406 U.S. 205, 245 (1972) (Douglas, J., dissenting). *See also* Ralph Mawdsley and Steven Permuth, "Home Instruction for Religious Reasons: Parental Right or State Option?" *West's Education Law Reporter* 4 (1982):948-49.

77. National Labor Relations Board v. Catholic Bishop of Chicago, 559 F.2d 1112 (7th Cir. 1977), *aff'd* 440 U.S. 490 (1979).

78. 559 F.2d at 1118 (7th Cir. 1977).

79. 440 U.S. at 503 (1979).

80. *Id.* at 506.

81. St. Martins Evangelical Lutheran Church v. South Dakota, 290 N.W.2d 845 (S.D. 1980), *rev'd and remanded*, 451 U.S. 772 (1981). There also has been considerable legal activity pertaining to social security tax exemptions for the Amish. While self-employed Amish and members of other religious groups, whose teachings oppose the social security system, are exempt from such taxes, 26 U.S.C. § 1402(g), in 1982 the Supreme Court ruled that this exemption does not apply to employers and employees. Noting the difficulty in distinguishing between the social security program and general tax programs, the court held that the overriding governmental interest in maintaining a sound tax system justified the limitation on free exercise rights of Amish employers and employees. The Court acknowledged that the payment of social security taxes and the receipt of benefits conflicts with Amish beliefs, but it concluded that the requested exemptions would "unduly interfere" with implementing the governmental tax program. United States v. Lee, 102 S. Ct. 1051 (1982).

82. Unemployment Insurance Letter No. 39-78 (30 May 1978), reprinted in *Unemp. Ins. Rep.* (CCH) § 21,522.

83. 451 U.S. at 788.

84. *Id.* at 777.

85. Alabama v. Marshall, 626 F.2d 366 (5th Cir. 1980); Luthern Church — Missouri Synod v. Bowling, 411 N.E.2d 526 (Ill. App. 1980).

86. Alabama v. Marshall, *Id.* at 369.

87. California v. Grace Brethren Church, No. CV 79-93 MRP, *reprinted* in J.S. App. 49, *vacated and remanded*, 102 S.Ct. 2498 (1982).

88. *Education Daily*, 4 September 1981, p. 2.

89. *Ibid.*, p. 1.

90. 102 S.Ct. at 2503. *See* Tax Injunction Act, 28 U.S.C. § 1341.

91. *Id.* at 2514-15 (Stevens, J., dissenting).

92. 42 U.S.C. 1981.

93. Runyon v. McCrary, 427 U.S. 160 (1976).

94. Brown v. Dade Christian Schools, Inc., 556 F.2d 310 (5th Cir. 1977).

95. *Id.* at 314.

96. Fiedler v. Marumsco Christian School, 631 F.2d 1144 (4th Cir. 1980).

97. 42 U.S.C. § 1983.

98. Monell v. Department of Social Services of the City of New York, 436 U.S. 658 (1978). *See also* Owen v. City of Independence, Missouri, 445 U.S. 622 (1980).

99. *See* Doe v. Renfrow, 631 F.2d 91 (7th Cir. 1980); Stoddard v. School Dist. No. 1, 590 F.2d 829 (10th Cir. 1979); Bertot v. School Dist. No. 1, Albany County, Wyoming, 613 F.2d 245 (10th Cir. 1979).

100. Rendell — Baker v. Kohn, 102 S. Ct. 2764 (1982).

101. *Id.* at 2772.

102. *Id.*

103. Bright v. Isenbarger, 314 F. Supp. 1382 (N.D. Ind. 1970), *aff'd per curiam*, 445 F.2d 412 (7th Cir. 1971).

104. Morgan v. St. Francis Preparatory School, 326 F. Supp. 1152 (M.D. Pa. 1971).

105. Huff v. Notre Dame High School of West Haven, 456 F. Supp. 1145 (D. Conn. 1978). However, in 1982 the Tenth Circuit Court of Appeals ruled that students could bring a Section 1983 suit against a private residential school, alleging that the school's practices violated their constitutional rights. The court reasoned that the school is operating under color of state law because it is partially state funded and some of the students have been placed in the school by state officials who were aware of its controversial behavior modification practices. Milonas v. Williams, 691 F.2d 931 (10th Cir. 1982), *cert. denied*, 51 U.S.L.W. 3720 (1983).

106. *See* Lugar v. Edmonson Oil Co., 102 S. Ct. 2744, 2754 (1982).

107. *See* Brown v. Strickler, 422 F.2d 1000 (6th Cir. 1970).

108. Bob Jones University v. United States, Goldsboro Christian Schools v. United States, 51 U.S.L.W. 4593 (May 24, 1983).

109. Green v. Kennedy, 309 F. Supp. 1127 (D.D.C. 1970).

110. Green v. Connally, 330 F. Supp. 1150 (D.D.C. 1971), *aff'd sub nom.* Coit v. Green, 404 U.S. 997 (1971).

111. 468 F. Supp. 890, 897 (D.S.C. 1978).

112. 639 F.2d 147, 151, 153 (4th Cir. 1980).

113. *Id.* at 154.

114. Goldsboro Christian Schools v. United States, 436 F. Supp. 1314 (E.D. N.C. 1977), *aff'd* 644 F.2d 879 (4th Cir. 1980).

115. The proposed legislation was criticized by several constitutional scholars and former Justice Department officials who asserted that such a measure was unnecessary because IRS already had authority to deny tax exemptions based on existing civil rights laws. *See* "Editorial on Administration's Tax-Exemption Actions," *The Chronicle of Higher Education*, 20 January 1982, p. 17; "Reagan's Bill on Tax Exemptions Wins Few Capitol Hill Adherents," *The Chronicle of Higher Education*, 10 February 1982, p. 11.

116. Wright v. Reagan, cited in *Education Daily*, 22 February 1982, p. 1.

117. *See* Cantwell v. Connecticut, 310 U.S. 296, 303 (1940); Reynolds v. United States, 98 U.S. 145, 164 (1878).

118. 51 U.S.L.W. 4593, 4598 (May 24, 1983).

119. *Id.* at 4599.

120. *Id.* at 4603 (Powell, J., concurring).

121. *Id.*

122. Ralph Mawdsley and Stephen Permuth, "Bob Jones University v. United States: Public Policy and Religious Educational Institutions," *West's Education Law Reporter* 1 (1982):748.

Chapter Eight

Some Concluding Observations

" "E"ver since the institutions of religion and of secular power were recognized as separate and distinct in human history, the two forces have competed for and struggled over human destiny."[1] The dual religious freedoms included in the First Amendment embody a uniquely American experiment to achieve religious liberty, but these provisions were not the invention solely of the amendment's drafters. They were the product of centuries of church-state conflict and efforts by minority sects to secure individual freedom of conscience. Colonists who fled to America were painfully aware that "cruel persecutions" had been "the inevitable result of government established religions."[2] Justice Brennan stated in 1963 that the two religion clauses of the First Amendment, "although distinct in their objectives and applicability, emerged together from a common panorama of history. The inclusion of both restraints . . . shows unmistakably that the Framers of the First Amendment were not content to rest the protection of religious liberty exclusively upon either clause."[3]

However, history supports that advocates of religious freedom often have changed their views when their sect has become the dominant religion. Early Christians pleaded for religious liberty but then persecuted heretics when Christianity became the state-established faith. John Robinson, a Pilgrim pastor, summarized the prevalent sentiment at the time of the founding of America: "Protestants living in the country of papists commonly plead for toleration of religions; so do papists that live where Protestants bear sway; though few of either, especially of the clergy . . . would have the other tolerated, where the world goes on their side."[4] More recently, Justice Prescott of the Maryland high court observed that the "desire to persuade, and failing in persuasion, to compel" others to adopt one's religious views is still evident in America.[5]

Fortunately, the church-state controversies in the United States have been mild when compared with those in many other countries. Religious wars have not been fought on American soil, and U.S. citizens have not been victims of the type of religious intolerance and persecution that has characterized nations where church and state are inseparable.[6] But our country has not totally escaped sectarian conflict or efforts to merge religious and political passions. The competing fears of state domination of religion and state extermination of religion have generated intense controversies and a growing body of litigation.

Precise interpretation of the First Amendment's religious protections has evaded the judiciary for two centuries. The Supreme Court has noted that "the language of the Religion Clauses of the First Amendment is at best opaque, particularly when compared with other portions of the Amendment."[7] Legal doctrines have evolved, but they are only starting points. Justices must apply the doctrines, weighing a variety of factors in the process. And no "test has been developed that will automatically weigh all the variables involved in sensitive First Amendment controversies."[8]

Substantial support exists for the notion that the religion clauses mandate a separation of church and state and that such a separation serves the best interests of sectarian as well as civil institutions. The Supreme Court has recognized that "the First Amendment rests upon the premise that both religion and government can best work to achieve their lofty aims if each is left free from the other within its respective sphere."[9] The Court also has noted that the "first and most immediate purpose" of the establishment clause rests "on the belief that a union of government and religion tends to destroy government and to degrade religion."[10]

The increasing secularization of governmental activities, including education, since colonial days does not suggest that the level of individual religious commitment among citizens in this nation has declined. De Tocqueville's nineteenth-century observation that the religious atmosphere of this country immediately strikes foreign travellers[11] probably remains true today. A recent Gallup Poll found the United State to be more religious than any other industrialized country in the world.[12] Also, a 1981 study conducted by the Connecticut Mutual Life Insurance Company indicated that the level of religious commitment among Americans "is a stronger determinant of our values than whether we are rich or poor, young or old, male or female, black or white, liberal or conservative."[13] Many have argued that religion has thrived in this country *because of* efforts to keep governmental and sectarian affairs discrete.

Religious leaders have been among some of the strongest advocates of a separation of church and state, asserting that evangelism cannot thrive in an environment of social conformity. A 1982 statement issued by six religious organizations, including the National Council of Churches and the American Jewish Congress, denounced governmental sponsorship of religion as a threat to religious liberty.[14]

From a practical standpoint, with over 250 different recognized religious sects in this nation, it seems imperative for sectarian institutions to maintain autonomy. John Dewey once observed that adherence to a separation of church and state does not infer hostility toward religion but rather respect for the diverse denominations represented in this country.[15] Leo Pfeffer also has asserted that religion has achieved "a high estate" in this nation, "unequalled anywhere else in the world," proving that "complete separation of church and state is best for the church and the state, and secures freedom for both."[16]

There is considerable sentiment that the wall of separation should be most preciously guarded in the educational domain because "the evils of inter-religious disharmony and oppression" are particularly manifest in connection with impairments of religious liberties in school settings.[17] In 1947 Supreme Court Justice Rutledge stated:

> Two great drives are constantly in motion to abridge, in the name of education, the complete division of religion and civil authority which our forefathers made. One is to introduce religious education and observances into the public schools. The other, to obtain public funds for the aid and support of various private religious schools. In my opinion both avenues were closed by the Constitution. Neither should be opened by this Court. . . . Now as in Madison's day it is one of principle, to keep separate the separate spheres as the First Amendment drew them; to prevent the first experiment upon our liberties; and to keep the question from becoming entangled in corrosive precedents. We should not be less strict to keep strong and untarnished the one side of the shield of religious freedom than we have been of the other.[18] [citations omitted]

However, this wall of separation, which the Supreme Court referred to as "high and impregnable" in 1947,[19] was called "a blurred, indistinct, and variable barrier" by the Court in 1977.[20] Supreme Court opinions over the past decade have provided more questions than answers in the church-state domain. Recent decisions have been characterized by dissension among the justices, with six or seven separate opinions becoming increasingly common. Instead of issuing strong guidance, the Supreme Court often has declined to review lower court decisions in this arena. Moreover, the Court has made it more difficult for plaintiffs to establish standing to sue in certain types of church-state controversies.[21] And the opinions the Supreme Court has rendered often have been difficult to reconcile with each other and with federal appellate court decisions. Philip Kurland has noted that there is "little quarrel, today, about the goals to be achieved by the religion clauses of the First Amendment," but "the problem that has bemused and confused" the Supreme Court has been "stating appropriate legal principles to serve as means to agreed-upon ends."[22]

Since schools are viewed as a primary vehicle to influence our nation's youth, it is understandable that educational issues have generated some of the most significant legal controversies over the relationship between sectarian and governmental affairs. Guiding constitutional principles seem particularly elusive in these church-state cases involving schools. The "conceptual chaos"[23] in establishment clause cases is illustrated by a comparison of some of the school activities that have been judicially permitted and prohibited under this clause. For example, public school schedules can be altered so that students can receive sectarian instruction in mobile units parked next to public school property during the regular instructional day,[24] but students cannot hold prayer meetings on public school premises before school starts.[25] One might argue that the former practice requires greater involvement of school officials in sectarian affairs and has a more significant impact on nonparticipating students than does the latter. Also, it seems inconsistent for the judiciary to condone prayers in public school graduation ceremonies because of their "fleeting" nature, but to disallow a brief prayer in a periodic school assembly.[26] Similarly, the decisions upholding the provision of federally funded auxiliary services for nonpublic school students on parochial school premises[27] are difficult to reconcile with decisions specifying that state-funded remedial and therapeutic services can be provided for parochial school students *only* at religiously neutral sites.[28]

Recent Supreme Court action cannot be easily classified into "separation" or "accommodation" categories. To illustrate, the Court has declined to review two cases in which state supreme courts reached somewhat different conclusions regarding the state's authority to regulate nonpublic school programs.[29] Also, the Court has struck down state income tax credits for tuition paid to private schools, but recently condoned state income tax deductions for private and public school expenses.[30] State aid for standardized testing programs in nonpublic schools has been upheld, but the loan of instructional equipment to such schools has not been allowed.[31] In 1980 the divided Supreme Court struck down the posting of the Ten Commandments in public school classrooms[32] but refused to address an appeal of a decision allowing religious holiday observances in public education.[33] The following year, the Court upheld the right of student religious clubs to hold devotional meetings on college campuses[34] but chose not to review a federal appellate court's decision disallowing such devotional meetings in a public secondary school.[35]

Lower court decisions have also reflected a range in interpretations of religious liberties, and the legality of various school activities fluctuates from one jurisdiction to the next. Considerable diversity exists among public school districts concerning practices such as the distribution of religious literature and the observance of religious holidays. Also, states vary greatly in their posture toward permissible public aid to sectarian schools and the state's role in monitoring such schools. One commentator has observed that the "acceleration in the number of court decisions, with the attendant lack of conceptual clarity in the resolution of issues presented, suggests that, in the area of constitutional adjudication, 'the machine is working in a way the framers of it did not intend'."[36]

Church-state issues involving schools are complex, defying simplistic resolution. They illustrate the tension between the free exercise and establishment clauses and raise sensitive questions regarding the scope of parental rights and governmental authority. Under what circumstances does the state's interest in assuring an educated citizenry override parental interests in directing the education of their children? Parents have a protected right to select private education as an alternative to public schooling, but does the free exercise clause exempt sectarian schools from governmental regulations designed to protect the welfare of the child and the state? Also, questions remain regarding how far public schools *must* go in excusing students from activities and requirements for religious reasons in order to respect free exercise rights, and how far they *can* go in making such religious accommodations without advancing sectarian concerns in violation of the establishment clause. Moreover, ambiguity surrounds the scope of parental rights to serve as religious censors, not only for their own children, but for *all* students. While the judiciary has upheld the authority of school boards to determine the curriculum over parents' religious objections, increasingly school boards are placing their stamp of approval on parental demands. How much latitude does the board have to restrict the curriculum in conformance with the dominant religious faith of the community before it runs afoul of the establishment clause?

In 1968 the Supreme Court made the following statement regarding the First Amendment's mandate of governmental neutrality toward religion:

> Government in our democracy, state and national, must be neutral in matters of religious theory, doctrine and practice. It may not be hostile to any religion or to the advocacy of nonreligion; and it may not aid, foster, or promote one religion or religious theory against another or even against the militant opposite. The First Amendment mandates governmental neutrality between religion and religion, and between religion and nonreligion.[37]

This eloquent statement, however, sheds little light on what specific practices impermissibly advance sectarian beliefs or exhibit hostility toward them. What constitutes proper state deference to free exercise rights and at the same time guards against governmental imposition of religion?

Perhaps the most troublesome questions facing the judiciary pertain to a determination of what constitutes a sincere religious belief and practice. Courts are being pressed to broaden the application of the First Amendment religion clauses to nontraditional faiths. Allegations that public schools are advancing the religion of secular humanism in violation of the establishment clause have particular implications for the future of public education. As discussed in chapter 4, almost all aspects of academic instruction have become vulnerable to the charge that an antitheistic belief is being established in public schools.[38]

Of course, if public schools are found to be unconstitutionally advancing a secular religion, it would be an inappropriate remedy to return theistic instruction and materials to the classroom, which would in effect substitute one constitutional violation for another. Judicial guidance is needed to clarify what practices advance an atheistic or secular religion, and such practices *should be disallowed* in public schools. But, neutral, nonreligious approaches to academic subjects should not be confused with antitheism, and the former should *not* be vulnerable to First Amendment challenge.

Some contend that if the fundamentalist attack on secular instruction should receive judicial endorsement, it will signal the demise of public education.[39] Conceivably, public schools would be replaced by state subsidies for private schools to enable parents to select the curricular orientation that conforms with their religious values. While this option might accommodate free exercise rights, it would be extremely difficult to reconcile such public assistance to religious institutions under establishment clause prohibitions. Nonetheless, the Supreme Court's recent endorsement of state tax deductions for educational expenses might be viewed as a step in this direction.

It is unfortunate that debates on church-state issues often have been characterized by irrationality and "a tendency to estrange rather than to reconcile the groups that compose American communities."[40] In 1962 a committee of the United Presbyterian Church reported:

> The branding of opponents of religious observance on public property as communists, the waging of telephone campaigns that invent and perpetrate slander, the evoking of racial and social fears, and the facile equation of 'Americanism' with 'Christianity' are the irrational accompaniments of much discussion of an issue whose solution demands unusual sobriety.[41]

Those who advocate removing sectarian influences from public schools are not necessarily atheists. Indeed, many of the well-established churches in this nation support the notion that prayer and other devotional activities do not belong in public education.[42] But the elimination of traditional religious—primarily Protestant—observances and instruction does not mean that the only alternative is for antitheism to take their place. Professor Martin Marty at the University of Chicago, a well-known commentator on the subject of religion and culture, has criticized the bifurcation between theists and humanists, asserting that society can benefit from "Christian humanism."[43] He has stated that "there is a danger that the religious right, in aiming its weapons at secular humanism, may also wound endeavors which it might embrace in the common struggle for the life, dignity, and freedom of all . . . persons."[44]

Nonetheless, groups contending that governmental sponsorship of the Christian faith is necessary to counteract the "atheist plot to stamp out religion"[45] are gaining increasing political influence. The new Christian Right has become a powerful political force in determining local, state, and even national elections. A 1981 study revealed a growing involvement of religion in politics, with candidates being pressed to take clear positions on moral and religious issues.[46] Without judicial intervention to protect constitutional guarantees, we may soon find that the rights of religious minorities are becoming contingent on the outcomes of elections.

In 1980 Justice White noted that the lack of unanimity on the Supreme Court on church-state issues might reflect the lack of societal consensus in this arena.[47] But public sentiments on these questions have always been mixed. There were loud objections when the Supreme Court barred Bible reading from public schools two decades ago, but such objections did not prevent the Court from protecting individual rights by enforcing First Amendment guarantees. In striking down state-sanctioned devotional activities in public education, the Court emphasized that the First Amendment prohibits "state action to deny rights of free exercise to *anyone*; it has never meant that a majority could use the machinery of the State to practice its belief."[48]

Public opinion should be irrelevant in judicial protection of individual liberties; the Bill of Rights was intended to "withdraw certain subjects from the vicissitudes of political controversy."[49] Yet, the judiciary recently has not provided clear guidance regarding the protections guaranteed by the religion clauses of the First Amendment. In the absence of guiding judicial precedent, activity has escalated to secure legislation codifying the religious values of the dominant faith.[50]

If the Supreme Court does not steadfastly safeguard religious liberties against governmental encroachment, other constitutional freedoms will likely be affected. Any infringement of our constitutional rights, "however well intended, takes something away from that aspect of our freedom that may never be recovered."[51] In 1971, Supreme Court Chief Justice Burger cautioned:

> A certain momentum develops in constitutional theory and it can be a "downhill thrust" easily set in motion but difficult to retard or stop. . . . The dangers are increased by the difficulty of perceiving in advance exactly where the "verge" of the precipice lies. As well as constituting an independent evil against which the Religion Clauses were intended to protect, involvement or entanglement between government and religion serves as a warning signal.[52]

Recent developments suggest that the warning has been sounded. The breach of neutrality which has been "a trickling stream" may indeed "become a raging torrent."[53] The judiciary—ultimately the U.S. Supreme Court—has an awesome charge to ensure that our constitutional liberties and the vitality of sectarian and educational institutions are not jeopardized.

Footnotes

1. Leo Pfeffer, *Religious Freedom* (Skokie, Ill.: National Textbook Co., 1977) p. 171.

2. Everson v. Board of Educ., 330 U.S. 1, 12 (1947).

3. School Dist. of Abington Township v. Schempp, 374 U.S. 203, 232 (1963) (Brennan, J., concurring).

4. M. Searle Bates, *Religious Liberty: An Inquiry* (New York: International Missionary Council, 1945), p. 155, quoting *Works of John Robinson I*, p. 40.

5. Horace Mann League of United States v. Board of Public Works, 220 A.2d 51, 59 (Md. 1966).

6. Philip Kurland, "Of Church and State and the Supreme Court," *University of Chicago Law Review* 29 (1961):96.

7. Lemon v. Kurtzman, 403 U.S. 602, 612 (1971).

8. James Burns, J. W. Peltason, and Thomas Cronin, *Government by the People*, 9th ed. (Englewood Cliffs, N.J.: Prentice Hall, 1975), p. 141.

9. McCollum v. Board of Educ., 333 U.S. 203, 212 (1948).

10. Engel v. Vitale, 370 U.S. 421, 431 (1962).

11. Alexis de Tocqueville, *Democracy in America*, vol. I (New York: Alfred A. Knopf, 1945), p. 308.

12. The 1976 international Gallup Poll conducted by the Charles Kettering Foundation indicated that 56% of adult Americans compared with 27% of adult western Europeans considered religion to be very important. *See* "The Impact of Belief," *American Association for Higher Education* (AAHE) *Bulletin* 34 (February 1982):3.

13. "The Impact of Belief," *ibid.*

14. *See Louisville Courier Journal*, 7 May 1982, p. A-2.

15. John Dewey, *Intelligence in the Modern World*, ed. J. Ratner (New York: Modern Library, 1939), p. 706.

16. Pfeffer, *Religious Freedom*, p. 172.

17. *Ibid.*

18. Everson v. Board of Educ., 330 U.S. 1, 63 (Rutledge, J., dissenting).

19. Everson, *id.* at 18.

20. Wolman v. Walter, 433 U.S. 229, 236 (1977).

21. *See* Valley Forge Christian College v. Americans United for Separation of Church and State, 102 S. Ct. 752 (1982); text with note 52, chapter 1.

22. Kurland, "Of Church and State and the Supreme Court," p. 96.

23. Jesse Choper, "The Religion Clauses of the First Amendment: Reconciling the Conflict," *University of Pittsburgh Law Review* 41 (1980):681.

24. *See* Smith v. Smith, 523 F.2d 121 (4th Cir. 1975), *cert. denied*, 423 U.S. 1073 (1976); Zorach v. Clauson, 343 U.S. 306 (1952).

25. *See* Brandon v. Board of Educ. of Guilderland Central School Dist., 635 F.2d 971 (2d Cir. 1980), *cert. denied*, 102 S. Ct. 970 (1981).

26. *Compare* Weist v. Mt. Lebanon School Dist., 320 A.2d 362 (Pa. 1974), *cert. denied*, 419 U.S. 967 (1974) *with* Collins v. Chandler Unified School Dist., 644 F.2d 759 (9th Cir. 1981), *cert. denied*, 102 S. Ct. 322 (1981).

27. National Coalition for Public Educ. and Religious Liberty v. Harris, 489 F. Supp. 1248 (S.D.N.Y. 1980) *appeal dismissed sub nom.* National Coalition for Public Educ. and Religious Liberty v. Hufstedler, 449 U.S. 808 (1980).

28. *See* Wolman v. Walter, 433 U.S. 229 (1977).

29. *Compare* Nebraska v. Faith Baptist Church, 301 N.W.2d 571 (Neb. 1981), *appeal dismissed sub nom.* Faith Baptist Church v. Douglas, 102 S. Ct. 75 (1981) *with* Kentucky State Bd. for Elementary and Secondary Educ. v. Rudasill, 589 S.W.2d 877 (Ky. 1979), *cert. denied*, 446 U.S. 938 (1980).

30. *Compare* Mueller v. Allen, 51 U.S.L.W. 5050 (June 29, 1983) *with* Committee for Public Educ. and Religious Liberty v. Nyquist, 413 U.S. 756 (1973).

31. *See* Committee for Public Educ. and Religious Liberty v. Regan, 446 U.S. 646 (1980); Wolman v. Walter, 433 U.S. 229 (1977).

32. Stone v. Graham, 599 S.W.2d 157 (Ky. 1980), *rev'd* 449 U.S. 39 (1980).

33. Florey v. Sioux Falls School Dist. 49-5, 619 F.2d 1311 (8th Cir. 1980), *cert. denied*, 449 U.S. 987 (1980).

34. Widmar v. Vincent, 102 S. Ct. 269 (1981).

35. Brandon v. Board of Educ. of Guilderland Central School Dist., 635 F.2d 971 (2d Cir. 1980), *cert. denied*, 102 S. Ct. 970 (1981).

36. Sidney Buchanan, "Governmental Aid to Sectarian Schools: A Study in Corrosive Precedents," *Houston Law Review* 15 (1978):789, citing Eakin v. Raub, 12 Serg. & Rawl. 330 (Pa. 1825) (Gibson, J., dissenting).

37. Epperson v. Arkansas, 393 U.S. 97, 103 (1968).

38. *See* text with note 95, chapter 4.

39. *See* Paul Freund, "Public Aid to Parochial Schools," *Harvard Law Review* 82 (1969):1685.

40. "Relations Between Church and State," A Report to the 174th General Assembly of the United Presbyterian Church in the United States, May 1962, p. 8, quoted in David Fellman, *Religion in American Public Law* (Boston: Boston University Press, 1965), p. 113.

41. *Ibid.*

42. *See* text with note 14.

43. "New Book Urges Christian Humanism," *Bloomington Herald-Telephone*, 18 September 1982, p. 14. In a recently released anthology of Christian writings, *Readings in Christian Humanism* (published by Augsburg Publishing House), an attempt is made to relate the Christian tradition to "the human adventure."

44. "New Book Urges Christian Humanism," *ibid.*

45. Kenneth Briggs, "Secular Humanists Attack a Rise in Fundamentalism," *The New York Times*, 15 October 1980, p. A-18.

46. "The Impact of Belief," *AAHE Bulletin*, p. 3.

47. Committee for Public Educ. and Religious Liberty v. Regan, 444 U.S. 646, 662 (1980).

48. School Dist. of Abington Township v. Schempp, 374 U.S. 203, 226 (1963).

49. West Virginia State Bd. of Educ. v. Barnette, 319 U.S. 624, 638 (1943).

50. Moreover, the proposed amendment to the U.S. Constitution to allow prayer in public schools would nullify the Supreme Court's decisions barring such devotionals and would cast serious doubt on the potency of the establishment clause to protect religious minorities from the imposition of majoritarian beliefs.

51. Ring v. Grand Fork Public School Dist., 483 F. Supp. 272, 274 (D.N.D. 1980).

52. Lemon v. Kurtzman, 403 U.S. 602, 624-25 (1971).

53. School Dist. of Abington Township v. Schempp, 374 U.S. 203, 225 (1963).